Electoral Systems and Political
Transformation in Post-Communist Europe

One Europe or Several?

Series Editor: **Helen Wallace**

The One Europe or Several? series examines contemporary processes of political, security, economic, social and cultural change across the European continent, as well as issues of convergence/divergence and prospects for integration and fragmentation. Many of the books in the series are cross-country comparisons; others evaluate the European institutions, in particular the European Union and NATO, in the context of eastern enlargement.

Titles include:

Sarah Birch
ELECTORAL SYSTEMS AND POLITICAL TRANSFORMATION
IN POST-COMMUNIST EUROPE

Sarah Birch, Frances Millard, Marina Popescu and Kieran Williams
EMBODYING DEMOCRACY
Electoral System Design in Post-Communist Europe

Andrew Cottey, Timothy Edmunds and Anthony Forster (*editors*)
DEMOCRATIC CONTROL OF THE MILITARY IN POSTCOMMUNIST EUROPE
Guarding the Guards

Anthony Forster, Timothy Edmunds and Andrew Cottey (*editors*)
THE CHALLENGE OF MILITARY REFORM IN POSTCOMMUNIST EUROPE
Building Professional Armed Forces

Anthony Forster, Timothy Edmunds and Andrew Cottey (*editors*)
SOLDIERS AND SOCIETIES IN POSTCOMMUNIST EUROPE
Legitimacy and Change

Andrew Jordan
THE EUROPEANIZATION OF BRITISH ENVIRONMENTAL POLICY
A Departmental Perspective

Valsamis Mitsilegas, Jorg Monar and Wyn Rees
THE EUROPEAN UNION AND INTERNAL SECURITY
Guardian of the People?

Helen Wallace (*editor*)
INTERLOCKING DIMENSIONS OF EUROPEAN INTEGRATION

One Europe or Several?
Series Standing Order ISBN 0–333–94630–8
(*outside North America only*)

You can receive future titles in this series as they are published by placing a standing order. Please contact your bookseller or, in case of difficulty, write to us at the address below with your name and address, the title of the series and the ISBN quoted above.

Customer Services Department, Macmillan Distribution Ltd, Houndmills, Basingstoke, Hampshire RG21 6XS, England

JN74.A75   BIR

Electoral Systems and Political Transformation in Post-Communist Europe

Sarah Birch
Reader, Department of Government, University of Essex, UK

First published 2003 by
PALGRAVE MACMILLAN
Houndmills, Basingstoke, Hampshire RG21 6XS and
175 Fifth Avenue, New York, N.Y. 10010
Companies and representatives throughout the world

PALGRAVE MACMILLAN is the global academic imprint of the Palgrave
Macmillan division of St. Martin's Press, LLC and of Palgrave Macmillan Ltd.
Macmillan® is a registered trademark in the United States, United Kingdom
and other countries. Palgrave is a registered trademark in the European
Union and other countries.

ISBN 0–333–98765–9

This book is printed on paper suitable for recycling and made from fully
managed and sustained forest sources.

A catalogue record for this book is available from the British Library.

Library of Congress Cataloging-in-Publication Data
Birch, Sarah, 1963–
     Electoral systems and political transformation in post-communist
Europe/Sarah Birch
          p. cm.
     Includes bibliographical references and index.
     ISBN 0–333–98765–9 (hardback)
     1. Elections – Europe, Eastern. 2. Elections – Europe, Central. 3. Europe,
Eastern – Politics and government – 1989– 4. Europe, Central – Politics
and government – 1989– I. Title

JN96.A95B56 2003
324.6'3'094091717—dc21   2003053609

10 9 8 7 6 5 4 3 2 1
12 11 10 09 08 07 06 05 04 03

Printed and bound in Great Britain by
Antony Rowe Ltd, Chippenham and Eastbourne

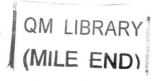

In memory of Freda Wilson

Contents

List of Tables

Preface

This study assesses the impact of electoral system design on political change in 20 post-communist European states between 1990 and 2002. In examining the *effects* of institutional structures, it is a companion volume to the collective monograph on their *causes* entitled *Embodying Democracy: Electoral System Design in Post-Communist Europe* (Birch *et al.*, 2002). In the dozen or so years since the collapse of communism in Central and Eastern Europe between 1989 and 1991, virtually all the states in the region have held at least three parliamentary elections, providing sufficient data for scholars to begin to examine patterns and discern emergent trends. The vast majority of the transitional states undertook significant electoral reform at the outset of the democratization process, and as documented in *Embodying Democracy*, the electoral institutions adopted at this point have remained largely unchanged in their broad outlines (despite considerable tinkering with the details). The aim of this study is to trace the multiple links between electoral systems and political change in order to establish patterns in the effects of electoral system design on post-communist developments. The focus will be on elections to lower or only chambers of the national parliaments, as these are bodies common to all states and these are the institutions central to the development of political party systems as effective mediators between the citizenry and political outcomes.

Research in the field of electoral systems has generated a corpus of well-substantiated findings as to the effect of electoral systems on representative structures and governance in liberal democracies. Not only do political scientists now have good grounds from which to predict the likely impact of electoral laws, but there are frequent suggestions that their findings would be of use to the framers of electoral regimes in democratizing countries. Indeed, this body of work has been influential in shaping the views of many of those who advise the leaders of such states as to what type of electoral system to adopt. Yet very little actual research has been done on the workings of electoral systems during transition. As the more cautious students of electoral systems note, the first few elections in a country are often not indicative of long-term trends. Nevertheless, the outcome of these elections are crucial in shaping the course of a transition process, and often in determining the fate of democratization itself.

Newly competitive political systems are especially susceptible to the influence of institutional design. The principal hypothesis to be tested in this study is that even in the early stages of democratization, electoral institutions have systematic effects that contribute in important ways to the shaping of representative structures. 'Party-enabling' aspects of electoral laws can be expected to foster popular inclusion in the electoral process and the institutionalization of policy-oriented party systems, whereas 'politician-enabling' rules will favour the development of weakly institutionalized systems and will result in popular exclusion from the electoral process.

Many of the analyses in this volume are quantitative in nature; it is thus desirable to have as large a case set as possible. For this reason the cases considered include all the Central and Eastern European states that have held open, competitive elections since their initial transitions from communism (with exception being made for the lapse from open competition that occurred in Albania in 1996, see Chapter 1 for details). The broad-brush focus of this investigation is designed to complement more detailed studies that rely on expertise in the politics of individual countries. Unless otherwise mentioned, all the data employed in the analyses undertaken here are drawn from the database of the Project on Political Transformation and the Electoral Process in Post-Communist Europe at www.essex.ac.uk/elections, which includes both an archive of relevant legislation and electoral results from the 1990–2001 period. Material from this database is supplemented with a range of sources listed by country in Appendix B. Summary election results for the 69 electoral events under analysis are presented in Appendix A.

This research was funded largely by a grant awarded by the Economic and Social Research Council (grant L213252021) as part of the 'One Europe or Several?' research programme. The Department of Government at the University of Essex was also generous in providing both the time and support necessary for the completion of the manuscript. The database on which this analysis is based was constructed as part of a joint project undertaken by the University of Essex, the International Foundation for Electoral Systems, and the Association of Central and East European Electoral Officials. Of the numerous individuals who helped to assemble and manipulate the data in this database, thanks are due in particular to Robertas Pogorelis for his painstaking collation of data and for his thoughtful comments on various aspects of the arguments developed here. I am also grateful to Kieran Williams for his patient replies to my many e-mails. Bernhard Kittel deserves thanks for his very helpful advice on the use (and avoidance) of pooled datasets.

Earlier versions of Chapter 6 were presented at the Annual Meeting of the American Political Science Association in Washington in September 2001, as well as at Nuffield College, Oxford in March 2002; I am indebted to the participants at these two events for their useful comments. Responsibility for errors of fact and interpretation remains mine alone.

Part I

Electoral Systems in Post-Communist Europe

1
Electoral Systems and Post-Communist Transition

A significant body of empirical theory has been developed over the past forty years to explain the effects of electoral laws on the party systems of established democracies, most of which have historically been located in Western Europe.[1] Research has also been undertaken on the comparative study of electoral regulations such as nomination procedures and campaign financing.[2] Yet it is not obvious that the effects of given electoral institutions in established democracies will be those they have during the introduction of competitive politics. Newly competitive political systems can be expected to be particularly susceptible to the influence of institutional design, especially when democratization involves the establishment of new party systems. The electoral regime affects democratic performance by influencing popular perceptions of the political process, by shaping the party system, and by determining the composition of governing organs. The way electoral institutions are designed can be expected to have a decisive influence on the success of political reform because they are among the principal institutional structures that mediate between popular demands and policy outcomes.

It is often argued that the effects of electoral laws do not become evident until electoral practices have become embedded in the political systems in which they operate and political actors have had time to 'learn' to use them. Though this argument is obviously valid as regards the long-term impacts of such laws, it neglects the effects they have on the transition process itself. As in many democratizing contexts, electoral reform was a relatively early aspect of the post-communist transitions. Regardless of how ephemeral or how enduring they turned out to be, these initial electoral settlements can be expected to play an important role in the subsequent course of the transition process. An understanding of *the transition-specific effects* of electoral systems is thus crucial to any explanation of the broader trajectory of post-authoritarian change.

Though it is generally acknowledged that open elections are the *sine qua non* of democracy, theorists of political change rarely fail to point out that the holding of 'free and fair' elections is not a sufficient criterion for a country to be considered democratic, and they caution against the fallacy of equating 'electoralism' with democracy. One of the consequences of the desire to avoid falling into the trap of 'electoralism' has been that the bulk of studies of democratization focus on the concomitants of democracy, whereas relatively little attention has been devoted to the role of elections as institutions. Despite the inherent importance of understanding the role of electoral systems in democratic transitions, only a limited amount of broad comparative research has been done on this topic.[3] Furthermore, though there have been detailed studies of the interactions between electoral system design and the dynamics of democratization in regions such as Latin America (CAPEIIJ, 1986; McDonald and Ruhl, 1989; Nohlen, 1993) and Africa (Nohlen *et al.*, 1999; Reynolds, 1999), work on the effects of electoral systems in Eastern Europe is limited to a handful of relatively short comparative analyses[4] and single country studies.[5]

This study will attempt to fill this gap in the aim of contributing to our understanding of electoral system effects in general and the relationship between electoral systems and democratization in particular. At the same time it will also seek to delineate the specific ways in which electoral laws shape post-communist politics. Recent theorizing about the development of party competition in the post-communist region has emphasized the factors which impinge on the structuring of choices offered to the electorate,[6] and the complex effects of electoral system design have been somewhat neglected. One of the main themes of the book will be that developments in patterns of electoral linkage between representatives and citizens constitute a central feature of political transformation in the region, and that electoral system design plays a crucial role in structuring these patterns.

Democratization includes (but is not restricted to) two key changes in the way political power is structured in society: the inclusion of the citizenry in the selection of leaders, and the establishment of accountability among the leadership chosen through democratic mechanisms. It goes without saying that neither of these tasks is ever complete, and that democratization is therefore an ongoing process. Nevertheless, there are points in the development of a state when rapid advances occur in other domains – points typically labelled 'transitions'. The concept of transition is more useful in some contexts than others, yet there can be little doubt that transitions from communism occurred during the later 1980s and early 1990 in post-communist Europe. However incomplete these transitions may in some cases have been, and whatever the deficiencies of the resulting competitive multi-party systems, there can be no disagreement that mechanisms of rule were fundamentally reshaped at this point, and that the introduction of electoral competition was an important component of the changes that took place during this period. The focus of this study will be on the impact of electoral institutions on inclusion and accountability via institutionalized multi-party politics.

Inclusion is in some sense the more tractable object of investigation, at least when this concept is understood in the electoral sense. We can count the number of people who vote, and we can establish how many votes contribute to the election of representatives. Comparative literatures have been developed on both topics, so it is possible to compare electoral inclusion in the post-communist states with inclusion in developed democracies as well as in other parts of the democratizing world. At the same time, it is important to bear in mind that the substantive importance of inclusion is different in the post-transition context from the meaning we might attach to it in a developed democratic setting. In one sense inclusion of the population in decision-making is the essence of democratization and the principal characteristic that distinguishes a democracy from a non-democracy. Yet inclusion in this sense is typically understood as a collective attribute. 'The people' as a whole are included in the job of ruling a polity. Individual-level inclusion – which will be the main object of investigation in this study – has a rather different significance. Some would argue that it is not necessary to include large numbers of individual citizens in the process of democratic decision-making in order to sustain democracy. Whatever the merits of this argument in the context of 'steady state' democracy, it is far less compelling with regard to polities at the point of democratization. Democratic consolidation is often seen as a process of getting all major players 'on board' and establishing democracy as the 'only game in town'. In this context it is vitally important that no major group in society be left out of democratic politics. The extent to which electoral mechanisms succeed in involving the people in voting and representation may be an important determinant of the likelihood that democracy will consolidate successfully.

Widespread electoral inclusion can thus be seen as a necessary condition for democratization; it is by no means a sufficient condition, however. Inclusion may be meaningless in practice if elected leaders cannot be held to account by the people. Most scholars agree that the principal mechanism of democratic accountability in modern societies is the political party, and that a relatively stable multi-party system is key to ensuring accountable leadership. Individual representatives have little chance on their own of influencing policy outcomes in even moderately large representative bodies. The only effective means of ensuring a meaningful link between electoral choice and policy outcomes is by means of strong and institutionalized political parties. The second main prong of this investigation will therefore focus on party development and party system development.

One of the most striking characteristics of the early post-communist transitions was the rapid proliferation of political parties. At the same time, independent political entrepreneurs also won substantial numbers of parliamentary seats in several states in the region, limiting the 'reach' of these emergent party systems. A second notable feature of post-communist party development was that as first elections led to second and third elections, we witnessed many spectacular defeats and virtual annihilations of newly established parties, which were replaced by new-comers. To some extent we can see both of these as healthy develop-ments, indicating that the societies in question are allowing open competition and that power-holders can be thrown out of office when the populace is dissatisfied with them.

At the same time, the presence of too many parties on the political scene may well be confusing for the people, especially if party names are similar and the programmatic differentiation among them is obscure. Likewise, change of government is one of the main hallmarks of democ-racy, but if the party system is completely reformed with each election, the basis for accountability is actually weakened. Successive parties may recognize that they have very little chance of being elected and may seek to grab what they can for themselves and their members while in office, with little consideration for the welfare of the population at large. Both multipartism and electoral volatility are, as with most things, best in moderation. Our interest in this investigation will be to determine which electoral institutions are conducive to establishing the conditions under which party system operation of this type can be fostered.

It is clear from the preceding discussion that the 'wish-list' of would-be democratizers is long: for democracy to have the best prospects for success, large sectors of the eligible population should be included in representative institutions via electoral mechanisms, the result-ant representative institutions should be structured around political parties rather than around individual politicians, those parties should be moderate enough in number to afford the electorate with meaningful and intelligible choice while at the same time facilitating the formation of parliamentary majorities. Finally, the party system should exhibit enough stability from one election to the next so that all major political actors become committed to the long-term persistence of the system and are willing to take the risk of losing one election in the knowledge that they will have a chance of winning again in several years' time. Such a long list immediately raises the question of the probable necessity of trade-offs among at least some of these desirables. The trade-off most commonly articulated is that between, on the one hand, 'representation', typically understood in terms of the range of political viewpoints represented in parliament, and 'effectiveness' or 'governability' on the other, most often articulated in terms of the ease with which stable governments are formed. As we shall see, however, the situation is somewhat more complex in the post-communist context, where a number of intervening variables work to multiply and structure relevant trade-offs.

It has become a truism that the sudden and simultaneous collapse of a relatively uniform form of rule in over two dozen states provided an ideal 'laboratory' for comparative analysis. Unfortunately, the peculiar features of communism also mean that generalizations reached on the basis of comparative analyses undertaken on post-communist cases cannot easily be applied to other parts of the world. The aim of this investigation is emphatically *not* to make generalizations about electoral systems and democratization on the basis of 20 rather peculiar cases. The aim is a more modest one of ascertaining the specific features of electoral systems under post-communism and developing hypotheses that can then be tested elsewhere. Comparative political science must perforce be about uncovering and explaining differences as much as it is about discovering similarities. If successful, this analysis will at the very least serve the purpose of helping us to understand what makes post-communism different.

Characteristics of the post-communist context

Communism was a complex political, social, and economic structure that left in its wake a situation in which the state, civil society, and the relations between them had to be reformed along new lines. A one-party system had to give way to an open electoral field where parties were free to form and compete; civil society had to be differentiated from the state; and tenure of political power had to be separated from tenure of economic power. The simultaneity of different types of change is widely acknowledged to be one of the hallmarks of post-communist transition and one of the features that distinguishes it from post-authoritarian transition elsewhere in the world. Furthermore, inasmuch as the collapse of communism also entailed the collapse of federalized states in Eastern Europe – the USSR, Yugoslavia, and Czechoslovakia – many post-communist societies were also having to deal with the complicated process of establishing (or re-establishing) the structures of sovereign political entities. Finally, certain of the transformations of the late 1980s and early 1990s included civil strife (Russia, Moldova, Georgia, Azerbaijan, and the Yugoslav successor states), and in these cases states were faced with the daunting task of undertaking political, economic, and social reforms while healing the wounds of conflict and striving to prevent new outbreaks of unrest.

Electoral reform was but one of a large number of changes required in the post-communist transition period. Yet it was a crucial change, as it structured the major decision-making institutions that were in charge of overseeing other aspects of reform. Electoral institutions were also the principal means used to manage the dismantling of the monopolistic parties that had served as the main engines and structuring devices of the communist socio-political and economic systems.

During the communist period, almost all Eastern European states had absolute majority single-member district (SMD) electoral systems in which candidate nomination was tightly controlled by the dominant or single parties, and there was no true competition among parties even in cases where more than one party existed. Moreover, individuals were required to rely in publicizing their candidacies on limited state-sponsored and state-controlled campaign resources, channelled mostly through a state-controlled media. All this meant that if there was competition at all, it was among personalities rather than ideologies.[7]

Since 1990, most of the electoral systems in the region have undergone considerable alteration, such that as of 2002 the modal system was proportional representation (found in Estonia, Latvia, Moldova, Bulgaria, Romania, Poland, the Czech and Slovak Republics, Slovenia, Croatia, Macedonia, Bosnia and Herzegovina, and FR Yugoslavia (Serbia and Montenegro)). Mixed proportional–single-member systems can be found in a further eight countries (Russia, Ukraine, Lithuania, Armenia, Azerbaijan, Georgia, Hungary, and Albania). Only Belarus has maintained a version of the single-member system for its lower-house elections,[8] though such systems also govern elections to the Polish and Czech senates.[9] In all cases state monopolies on nomination, campaign finance, and media regulation have been relaxed, such that the electoral campaigns which take place in the post-communist region do so on the basis of open or semi-open competition. These changes have been brought about through reforms of legislation, operating procedures, and attitudes toward elections.

When assessing the role of electoral institutions in the post-communist democratization process, it is useful to compare this process with the 'first wave' democratic transitions that took place in Western Europe in the late nineteenth and early twentieth centuries. Several aspects of the development of democracy in Western Europe distinguish it from post-communist democratic transition. First, most of today's established democracies were firmly established as states at the time of democratization. This meant that they were relatively integrated geographically when democratization occurred, and a core group of political parties could claim support in most parts of the country. Second, democratization involved a gradual increase in the role of the state in regulating everyday life, a role that was at the outset minimal. Third, and perhaps most importantly, party systems were formed in Western European states prior to the expansion of the franchise (Lipset and Rokkan, 1967; Carstairs, 1980).

In most of Eastern Europe, by contrast, enfranchisement and competitive electoral politics pre-dated or occurred simultaneously with autonomous state formation. The majority of the post-communist states are new states, and many of them are relatively poorly integrated. Questions of national, regional, and ethnic identity interact in important ways with electoral dynamics. At the same time, most of those states that survived the communist collapse intact are in line to join the European Union in the first wave of expansion in 2004. This commitment also raises questions of sovereignty and the relationship of the state to alternative loci of political authority. In both cases the state has had to be fundamentally reinvented since the demise of communism. State integration and autonomy are important shapers of patterns of political organization in as much as they influence socio-political identifications and perceptions of institutional roles (Rustow, 1970; Dahl, 1989; Linz and Stepan, 1996). The fluid nature of post-communist statehood during the democratization process marks this region off from the dominant Western European pattern.

The scope of the state was also much greater in Eastern Europe at the time of transition than it was during the 'first wave' democratizations in the Western portion of the continent. Radical territorial dislocations notwithstanding, the elements of state organization inherited by the post-communist societies represented well-developed institutional models (if not particularly efficient de facto structures). With democratization has come a significant reduction of the role of the state in most spheres. This downsizing has had major consequences for popular expectations of the representative process and for elite mobilization strategies (Przeworski, 1991).

Finally, the role of parties and party systems in the post-communist transitions was distinctive. Whereas the events which precipitated party alignment in Western Europe were associated with the expansion of the *electorate*, in the East they have involved the expansion of the *party system*. In Western European countries existing political parties were able to provide a framework along which newly enfranchised electorates could align. In some cases enfranchisement made possible the creation of new parties, but the basic system was already in place, as were the institutional mechanisms through which it operated. This was not true for Eastern Europe. Here the demonopolization of the political system involved the effective inauguration of partisan competition.

Though it might be tempting to think that many of the post-communist states had by the late 1990s reached a level of democratization where their electoral systems could be expected to perform in much the same way as similar electoral systems in established Western democracies, this may well not be the case. There are fundamental differences between the Western and Eastern European experiences of electoral liberalization as regards both the characteristics of the state and the relationship between citizens and political élites. Changing state identities, declining state capacity, and lack of established party systems distinguish the bulk of the post-communist transitions from those that took place a century before. These differences can be expected to be important in influencing the two main objects of investigation in this study: the differential ability of electoral regimes to include the citizenry in the representative process, and strategies and structures of political intermediation. These two topics will be considered in turn.

Inclusion and electoral systems

It was argued above that inclusion of the citizenry in electoral and representative processes is vital for the consolidation of democracy in post-transition settings. The most obvious means of ensuring that citizens participate in the democratic mechanisms available to them is to require them to exercise their right to vote. Such requirements have been institutionalized in the form of compulsory voting in a wide variety of polities, from established democracies such as Australia and Belgium to democratizing countries in Latin America.[10] Yet compulsory voting was effectively off-limits politically following the collapse of communism, due to the association between this institution and the enforced participation under the totalitarian (and quasi-totalitarian) *anciens régimes*. Many citizens took the opportunity of political liberalization to retreat from the public sphere back into their private lives, and declining levels of political participation began to be viewed as an acute problem (see Chapter 3). At the same time, the relatively high thresholds embedded in some of the electoral systems adopted in the region led to large numbers of 'wasted votes' as small parties were excluded from seat allocation. Thus from a normative perspective, the quality of democratic involvement experienced by the many citizens during the immediate post-communist period was suboptimal.

Interestingly, politicians and political commentators demonstrated only a weak grasp of the impact of electoral system design on participation and inclusion. The detailed analyses of electoral reform in eight post-communist countries undertaken in *Embodying Democracy* suggest that electoral turnout was virtually never considered in connection with debates over electoral laws (Birch *et al.*, 2002), despite ample cross-national evidence that electoral regulations do have an impact on participation rates, and despite evidence – presented in Chapter 3 below – that similar effects were at work in the post-communist region.

There was a greater awareness among post-communist élites of the role of thresholds in including or 'wasting' votes. At the same time, the analyses undertaken in Chapter 4 show that thresholds actually have a relatively marginal role in determining overall rates of electoral inclusion. The important factor is district size, with SMDs having a powerful reductive impact on the number of votes that contribute toward the election of parliamentary representatives. Again, there seems to have been little awareness of this effect among political actors involved in debates on electoral laws (Birch *et al.*, 2002). It can be speculated that this is at least partly due to the fact that the impact of thresholds is more visible than that of district size, especially given that aggregate single-member district vote percentages are often not released by electoral authorities in the region; in order to discover the extent to which SMDs exclude citizens from representation, the curious citizen would need to add together vote totals for all parties from dozens if not hundreds of districts (see Birch, 2001).

The relative lack of discussion of inclusion by politicians debating electoral laws can in all probability be explained with reference to the élite-dominated nature of the political systems that developed during the early post-communist years. As more and more ordinary citizens withdrew from politics – either due to relief at no longer being compelled to contribute or through disillusionment with the new political order that had come into being – politicians and those who aspired to elected office came to be distanced from those they would represent.[11]

Yet the absence of this topic from post-communist political discourse is by no means grounds for neglecting it. As detailed in Part II, there is every reason to expect that electoral systems will influence inclusion in post-communist states in much the same way as they have been found to do in established democracies. Systems of proportional representation can be expected to raise turnout and widen the range of electoral options that are successful in winning representation. In so doing they will encourage larger numbers of voters to participate in electoral activities.

Increasingly electoral competition and participation is being thought of by scholars in terms of the mobilization tactics employed by élites (which will be considered in greater detail in the next chapter). Electoral institutions such as the availability of a personal vote and campaign finance rules shape mobilization strategies by structuring the strategic incentives faced by parties, in as much as they help to determine the resources parties have at their disposal. If candidates have an incentive to compete for a personal vote, this will represent 'human resources' for parties. If the state provides funds for the campaign, that translates into material resources. We can therefore anticipate that inclusion of the electorate in representative institutions will be shaped by a variety of different aspects of the electoral regime.

Political intermediation and electoral systems

As we have seen, effective political intermediation via strong political parties is important for the establishment of accountable representative structures. The question to be considered here is which types of electoral institutions are most likely to achieve this end. In characterizing the relations between parties and their supporters, Kay Lawson distinguishes between policy-responsive linkage and linkage by reward (Lawson, 1980). As an ideal type, parties whose ties to their constituents involve policy-responsiveness aggregate the policy preferences of those they represent and promote positions on political issues that correspond to those preferences. Parties that maintain ties with citizens on the basis of reward provide those citizens with particularistic benefits, including material goods and access to useful 'connections'. This type of linkage is generally understood as a relationship between patrons and clients in which client voters support politician patrons or their proxies (see, for example, Rouquié, 1978; Etzioni-Halevy, 1979; Schmidt, 1980).

In the electoral situation voters face the elemental collective action problem: to influence the policy process they need to coordinate, but in order for this to be possible, there must exist institutions which make such co-ordination efficacious. Votes are perishable goods in the sense that they cannot be cumulated from election to election and cast in bundles; voters are thus not at liberty to wait until such time as the electoral situation is propitious to the effective aggregation of their demands. Without reliable aggregative institutions which would enable them to influence policy-making, they have an incentive to trade their votes instead for the more immediate and tangible rewards of clientelistic relations.

This makes it likely that, in the absence of established parties with a proven ability to realize policy in accordance with the preferences of the electorate, voters will be prone to accept – or even to demand – linkage with their representatives that focuses on reward rather than policy preference aggregation. Politicians, for their part, will be all the more willing to supply such linkage if existing authoritarian-era political ties are structured along the lines of patronage networks. Adapting such networks to the circumstances of competitive electoral politics will then simply be a matter of reorganizing and extending existing structures to include relevant sectors of the voting citizenry.

Both the conditions likely to make voters accept linkage by reward and the circumstances that enable politicians to supply such linkage were characteristic, to varying degrees, of the immediate post-communist environment. At the time of the communist collapse the communist party was in each state the only political organization with a proven record of supplying any policy in recent memory, and responsiveness to popular preferences was not a prominent characteristic of the policy process in most communist systems. The alternative political groups that had in most states formed to contest communist power were typically loosely organized, politically inexperienced, and often not even willing to label themselves 'parties'. Public identification with and trust in political parties of all types was therefore almost universally low at the outset of the transition process (Rose and Mishler, 1994; Rose, 1995; Wyman *et al.*, 1995).

Moreover, many communist systems were characterized by patron–client links among élites, which was reflected among the population at large in modes of social organization in which personal connections were essential not only to career success but also to the acquisition of basic material necessities (Jowitt, 1983; Willerton, 1988; Ekiert, 1991;

Kitschelt, 1995; Kitschelt *et al.*, 1999). This was partly a means of compensating for the inability of the command economy to service people's needs, and partly an inheritance of previous political regimes in which patron–client relations had also been prominent. It is therefore not surprising that in many cases informal relations of this type should have been able to weather the transition from communism to competitive multi-party politics (Vorozheikina, 1994; Kitschelt, 1995; Agh, 1996; Birch, 1997; Golosov, 1997; Kitschelt *et al.*, 1999).

We can expect that the advent of political competition will have led to a diversification in types of patron–client relations as political parties form to attract different groups, and they exist side by side with independent political entrepreneurs who have weak or non-existent ties to formal political organizations. Patronage parties can also be expected to compete within party systems with parties which have a stronger policy-orientation. Policy-oriented, or 'programmatic' parties, are more institutionalized than patronage parties, in the sense that individual politicians within the party are subordinated to the party as an organization rather than vice versa. The establishment and development of such parties can therefore be expected to lead to a more institutionalized party system with stable patterns of competition that are not thrown into disarray by personal quarrels or leadership turnover. Where patronage relations dominate, the party system can be expected to exist side by side with personal political fiefdoms established and maintained without recourse to the formal trappings of partisan institutionalization.

In the immediate context of post-communism many parties were formed by élites who sought to project support bases rather than to aggregate existing interests. The linkage patterns that have developed between parties and electorates in the post-communist region are therefore rather different from those that have developed in the West. Though there is considerable variation across states in the region, even parties not based primarily on patronage tended in the early stages of the transition process to be weakly institutionalized, centralized, and élite-led (Wightman, 1995; Lewis, 1996). They have also had relatively weak hold over individual representatives, who were prone to mid-term defections. There was thus considerable fluidity in the party systems as new parties formed to test the electoral waters and the less successful among them sought to establish coalitions to boost their chances (e.g. Cotta, 1996; Mair, 1996). Under these circumstances it is likely that institutions will have been more sensitive to electoral system design than is the case where parties' links with their supporters are long-established, dense, multifaceted, and slow to change.

Electoral rules can be divided for the purposes of this analysis into 'party-enabling' institutions and those that enable individual politicians. Party-enabling rules allow party hierarchies to have exclusive control over the candidate nomination process; they channel campaign resources exclusively through parties; and they give parties maximum control over the ultimate victors. 'Politician-enabling' rules, on the other hand, provide individuals with access to competition outside the framework of the party; they refrain from distributing resources to parties and/or allocate them to individual candidates; and they afford voters maximum direct influence over the electoral fortunes of individual candidates.

Our main hypothesis *vis-à-vis* party structures can be summed up as follows. Party-enabling rules can be expected to lead to party institutionalization and a strengthening of the party system and the encouragement of parties with relatively stable bases of support. Politician-enabling rules will most likely tend, by contrast, to generate weak, fragmented, and unstable party systems. The potential attractions of party organization will undoubtedly not be lost on powerful individual politicians, and they will, at the same time, find it harder to co-ordinate sufficiently to agree on measures which would limit the control of parties over the electoral process. Faced with this possibility, clever party leaders need only offer the strongest of the politicians choice slots at the next election to hinder any efforts to legislate to their disadvantage.

One of the ironies of democratization is that while strong parties will help in the long run to provide policy accountability to voters, in the short term it may have the effect of limiting voters' input into the electoral process. Declining levels of electoral participation in the wake of communism represented a challenge to politicians. It may be expected that voters can be attracted to participate by means of electoral institutions that maximize their influence. These include rules that allow ordinary voters a role in candidate nomination, campaign finance regulations that give an incentive to parties to seek individual donations, and seat allocation rules that maximize the likelihood that individual votes will contribute to the election of one or more candidates. Such rules can be expected to contribute to the legitimation of the new political regime, yet they may at the same time hinder the development of accountable parties.

Two caveats are in order at this point. First, the contrast between personalized political systems and systems dominated by institutionalized parties is not unique to the post-communist context. Allowing voters a greater direct say in the allocation of elected power will ipso facto reduce the influence of party structures and increase the ability of politicians to establish direct relationships with groups of voters. There is a tendency in Western Europe to view parties as having become too strong; Italians talk of the *partitocrazia*, and theorists of party system change speak of professionalized parties or party cartels, cut off from their grass-roots (Panebianco, 1988; Mair, 1994; Katz and Mair, 1995). But there are reasons to believe that this contrast will be especially keenly felt in the post-communist context. Varying degrees of personalization in the power structures of all the *anciens régimes* will be magnified as communist leaders seek to shed the unpopular ideological baggage of communism and reinvent themselves as 'experienced', 'competent', 'professional' politicians (Ishiyama, 1998, 2000; Grzymala-Busse, 2002). Moreover, initial popular disillusionment with parties in general means that party leaders will have faced an uphill battle in convincing voters that the institution of the party was best suited to representing them – a battle they will have had to fight in addition to that of winning sufficient sectors of the electorate round to their particular brand of politics. Without direct experience of effective interest representation via hierarchically structured political organizations, voters will understandably be wary of the 'iron law of oligarchy' and its potential to sideline their true interests. Representative multi-party democracy is a relatively abstract concept that makes sense to those who have been brought up with it and can see its effects, but for those who do not have the benefit of years of experience, trust in multi-party representative institutions involves a leap of faith. This is especially true under the circumstances of economic hardship and rapidly increasing wealth differentials that accompanied the transition from a command economy.

Second, it must be acknowledged that electoral systems are far from being the only factors that influence the nature of the political system; executive type, economic structure, and historical legacy have also been demonstrated to have important influences on the representative systems that will develop in a country following a transition period.[12] Not only is it necessary to acknowledge these other factors, but the analysis in the chapters which follow will need to consider the possibility that they interact with electoral system design. Presidentialism has been found on other contexts to have a fragmenting effect on the parliamentary electoral system (Shugart and Carey, 1992; Jones, 1995). Economic crisis may have a similar impact, inasmuch as the population become disillusioned with the range of parties on offer and political entrepreneurs are able to build partisan support bases by founding new parties. For the same reasons, economic dislocation can also be expected to generate increased electoral volatility. Previous experience of democracy is an additional factor that will undoubtedly influence the way in which political competition is structured. States with relatively recent and relatively lengthy histories of multi-party electoral competition may well find it easier to refound and instituitonalize stable party systems than new states with no 'useable' history of democracy.

Electoral systems as causes and effects

The ability to make predictions about the likely effects of electoral laws is obviously not the exclusive domain of political scientists. Political actors in the post-communist world – as elsewhere – have sought to discover what electoral reforms would mean for their political fortunes, and they have sought to manipulate electoral institutions to their benefit. In a situation where existing institutions have been largely discredited and the rules of political competition are essentially 'up for grabs' it is not surprising that many actors have found it more convenient and more fruitful to shape those rules to their advantage rather than shaping their strategies to the rules. Our predictions must therefore be tempered with consideration of how the formation of electoral systems will be related to their impact.

Inasmuch as parliamentary electoral institutions govern the formation of bodies that generate policies, including the very laws that regulate the electoral process itself, electoral systems can be understood as both causes and effects of political outcomes. It is perhaps for this reason that the study of electoral systems is so fascinating, but this complex causal structure also raised problems for those who would seek to isolate either the causes or the effects. This is the so-called 'endogeneity problem': if we find an association between a certain electoral system type and a certain type of partisan configuration in the resulting parliaments, it can be difficult to establish the direction of causality. It may be, for example, that proportional representations generate party system fragmentation, as Duverger's famous formulation would have it, but it may also be that fragmented party systems generate a demand for proportional representation in order to enable the newly established parties to be represented in parliament, a demand that is then met by means of electoral reform (as appears to have been the case in Western Europe at the turn of the last century; Rokkan, 1970). How do we disentangle these two effects? In one sense the problem is an illusion, as electoral outcomes cannot in and of themselves 'cause' electoral reform in isolation from perceptions of the likely effects of that reform (Cox, 1997; Moser, 2001a). Politicians will only seek to redesign electoral systems to achieve certain ends if they believe in the causal efficacy of electoral systems themselves. If they are correct in anticipating the outcomes of reform (which is often not the case), then the causal efficacy of electoral systems is validated. If they are incorrect, and electoral reforms have consequences they have not anticipated, then the problem disappears. The endogeneity problem can thus be restated as follows: we have reason to believe that electoral systems have discernable impacts on political outcomes; what we do not know is whether over a period of time those outcomes can feed back into the process of electoral system design, generating a reciprocal causal structure. A second aspect of the problem is that if electoral systems are largely outcomes of variations in the partisan configuration of forces, then that configuration of forces may have other systematic effects on the political process that would then be associated with electoral system design. Indeed, some scholars have claimed that post-communist electoral laws are largely the product of the political context in each state at the start of the transition process (or prior to it), and that it was this context that subsequently shaped a range of political outcomes, electoral systems being one of many (e.g. Kitschelt *et al.*, 1999). Were this the case, we would observe spurious associations between electoral systems and other aspects of post-communist political development.

Anticipating this problem at the start of the research project of which this study is a product, the author initiated a collaborative study of the factors that influenced electoral system design in eight of the countries incorporated into the current analysis: Poland, Hungary, the Czech Republic, Slovakia, Bulgaria, Romania, the Russian Federation, and Ukraine. This study – based on primary source material in eight languages – enabled a fine-grained appreciation of general trends across the region and the individual characteristics of the design process. The results of this analysis will facilitate the identification of possible areas of reciprocal or spurious causality in the current investigation.

These results – described in far greater detail in *Embodying Democracy* (Birch *et al.*, 2002) – can be summarized as follows. Electoral laws were shaped by three embedded processes: the initial menu of options from which politicians selected electoral design elements was shaped by commonly held perceptions of the sorts of institutions that were appropriate to the state in question. The choice was typically narrowed down with reference to aspects of the immediate context in which the law was being implemented – the desirability of preventing ex-communists from winning elections, the perceived benefits of a smaller party systems, and so on. Finally, remaining disagreements over laws were worked out by means of bargaining among major actors along the lines of perceived self-interest. Despite much interest-based activity, actors in many cases took a long-term view, opting not only for personal or party advancement in the narrow sense of a system that would maximize their own chances of success, but also for democracy – generally understood in terms of electoral systems that would promote party development, allocating seats according to the proportional share of party votes; such explicit foregrounding of parties as vote-winners was linked to the principle of political pluralism. The reasons for this 'socio-tropic' turn are threefold. First, at this critical juncture the euphoria of transition enabled many to transcend their personal interests and make historical decisions; but there was also a more practical consideration involved: the high degree of uncertainty surrounding first elections meant that politicians were acting behind a 'veil of ignorance'; they often were not in a position to know which electoral system type would benefit them personally. Collective interest was a default choice. Parties of all stripes had an interest in a system that would benefit parties, as opposed to single-party rule. The communist institutional structure was identified by the opposition as the main obstacle to democratization; its institutional features were therefore discredited by association. A final factor was the desire to spread the blame for hard choices by choosing an electoral system that would be likely to result in coalition governments.

One of the main factors that accounted for variations in electoral institutions across states was the role of popular movements in bringing down the communist regime. Where there was widespread mobilization behind a popular movement against the communist system, the parties that emerged from that movement had better developed grass-roots structures that they could transform into party infrastructures. The élite-level organization entailed by a sustained movement also helped to build decision-making capacity within the movement that gave it enhanced leverage in the early stages of the bargaining process over electoral rules.

A related factor was the enduring strength of the ex-communist party and its ability to control the legislative process (or at the least to block reform efforts). Given that the communist parties were initially in rather different strategic positions from the newly established opposition parties, the communist successors had different preferences as to electoral system design in the early stage of the transition. Paradoxically, it was these more institutionalized parties that promoted the least party-enabling electoral rules, and vice versa. The post-communist parties were, at the outset of the transition, the only organizations that could be deemed 'true' parties with well-articulated organizational apparatuses and wide networks of regional structures. Nevertheless, the general popular antipathy towards these institutions and the weak ideological commitment on the part of many of their leaders made most favour electoral structures that enhanced the role of the individual politician, such as single-member districts. Conversely the anticommunist oppositions, despite the fact that they did not have strong party structures, called for electoral institutions such as proportional representation which benefited parties (cf. Geddes, 1996; Elster *et al.*, 1998; Jasiewicz, 1998; Kitschelt *et al.*, 1999).[13]

One of the most noteworthy general conclusions to be drawn from the investigation of post-communist electoral reform was the high degree of stability of the overall shape of the electoral systems in the region. Most decisions about the architecture of the electoral system were made relatively early in the reform process, and by the end of the initial transition, all but three of the 20 countries considered here had in place the basic outlines of the electoral systems that were to serve them for the following decade or more. The three exceptions are Ukraine, Macedonia, and Croatia which moved toward more proportional electoral systems at various points over the period under investigation. But by and large, the question of reciprocal causality is non-existent in relation to the states examined in this study, because reform preceded the development of fully fledged party systems. It is also worth noting that the novice electoral engineers who forged the basic principles on which the post-communist electoral systems were built often had highly inaccurate beliefs as to the likely effects of those systems, and in some cases the designs that emerged were products of uncertainty rather than the result of positive efforts to achieve given ends. We can also be fairly sure that certain factors were not on the minds of electoral systems designers when they considered alternative institutional options. Participation and representative inclusion have already been mentioned in this context.

Electoral thresholds were the one area in which there was considerable change over the period in question and where electoral reformers did have fairly clear notions of what the outcome of change was likely to be. A relatively large proportion of the changes made to electoral laws between 1990 and 2002 involved increases in the threshold of representation for the distribution of proportional representation seats. In view of the possible dangers associated with interpreting associations between thresholds and party system outcomes, this study will avoid relying heavily on an analysis of thresholds and will focus instead on those aspects of electoral system design that were more stable: overall system architecture, the availability of a personal vote, and the provision of state financing for electoral campaigns. The danger of making spurious causal claims is a problem that dogs most social science research, not one confined to the study of electoral systems. This danger can be reduced by means of careful theorizing, with attention to existing knowledge regarding the intentions of electoral architects. It will also be necessary in some contexts to control for the other contextual factors, such as communist heritage, economic change, and various aspects of constitutional design. We can anticipate that the effects of electoral laws will also vary somewhat from state to state according to idiosyncratic aspects of the state's political development; nevertheless, previous research suggests that the broad overall impact of different types of electoral regulatory devices should be relatively constant across states. It is to the details of these institutional structures that we now turn.

An integrated approach to electoral systems

In most of the existing literature on electoral institutions, different aspects of electoral system design have been considered separately. The two sub-fields of analysis that have generated the largest body of empirical work have been the study of district design and vote-to-seat conversion formulae (the 'electoral system' in the narrow sense) and the examination of campaign finance regulatory structures (usually in the context of analyses of party development). These two streams of investigation have rarely been combined, despite the fact that they are aspects of electoral systems that can be expected to impact on similar types of political outcome.[14] It makes sense in the post-communist context to take an integrated approach to the analysis of electoral systems. The effects of these two important aspects of the electoral regime will be considered in turn.

(1) *The electoral formula.* Existing research on electoral results in Eastern Europe questions the common belief that list-PR (proportional representation) systems allow a wider range of parties to enter parliament than single-member district (SMD) systems. In diverse and new states such as Armenia, Georgia, Russia, and Ukraine it is the single-member systems and the single-member components of mixed systems that have led to the representation of the largest absolute number of parties, and the list systems, with their typically high thresholds, have been most exclusionary. Likewise, the characteristic tendency in established

democracies for single-member systems to generate small numbers of parliamentary parties does not appear to be operative throughout the region (Moser, 1997, 1999; Birch, 2000). Under circumstances of weak state and party system formation, single-member systems and the single-member components of many of the region's mixed systems encourage candidacies by small groups, because they focus on strategy at the district level. This leads to divisions within party camps and it exacerbates what may already be considerable regional heterogeneity of party organization, especially in new and weakly integrated polities. In the terms elaborated above, PR systems are 'party-enabling' institutions, while single-member laws tend in the circumstances of post-communism to be 'politician-enabling' devices. The above analysis suggests that this qualitative distinction may be of equal or greater significance to the nature of party systems as the quantitative attributes of party system size and proportionality. The availability of a personal vote should also be important. The option of voting for an individual candidate is clearly a device that will personalize the electoral process. Personal votes are available in all SMD systems, but also in a large number of PR lists. Open lists are found in the PR systems of Bosnia and Herzegovina (from 2000), the Czech Republic, Estonia, Latvia, Poland, and Slovakia. We may hypothesize that these will be politician-enabling features, inasmuch as they take control over the electoral process away from party apparatuses and provide politicians with the incentive to use whatever means they have at their disposal to cultivate personal votes (Katz, 1980, 1986, 1997; Carey and Shugart, 1995). In as much as the personal vote enables candidates to establish ties on the basis of their own characteristics (as opposed to the characteristics of the party alone), they will be less beholden to their party. If they are less beholden to their party, they are more likely to defect from it and either join a new party or found their own political organization. Moreover, voting for individuals rather than parties may mean that voters fail to consider the electoral prospects of the party to which the individual belongs. Individual loyalty and other types of personalistic bonds may thus serve to fragment the party system by hampering strategic co-ordination around a small number of viable alternatives.

(2) *Campaign finance regulation.* Many aspects of campaign activity could in theory be analysed, but the existing literature points to three types of regulation that most often have a significant impact on the variables under consideration here: (1) the extent and form of public subvention of campaign expenses; (2) spending limits in electoral campaigns, including the level and types of expenditure limited; and (3) income and/or expenditure disclosure requirements. Regulatory

regimes covering campaign resources are linked to a country's party traditions (or lack thereof), its political culture, and its economic structure. They influence matters such as who competes, who wins, and how secure is their margin of victory. The economic dislocations that have accompanied the transition from state socialism in post-communist Europe have resulted in substantial redistributions of wealth. These have a significant bearing on the opportunities available to individuals and groups to engage in effective political action.

One of the most important political legacies of communism is the fact that political parties were distrusted by large sectors of the Eastern European electorates in the wake of the initial transitions. At the same time, many of the new parties that formed suffered from lack of material resources. The combination of these two factors made the establishment of new parties at first difficult. In most cases the only political organizations that managed to build mass support bases in the early post-communist years were the former communist parties, which could rely not only on a solid core of dues-paying rank-and-file members, but also on considerable organizational resources, equipment, and experienced personnel. The disadvantaged position of the new parties explains in part why many of the post-communist states, especially those of Central Europe, have opted for the public financing of political parties. The former Soviet states have been more hesitant in taking this route, however, concentrating mainly on subsidies in kind and the attempted limitation of campaign expenditure (see Lewis, 1998, 2000; Gel'man, 1998). These differences in approach to campaign financing can be expected to have significant consequences for party formation and organization, for patterns of political recruitment, and for the establishment of lines of accountability between elected representatives and voters.

The literature on campaign resource regulation has mostly taken the form of case studies of established democracies or comparisons of a small number of cases (e.g. Alexander, 1979, 1989; Gunlicks, 1993; Alexander and Shiratori, 1994). Until recently there was relatively little examination of the effects of such regulatory devices in democratizing states. Analyses of established democracies suggest that the introduction of public subsidies and other forms of campaign regulation has the effect of petrifying the party system, while changing parties to the 'cartel' type (Katz and Mair, 1995). This is true for a variety of reasons, not least that those who have already been successful in gaining political power design the regulations. Eligibility criteria for public subsidies are typically based on retroactive electoral performance; spending limits benefit those who can draw on non-material resources such as prestige and experience, restrictions on the use of non-state media tend to privilege those more closely connected with the state apparatus.

It is important to note that state funding and reforms of electoral campaign financing were introduced relatively late into Western party systems. In the context of an emerging party system, regulations of this type may be highly 'party enabling', but they may by the same token inhibit the formation of durable links between parties and distinct sectors of the electorate. These links generally formed in established democracies before the age of mass communications when face-to-face contact was a crucial factor in the mobilization of support. Party systems born in the age of mass media advertising and televised debates may be pressured from the start into becoming what Panebianco (1988) describes as 'electoral-professional' parties. The fact of public funding from the outset in some East European countries may exacerbate this tendency and positively discourage the establishment of grass-roots organization.

There has recently been increased attention to campaign financing in new democracies, and in particular to post-communist states (Burnell and Ware, 1998; Krasovec, 2001; van Biezen and Kopecky, 2001; Szczerbiak, 2001; Ikstens *et al.*, 2002; Roper, 2002). The prevalence of state financing has been noted and linked to the 'cartelization' of party politics in the post-communist region (though with some important reservations; Lewis, 2000; Szczerbiak, 2001). Yet there has been virtually no systematic attempt to link party finance laws to the size, shape, or stability of the party system. We can expect the provision of state resources for electoral competition to have a 'freezing' effect on the party system, in as much as state financing is almost invariably linked to electoral success. If the state 'reward' for electoral success takes the form of resources that increase the chances of an electoral competitor improving its position at subsequent elections, newcomers will be at a distinct disadvantage and may be effectively 'locked out' of the system. This should result in both a limitation of the numbers of parties that achieve electoral success and also a relative stabilization over time. If, on the other hand, private finance is allowed to dominate, and if there are no limits on campaign spending, those who manage to enrich themselves stand a good chance of winning elections. In as much as wealth changes hands relatively rapidly during the economically volatile period following the introduction of a market economy, the new rich will be a constantly changing group. If such economic victors decide to move into the political sphere, there will be a pool of political newcomers at each successive election, adding to the range of parties on offer and increasing electoral volatility.

We can therefore expect that electoral institutions will influence political outcomes in a variety of distinct ways. They will influence both the extent to which the electorate is effectively incorporated into the new democratic structures and the degree of accountability that is provided by the party system. It remains to define the geographic and temporal parameters of the investigation and to outline the organization of the chapters to follow.

The scope and structure of the study

In view of the foregoing considerations, emphasis will be given in this study to two main sets of outcome variables: the degree of inclusion of the citizenry in the electoral process and party system institutionalization. The focus of the analysis will be on elections to lower or only chambers of the national parliaments of post-communist states during the 13-year period between 1990 and 2002. The study will be based on 20 post-communist states, representing virtually the entire range of democratic electoral experience in the European portion of the former communist lands. These include the former Soviet states of Armenia, Estonia, Georgia, Latvia, Lithuania, Russia, Ukraine, and Moldova, the Central European countries of Poland, the Czech Republic, Slovakia, Hungary, Romania, and Bulgaria, the former Yugoslav states of Bosnia and Herzegovina, Croatia, Macedonia, Slovenia, and FR Yugoslavia (Serbia and Montenegro), and finally, Albania.

The cluster of states on the Western border of 'Eastern Europe' – Poland, the Czech Republic, and Hungary – have, together with Russia, received a disproportionate share of the scholarly attention that has been devoted to the study of post-communist parties, despite the fact that they together constitute only a fraction of the states that make up the region. One of the objectives of this study is to examine a wider range of states in order to evaluate whether conclusions that have been drawn from smaller N studies hold more generally. However, Azerbaijan, Belarus and pre-2000 Yugoslavia (Serbia and Montenegro) have had to be excluded on the grounds that their elections have not been democratic enough by international standards; given that the electoral system effects posited in this study are predicated on relatively open, multi-party competition and fraud-free electoral administration, we would not expect to observe such effects in states that do not meet these criteria. Though the quality of electoral administration has been at times questionable in several of the states considered here, levels of outright corruption appear to have been considerably lower, as were limitations on open competition.

The 1990 republic elections held in the Soviet Union and Yugoslavia will not be included. Though these were the electoral arenas in which multi-party politics was born in Bosnia and Herzegovina, Croatia, Macedonia, Slovenia, Yugoslavia, and to a lesser extent Estonia, Latvia, Lithuania, and Georgia, the fact that they were still (formally, at least) sub-national elections to parliaments with limited immediate policy-making power suggests that the factors that condition the strategies of both citizens and élites may have differed in significant ways from those at work in the context of elections to the parliaments of sovereign states. The transitions were also incomplete at the time of both sets of republic elections, making them transitional rather than fully democratic events. The semi-competitive Polish elections of 1989 are excluded from analysis on the same grounds; they were also transitional events in which the full play of electoral forces was yet to be evident.

A final word is in order about two particular cases; data from elections to the Czech and Slovak national Councils of 1990 and 1992 were employed rather than that from the federal elections that took place in these years. This may seem to contradict the principle that only elections from sovereign states are to be considered, as Czechoslovakia was still united at this point. Yet the fact that the elections at the two levels were held concurrently meant that the results were very similar, and it is desirable to respect the continuity in institutional structure between the national councils and the parliaments of the states that emerged from the Czecho–Slovak divorce. The alternative would be to leave the 1990 and 1992 elections out of the dataset entirely, but this would considerably distort the results of the analysis, in that the transition from communism had already been made in 1990. The other tricky case is that of Albania, which experienced a period of democratic breakdown in the mid-1990s following a period of economic and political crisis in which weapons stores were looted and the country sank temporarily into a state of virtual anarchy. By all accounts, the parliamentary elections of 1996 failed to live up to even the minimum standards necessary for them to be classified as 'free and fair', and repeat polls were held the following year. After careful consideration, it was decided best to exclude the 1996 elections from the dataset rather than to lose the Albanian case altogether. The 1997 elections will therefore be referred to in subsequent chapters as the 'third' Albanian elections (following the electoral events of 1991 and 1992).

The investigation will comprise three parts, each of which will build upon the preceding one, but each of which will also represent discrete studies of different aspects of electoral system effects under post-communism. Chapter 2 will provide a descriptive overview or electoral system design in post-communist Europe and will establish the methodological tools necessary to carry out the investigation. This will involve developing coding schemes for each of the electoral institution dimensions to be examined, as well as measures of the dependent variables of interest. The second part of the study will examine the extent to which electoral systems have succeeded in including the citizenry in the electoral process. Citizens are included first and foremost by voting, and Chapter 3 will analyse the institutional and other factors that influence electoral participation in the post-communist region. Chapter 4 will assess inclusion from the point of view of representation; citizens can be seen as being effectively included in democratic structures if their vote contributes to the election of representatives. The link between electoral institutions and representational inclusion will be examined both cross-sectionally and over time. The relationship between electoral systems and party systems will be addressed in the third part of the volume; the size and shape of successive post-communist party parliamentary systems will be the subject of Chapter 5, while Chapter 6 will investigate patterns of stability and change in the party systems over time. A brief conclusion will draw together the strands of the analysis and trace the links among the individual chapter findings.

2
An Overview of Post-Communist Electoral Systems: Design and Measurement

The purpose of this chapter is to provide a descriptive overview of the range of electoral system designs in post-communist Europe and to elaborate ways of measuring them. The chapter is divided into three parts. The first section will review the general trends in electoral system design in the region, while the second section will be devoted to providing brief details of major changes in electoral institutions in each of the 20 states, together with a more detailed description of peculiarities specific to each system. The third section will discuss issues associated with the measurement of electoral systems and their impacts. The chapter will close with a brief note on the statistical methods used in this study.

Electoral institutions in post-communist Europe at a glance

When most people think of 'electoral systems', they think of districting and seat allocation rules, and indeed these are the electoral institutions that were first reformed following the collapse of communism. A schematic overview of the district format and vote-to-seat conversion formulae of the 20 states is presented in Table 2.1. Electoral reform in the Central and Eastern European region was marked by a number of common features; first a move away from the SMD absolute majority systems operative under communism, and subsequent gradual increases in barriers to entry, with graduated thresholds distinctive of the region introduced at various points in Albania, Croatia, the Czech Republic, Poland, Romania, and Slovakia. The only case of a threshold being lowered was the decrease from 4–2 per cent in Albania at the time of the

Table 2.1   Details of electoral system format in 20 post-communist states

Country	Size of chamber	Number of districts (lower + upper tiers)	Number of upper-tier seats	Proportion PR seats (%)	Single-party threshold (first tier PR seats)♣ (%)	Preferences in PR list voting?	Success requirement in single-member seats
Albania 1991	250	250	None	0	—	—	Abs. maj.
Albania 1992	140	100 + 1	40	29	4	—	Abs. maj.
Albania 1997	155	115 + 1	40	26	2	—	Abs. maj.
Albania 2001	140	100 + 1	40	29	2.5♣	No	Abs. maj.
Armenia 1995	190	150 + 1	40	21	5	No	Plurality (and at least 25%)
Armenia 1999	131	75 + 1	56	43	5	No	Plurality
Bosnia & H. 1996	42	2	0	100	None	No	—
Bosnia & H. 1998	42	2	0	100	None	No	—
Bosnia & H. 2000	42	8 + 1	12	100	None	Yes	—
Bosnia & H. 2002	42	8 + 1	12	100	None	Yes	—
Bulgaria 1990	400	200 + 1	200	50	4	No	Abs. maj.
Bulgaria 1991	250	1*	None	100	4	No	—
Bulgaria 1994	250	1*	None	100	4	No	—
Bulgaria 1997	250	1*	None	100	4	No	—
Bulgaria 2001	250	1*	None	100	4	No	—
Croatia 1992	138	60 + 1 + 18 minority seats	60	43	3	No	Plurality
Croatia 1995	127	28 + 1 + 19 diaspora and minority seats	80	63	5♣	No	Plurality
Croatia 2000	151	10 + 11 diaspora and minority seats	None	100	5	No	—
Czech Rep. 1990	200	8 + 1	Variable	100	5	Yes	—
Czech Rep. 1992	200	8 + 1	Variable	100	5	Yes	—
Czech Rep. 1996	200	8 + 1	Variable	100	5♣	Yes	—
Czech Rep. 1998	200	8 + 1	Variable	100	5♣	Yes	—
Czech Rep. 2002	200	14	None	100	5♣	Yes	—
Estonia 1992	101	12 + 1	Variable	100	None**	Yes	—
Estonia 1995	101	11 + 1	Variable	100	None**	Yes	—
Estonia 1999	101	11 + 1	Variable	100	None**	Yes	—

30 Electoral Systems and Political Transformation

Table 2.1   (Continued)

Country	Size of chamber	Number of districts (lower + upper tiers)	Number of upper-tier seats	Proportion PR seats (%)	Single-party threshold (first tier PR seats)♣ (%)	Preferences in PR list voting?	Success requirement in single-member seats
Georgia 1992	235	84 + 10 + 1 + 1	150	64	None	Yes	Abs. maj.
Georgia 1995	223***	73 + 10 + 1	150	67	5	No	33% maj.
Georgia 1999	225***	75 + 1	150	67	7	No	33% maj.
Hungary 1990	386	176 + 20 + 1	210	54	4	No	Abs. maj.
Hungary 1994	386	176 + 20 + 1	210	54	5	No	Abs. maj
Hungary 1998	386	176 + 20 + 1	210	54	5	No	Abs. maj.
Hungary 2002	386	176 + 20+ 1	210	54	5	No	Abs. maj.
Latvia 1993	100	5	None	100	4	Yes	—
Latvia 1995	100	5	None	100	5	Yes	—
Latvia 1998	100	5	None	100	5	Yes	—
Latvia 2002	100	5	None	100	5	Yes	—
Lithuania 1992	141	71 + 1	70	50	4	No	Abs. maj.
Lithuania 1996	141	71 + 1	70	50	5	No	Abs. maj.
Lithuania 2000	141	71 + 1	70	50	5	No	Plurality
Macedonia 1994	120	120	None	0	—	—	Abs. maj.
Macedonia 1998	120	85 + 1	35	29	5	No	Abs. maj.
Macedonia 2002	120	6	None	100	None	No	Abs. maj.
Moldova 1994	104	1	None	100	4	No	—
Moldova 1998	101	1	None	100	4	No	—
Moldova 2001	101	1	None	100	6	No	—
Poland 1991	460	37 + 1	69	100	None	Yes	—
Poland 1993	460	52 + 1	69	100	5♣	Yes	—
Poland 1997	460	52 + 1	69	100	5♣	Yes	—
Poland 2001	460	41	None	100	5♣	Yes	—
Romania 1990	385 (+9 minority seats)	41 + 1	Variable	100	None	No	—
Romania 1992	328 (+13 minority seats)	42 + 1	Variable	100	3	No	—
Romania 1996	328 (+15 minority seats)	42 + 1	Variable	100	5♣	No	—
Romania 2000	327 (+18 minority seats)	42 + 1	Variable	100	5♣	No	—

Table 2.1   (Continued)

Country	Size of chamber	Number of districts (lower + upper tiers)	Number of upper-tier seats	Proportion PR seats (%)	Single-party threshold (first tier PR seats)♣	Preferences in PR list voting?	Success requirement in single-member seats
Russia 1993	450	225 + 1	225	50	5	No	Plurality
Russia 1995	450	225 + 1	225	50	5	No	Plurality
Russia 1999	450	225 + 1	225	50	5	No	Plurality
Slovakia 1990	150	4	Variable	100	3	Yes	—
Slovakia 1992	150	4	Variable	100	5♣	Yes	—
Slovakia 1994	150	4	Variable	100	5♣	Yes	—
Slovakia 1998	150	1	None	100	5♣	Yes	—
Slovakia 2002	150	1	None	100	5♣	Yes	—
Slovenia 1992	90	8 + 1 (+2 minority seats)	Variable	100	None	Yes	—
Slovenia 1996	90	8 + 1 (+2 minority seats)	Variable	100	None	Yes	—
Slovenia 2000	90	8 + 1 (+2 minority seats)	Variable	100	4	Yes	—
Ukraine 1994	450	450	None	0	—	—	Abs. maj.
Ukraine 1998	450	225 + 1	225	50	4	No	Plurality
Ukraine 2002	450	225 + 1	225	50	4	No	Plurality
Yugoslavia 2000	138	27	0	100	5 (district-level)	No	—

* Bulgaria is divided into 31 districts, but seat allocation among parties is effected at the national level without regard for district boundaries.

** A 5 per cent threshold is imposed for seat distribution in the upper tier.

*** The SMD seats in Abkhazia were not subject to re-election in either 1995 or 1999 and are therefore excluded from the figures reported here (there were 12 such seats in 1995 and 10 in 1999).

♣ Graduated threshold structure; higher levels for coalitions.

1997 elections (with a subsequent rise to 2.5 per cent in 2001).[1] Thresholds in Central and Eastern Europe are high by international standards; the average single-party lower-tier threshold in West European PR systems was 1.23 at the millennium, as compared with an average of 4.25 in 20 Central and East European states at the same point in time (Birch, 2001: 367–8).

A second distinctive feature of electoral system design in the post-communist states is the use of mixed systems, especially of the unlinked (parallel) variety. Mixed systems proved popular with post-communist electoral system reformers for a variety of reasons; they were a sensible way of hedging bets under conditions of uncertainty, and they represented logical bargaining outcomes (see Shugart and Wattenburg, 2001; Birch *et al.*, 2002).[2] The very fact that so many of the states in the region adopted mixed systems is noteworthy; they were the initial system of choice in Armenia, Bulgaria, Croatia, Georgia, Hungary, Lithuania, Russia, and Yugoslavia (as well as in Azerbaijan). Mixed systems were subsequently adopted in Albania, Ukraine, Macedonia and further east in Tadjikistan, Uzbekistan, and Kyrgzstan.

In designing mixed systems, the post-communist electoral engineers innovated. The main model for the mixed system prior to the communist collapse was the German linked (compensatory) system. The first post-communist state to experiment with the mixed system was Hungary, which adopted a linked system considerably more complex than the German model, but not dissimilar in principle. The Albanian system adopted in 1991 was also of the linked variety, though it was unusual in being based on a single vote rather than two separate votes for the two component parts of the system. The *unlinked* mixed system most distinctive of the post-communist region was first adopted in Bulgaria in June of 1990, before spreading to Georgia (October 1990), Croatia (1992), Lithuania (1992), Yugoslavia (1992), Russia (1993), Armenia (1995), Ukraine (1998), and Macedonia (1998). Since its 'invention' in Eastern Europe, the unlinked mixed system has been taken up by states as diverse as Japan, Taiwan, Cameroon, Guatemala, and others, making it the fastest-growing electoral system type in the world today.

A final distinctive feature of electoral system design in post-communist Europe is that a relatively high percentage of the electoral systems in the region are in some way constitutionally entrenched. The Czech, Georgian, Polish, and Slovenian electoral systems are designated in the constitutions of those states. In Slovenia even a national referendum in 1996 on the adoption of a majoritarian electoral law failed to dislodge the PR system, as the Constitutional Court held that the provisions of the Constitution took precedence over the popular will (see Matic, 2000). In Hungary the electoral system can only be changed by three-fifths majority. This constitutional entrenchment in part explains the relative stability of electoral systems in the region.[3]

Though this volume focuses on elections to lower or only houses of parliament, many of the states have other elected bodies at the national level. As will be argued in later chapters, the existence of such bodies can be expected to shape electoral patterns in lower chamber parliamentary elections in certain ways, by providing alternative incentive structures and conditioning institutions for voters and electoral contestants alike. Table 2.2 provides an overview of these other institutions and the methods employed to form them. As can be seen from a cursory glance at the data in this table, the proportional methods prevalent among electoral institutions at the lower chamber level are in some cases counterbalanced

Table 2.2   Additional national-level elected bodies

Country	Upper chamber	Directly elected president
Albania	No	Yes
Armenia	No	Yes
Bosnia and Herzegovina	House of the People, elected indirectly	Yes
Bulgaria	No	Yes
Croatia	House of the Counties, elected in 3-seat districts by PR	Yes
Czech Republic	Senate, elected by absolute majority in SMDs	No
Estonia	No	No
Georgia	No	Yes
Hungary	No	No
Latvia	No	No
Lithuania	No	Yes
Macedonia	No	Yes
Moldova	No	Yes*
Poland	Senate, elected by absolute majority in SMDs	Yes
Romania	Senate, elected by PR	Yes
Russia	Federation Council, elected according to varying procedures established in each of Russia's 89 regions	Yes
Slovakia	No	Yes**
Slovenia	State Council, elected indirectly	Yes
Ukraine	No	Yes
Yugoslavia	Chamber of the Republics, elected by PR	Yes

* The Moldovan president was directly elected during the period under consideration in this study. Following the parliamentary elections of 2000, Moldova switched to a parliamentary form of government.
** The Slovak president has been directly elected since 1999.

by majoritarian institutions elsewhere, either in the form of upper chambers elected via a majoritarian formula as in Poland and the Czech Republic, or, more commonly, by directly elected presidents (all states in the region except the Czech Republic, Estonia, Hungary, and Latvia). Also noteworthy is the fact that virtually all the directly elected presidents in the region are chosen by absolute majority in two rounds (if necessary), and that almost all these states also have prime ministers (they are thus semi-presidential systems, with the exception of Slovakia and Bulgaria, which are parliamentary systems in that the presidents, though directly elected, do not have executive powers).

The second main element of electoral system design to be considered in this investigation is campaign finance rules. Political finance is closely linked to the normative ideal of democracy; in as much as electoral competitors differ in their ability to raise funds, the 'level playing field' that is supposed to underlie democratic elections is tilted in favour of the rich. The distribution of state funds to electoral hopefuls is one way of potentially overcoming this problem. The laws that would establish systems of this type are enacted by those who stand to be most affected by them, and it should not surprise if reflexive legislation of this sort has outcomes that are skewed to the benefit of those who already command the greatest amount of political power.

Table 2.3 presents details of regulations relevant to campaign finance, including sources of state support, limits on campaign spending, and disclosure requirements. Some states provide parties with regular financing which may then be used to fund electoral campaigns. In other cases, funds are allocated only at the time of the election itself, typically with some built-in restrictions or threshold. This threshold is often retrospective, being based on the party's performance at the previous election; in other cases it is prospective, and parties' expenses are reimbursed by the state if they win a certain number of votes (or seats) in parliament. Elsewhere the state provides virtually no support. In general there has been extensive state funding of parties in Central Europe, and less provision in the former Soviet countries, where private finance (frequently alleged to be derived from murky sources) has been the rule.

Though public finance may have the effect of helping fledgling parties to establish themselves during the immediate post-transition years, it may limit the incentives parties face to strengthen their support. The provision of public funds may inhibit the formation of links between parties and distinct sectors of the electorate, which may be particularly problematic in the context of democratization where new parties are seeking to gain popular confidence. If parties are not obliged to appeal

Table 2.3   Details of party and campaign finance rules

Country	State financing of parties or electoral campaigns (lowest applicable vote share threshold)*	Limits in campaign spending	Finance disclosure requirements
Albania 1991	No	No	No
Albania 1992	Yes (3%)	No	No
Albania 1997	Yes (2%)	No	No
Albania 2001	Yes (2.5%)	No	No
Armenia 1995	N/A	N/A	N/A
Armenia 1999	No	Yes	Yes
Bosnia & H. 1996	No	No	No
Bosnia & H. 1998	No	No	No
Bosnia & H. 2000	No	Yes	Yes
Bosnia & H. 2002	No	Yes	Yes
Bulgaria 1990	Yes (4%)	Yes	Yes
Bulgaria 1991	Yes (4%)	Yes	Yes
Bulgaria 1994	Yes (4%)	Yes	Yes
Bulgaria 1997	Yes (4%)	Yes	Yes
Bulgaria 2001	Yes	Yes	Yes
Croatia 1992	Yes (SMD: 6%; list: 3%)	No	No
Croatia 1995	Yes (SMD: 5%; list: 5%)	No	Yes
Croatia 2000	Yes (5% of district vote)	No	No (pre-election intended expenditure only)
Czech Rep. 1990	Yes (2%)	No	No
Czech Rep. 1992	Yes (2%)	No	No
Czech Rep. 1996	Yes (3%)	No	Yes
Czech Rep. 1998	Yes (3%)	No	Yes
Czech Rep. 2002	Yes (1.5%)	No	Yes
Estonia 1992	No	No	Yes
Estonia 1995	No	No	Yes
Estonia 1999	No	No	Yes
Georgia 1992	N/A	N/A	N/A
Georgia 1995	N/A	N/A	N/A
Georgia 1999	Yes	Yes	Yes
Hungary 1990	Yes (1%)	No	Yes
Hungary 1994	Yes (1%)	No	Yes
Hungary 1998	Yes (1%)	Yes	Yes
Hungary 2002	Yes (1%)	Yes	Yes

Table 2.3   (Continued)

Country	State financing of parties or electoral campaigns (lowest applicable vote share threshold)*	Limits in campaign spending	Finance disclosure requirements
Latvia 1993	No	No	No
Latvia 1995	No	No	Yes
Latvia 1998	No	No	Yes
Latvia 2002	No	No	Yes
Lithuania 1992	Yes	Yes	Yes
Lithuania 1996	Yes	Yes	Yes
Lithuania 2000	Yes	Yes	Yes
Macedonia 1994	Yes (elected candidates)	No	No
Macedonia 1998	Yes (elected candidates)	Yes – for incumbents	Yes
Macedonia 2002	Yes (elected candidates)	Yes	Yes
Moldova 1994	Yes	No	Yes
Moldova 1998	Yes	No	Yes
Moldova 2001	Yes	No	Yes
Poland 1991	No	Yes	Yes
Poland 1993	Yes (5%)	No	Yes
Poland 1997	Yes (3%)	No	Yes
Poland 2001	Yes (3%)	Yes	Yes
Romania 1990	Yes	No	Yes
Romania 1992	No**	No	Yes
Romania 1996	Yes (2%)	Yes (annual income limit)	Yes
Romania 2000	Yes (2%)	Yes (annual income limit)	Yes
Russia 1993	Yes	Yes	Yes
Russia 1995	Yes	Yes	Yes
Russia 1999	Yes (SMD: 5%; list: 3%)	Yes	Yes
Slovakia 1990	Yes	No	No
Slovakia 1992	Yes	No	No
Slovakia 1994	Yes (3%)	No	No
Slovakia 1998	Yes (3%)	No	No
Slovakia 2002	Yes (3%)	No	No
Slovenia 1992	No	No	No
Slovenia 1996	Yes (2% nationally or 6% in one district)	Yes	Yes
Slovenia 2000	No	No	No

Table 2.3   (Continued)

Country	State financing of parties or electoral campaigns (lowest applicable vote share threshold)*	Limits in campaign spending	Finance disclosure requirements
Ukraine 1994	Yes	Yes	Yes
Ukraine 1998	Yes	No	Yes
Ukraine 2002	Yes	Yes	Yes
Yugoslavia 2000	Yes (in proportion to candidates elected)	No	No

* All the states in question provided at least some free media access to electoral contestants. The state financing noted here includes the provision of electoral campaign resources (in cash or kind) other than free media access.
** Though the electoral law made provision for state finance, the necessary enabling legislation was never passed and state funds were not distributed to electoral competitors (Roper, 2002:182–3).

to the electorate for contributions, they may never have the incentive to build firm support bases, but may rely instead on the flux of 'floating voters', with all the negative implications this has for party system stabilization and institutionalization. The relative importance of state finance in Central Europe has led some to describe the party systems in these states in terms of the 'cartel' model developed by Katz and Mair (1995). With qualifications, some scholars have seen these party systems to have been 'cartelized' from the outset, due to the heavy reliance of most major parties on state funds (Kopecky, 1995: 519; Lewis, 1998; Lewis, 2000: 107). Public funding makes parties less dependent on rich donors, but also less dependent for support on members of the voting public, and therefore less likely to cultivate the grass roots.[4] This dependency has further reinforced the élite nature of the party systems and weakened links with mass memberships, which tend to be low (Mair and van Biezen, 2001).

As can be seen from the data in Table 2.3, there is a great degree of variety across the region not only in the type of regulatory mechanisms imposed on campaign finance, but also the extent to which this area is regulated at all, from virtually no regulation in the first two Bosnian elections, to the Russian law of 1999 which devotes six articles and 60 sub-sections to electoral finance (a text stretching to nearly 8000 words). There is also variety in the types of activities that are regulated and the sorts of support provided by the state. In all of the post-communist countries the state provides free media time/space to electoral contestants. In 15 of 20 cases the state was by the end of the first decade after the transition providing some additional financial support to parties on a regular basis and/or at election time. This support was typically linked to a minimum vote share in parliamentary elections, and increased with increasing levels of electoral support (a 'proportional' rather than a 'flat' criterion of allocation (Katz, 1996: 130)). Interestingly, unlike with seat allocation thresholds, there have been no obvious increases in the electoral thresholds below which parties receive no support (or must refund the aid they are allocated). The threshold rose in the Czech Republic before being lowered in 2002 (as part of a complex series of changes in the party funding regime). In Albania the opposite was observed: the threshold fell in 1997 and was raised marginally in 2001. In Poland the funding cut-off was reduced from 5–3 per cent prior to the 1997 elections.

The regulation of private finance is the second key element in the regime governing the use of electoral campaign funds. In the Eastern European context, private finance has provided a mechanism whereby the newly established anti-communist parties can overcome the advantages retained by the communist successors. The parties of the former ruling élite may have lost the confidence of the bulk of the electorate in the immediate post-transition years, but they still had a distinct advantage in material and organizational terms, allowing them to mobilize the vote of many who became disillusioned with the socio-economic changes that occurred during the process of marketization. Though the communist successor parties were in virtually all cases stripped of other channels of access to state resources at the time of the transition, they retained extensive grass-roots networks, a pool of experienced activists on which to draw, and in many cases buildings and equipment that enabled them to launch relatively professional and well-coordinated campaigns, while the new parties often struggled to establish their presence outside the immediate social or geographic context from which they emerged. In this situation, private finance was the key to electoral success.

Under these circumstances, it is not surprising that private finance has everywhere been allowed. The differences among states pertain to the restrictions they impose on campaign spending and the disclosure of income. Far fewer states impose limits on electoral campaign spending.[5] By 2002 only just over half the cases in this dataset (11) capped the amount parties could spend to publicize themselves at election time. Most, however, require disclosure of campaign-related (or general) expenses, which is not surprising given that the parties are to a large extent funded by public money.

Campaign finance regulations differ from many other aspects of the electoral regime in that they are more difficult to institutionalize effectively. A seat allocation formula provides a counting rule that is transparent and relatively difficult to avoid implementing without resorting to outright fraud. The situation is entirely otherwise when it comes to regulations designed to govern how money is raised and spent during the course of an electoral campaign. Money is more difficult to trace than votes, and the electoral administration does not have direct control over campaign funds. Even in established democracies, leaders have been reluctant to create strict compliance procedures and there has been systematic underfunding of compliance bodies (Alexander, 1979; Paltiel, 1979; Castillo, 1989).

In post-communist Europe the success of implementation of campaign finance laws has been variable (Gel'man, 1998; Lewis, 2000: 110–12; Krasovec, 2001; Roper, 2002), and many states in the region have been wracked with party finance scandals. The access of ex-communist parties to state resources has been especially contentious (Lewis, 1998; 2000). Spending limits and disclosure requirements have often been flagrantly violated, and sanctions – where they exist – have frequently been ineffective. It is therefore unclear whether these regulations will have a significant impact on electoral outcomes. It does not make sense to ignore them entirely, however, because these sorts of formal rules may well serve to shape party strategies, even if they are not followed to the letter. The most we can say at this point is that the impact of campaign finance regulations is an empirical question that can only be resolved by means of empirical analysis.

The wave of campaign finance reforms that swept Western Europe and North America between the 1950s and the 1970s had a number of unexpected consequences, but Eastern European reformers could rely on a wide range of Western experience when it came to crafting their electoral finance regimes. This experience suggests that disclosure requirements on income and expenditure may be more effective means of controlling abuse than formal limits, because campaign expenditure is typically visible. Its primary purpose being publicity (and discounting outright bribery), it is often possible for the state (or investigative journalists) to spot when a party has spent more than it claims to have done. The parties therefore have an incentive to provide (relatively) accurate accounts of the money they have spent; it is then up to the voters to judge parties at least in part on the basis of where they have derived their money and how much they have spent. A lesson from the comparative literature is that spending limits tend to benefit incumbents, because they shift the relative weight of experience and publicity in favour of the former. Incumbent deputies and parties benefit from the exposure they get by being in office and the contact they have with the electorate during the normal course of their parliamentary duties. Newcomers are therefore at a significant disadvantage that can often only be overcome by spending money on campaign publicity. Thus while spending limits might appear at first glance to be an anti-élitist measure, they in fact benefit those who have been most successful in the past (Jacobson, 1979; Nassmacher, 1989).

Campaign finance regulation is a complex phenomenon whose effects often differ from the intentions of those who introduce them. During times of economic dislocation such as those experienced by the post-communist states of Central and Eastern Europe, the importance of these institutions is likely to be significant. Though there are certain common features to the regulatory structures put in place across the region, there are also sufficient differences to warrant close comparative analysis of their impact.

Changes in electoral system design in individual states

The 20 countries under consideration here can be divided into three broad categories; those that adopted PR early, those that adopted mixed systems and stuck with them, and those that shifted toward greater proportionality. Despite efforts to move back toward majoritarianism in countries such as Romania, Slovakia, the Czech Republic, Poland, Ukraine, Latvia, and Slovenia, no state has yet done so. Those that made an early transition to PR constitute a plurality of our 20 cases; they include the Central European states of Bosnia and Herzegovina, the Czech Republic and Slovakia, Poland, Romania, and Slovenia, as well as the ex-Soviet countries of Estonia, Latvia, and Moldova.

The Czech Republic   In 1990, Czechoslovakia was the first state in the region to make the move to full proportionality. This system has been retained in the Czech and Slovak republics, despite moves in each toward the reintroduction of majoritariansim. Between 1990 and 1998 elections for the Czech parliament were conducted in regional districts with an upper tier for remainder seats. Prior to the 2002 elections this system was altered so that there are 14 regional districts. A 5 per cent threshold for single parties has applied throughout the period, with a graduated structure of higher thresholds being in force since 1996.

Estonia   The 1990 elections were conducted under the single-transferable vote system in Estonia. This system was abandoned at the time of the first post-Soviet elections (1992) in favour of an unusual PR system (not dissimilar to that employed in Finland) in which citizens vote in 11 multi-member districts for single candidates (candidates being arranged on the ballot in party lists). A simple quotient is then calculated for success in each district, and the candidates that have individually achieved this quota are declared elected. The majority of seats are decided, however, at a second stage of seat allocation in a pooled upper tier, in which seats are distributed proportionally, with a 5 per cent threshold.

Latvia Following the retention of the Soviet the single-member absolute majority system for the 1990 republican elections, the Latvian electoral system has since 1993 been a system of regional proportional representation in which the 100 seats in the assembly are distributed among five districts. A 4 per cent national threshold applied to the 1993 elections; this was subsequently raised to 5 per cent for the 1998 contest.

Moldova Like Latvia, Moldova retained its single-member absolute majority electoral system for the Soviet republic elections of 1990. After that it adopted PR with a 4 per cent threshold, raised to 6 per cent for the 2001 elections. Due to difficulties holding elections in breakaway Transdnistria, a single electoral district has been employed since 1998 for the allocation of all 101 seats in the parliament.

Poland The semi-competitive Polish elections of 1989 that inaugurated the process of political change across Eastern Europe were conducted according to the communist-era single-member absolute majority electoral system. At the time of the next Sejm elections in 1991, a regional PR system was adopted, in which most parliamentary deputies were elected in 37 districts, and 69 from a national list. There was no threshold at either level, resulting in a highly fragmented parliament. Prior to the following election in 1993, a graduated threshold was introduced, 5 per cent for single parties and 8 per cent for coalitions. At the time of the 2001 elections, the national list was abolished, and PR employed in 41 regional districts.

Romania Romanian elections are perhaps the least institutionalized in the region – the 1990 elections were regulated by decree, and unlike all the other states considered here, Romania still had not as of 2002 introduced a permanent electoral commission. Nevertheless, the Romanian electoral system has undergone the least change. Elections have since 1990 been held in 42 regional districts with an upper tier for pooled remainder seats. A variable number of seats has been allocated through separate procedures to ethnic minorities. The most important change to have taken place over this period was the introduction of a 3 per cent national threshold in 1992, and its increase in 1996 to a graduated threshold starting at 5 per cent for individual parties.

Slovakia   As in the Czech Republic, elections to the Slovak National Council were held between 1990 and 1994 in four regional districts, with a 3 per cent national threshold in force in 1990, raised to a sliding scale starting at 5 per cent for the 1992 elections. A single nationwide district was introduced prior to the 1998 polls, and this was retained for the 2002 elections.

Slovenia   Slovenian elections have since the 1990 republican elections been held under proportional electoral system in eight regional districts with a pooled tier for remainder seats. A threshold of 2.5 per cent, introduced for the 1990 elections, was abolished prior to the 1992 contest, but a 4 per cent threshold was reintroduced by constitutional amendment prior to the 2000 race. An unusual feature of the Slovenian electoral system is that parties are obliged to allocate members of their lists to 'units' within the eight multi-seat districts. Though these sub-district units have no relevance for the allocation of seats among parties, they are important in voting, as voters vote for individual candidates who have been allocated to their territorial 'unit'. A further two seats are filled by representatives of minority groups through separate processes.

Bosnia and Herzegovina   Following the Dayton Accords of 1995 that ended the war in Bosnia and Herzegovina, elections were run by the Organization for Security and Co-operation in Europe (OSCE). Over the course of the following six years, electoral management was gradually handed over to national (Bosnian) administrators, such that by 2002 the OSCE had largely withdrawn from direct involvement in the process. Elections to the 42 seats of the lower house of the parliament of Bosnia and Herzegovina were conducted in 1996 and 1998 by proportional representation in two districts corresponding to the two territorial 'entities' that make up the post-Dayton state: the Republika Srpska and the Federation of Bosnia and Herzegovina. From the year 2000, eight regional districts were created together with an upper tier of 12 compensatory seats. Preferential voting was also introduced at this point. The Bosnian electoral system is unusual in not employing a formal threshold, though the small size of the chamber has a limiting effect on the number of parties that can win seats.

Hungary, Georgia, Lithuania, Russia, and Armenia adopted mixed systems early on and have stuck with them.

Hungary   The Hungarian electoral system is notorious for being the most complex system in the world. It is a two-vote mixed system in three tiers. The bottom tier consists of 176 single-member district seats elected by absolute majority in two rounds. In addition to an SMD vote, the voter also votes for a regional list (in one of the 20 regional districts). The list seats are distributed according to a complex semi-compensatory two-tier formula, with a national threshold (4 per cent in 1990, 5 per cent ther after).

Georgia Georgia was the second country after Bulgaria to adopt an unlinked mixed system. Following the postponement of the republic elections initially scheduled for March 1990, the electoral law was redrafted and elections were conducted in October under a mixed system. The basic outline of this system was retained for the first post-independence elections in 1992. The 1992 law prescribed a multilayered seat allocation procedure. Of the 235 seats, 84 were elected by absolute majority in single-member districts. A further 150 seats were elected by proportional representation from 10 regional districts, with an upper tier for pooled remainder seats. On the PR ballot, each voter was allowed to rank order up to three parties (by selecting individual candidates from party lists). The seats were then distributed among parties by means of a quota system based on a complex weighting procedure for first, second, and third preference votes. Finally, the chairman of the parliament was directly elected from a single nationwide district. This system was simplified somewhat prior to the 1995 elections: the PR seats were henceforth elected via a more conventional one-vote mechanism (still in ten districts), and subject to a 5 per cent threshold. At the same time the majority requirement for the single-member districts was lowered from 50 to 33 per cent. In 1999 a single PR district replaced the ten regional ones, and the threshold was raised to 7 per cent (the highest in the post-communist world).

Lithuania Lithuania retained the Soviet absolute majority system for its republic elections of 1990 (which were conducted on a competitive semi-partisan basis). Since 1992, 71 of the seats in Lithuania's 141-seat parliament have been elected in single-member districts, by absolute majority in 1992 and 1996, by plurality in 2000. The remaining 70 seats are elected from nationwide lists by PR with a threshold of 4 per cent in 1992, raised to 5 per cent in 1996.

Russia Russia's mixed electoral system was developed during the turbulent days of the 1993 conflict between President Boris Yeltsin and the Russian Duma (parliament), which resulted in the forcible dissolution of the latter. Despite its origins, the system has survived more or less unchanged. Half of the 450 seats in the Duma are elected by plurality in SMDs, and half by PR from nationwide lists with a 5 per cent threshold.

Armenia   The Armenian republic elections of 1990 were held under a SMD absolute majority law. Prior to the 1995 elections, a mixed system was introduced according to which 40 of the 190 seats in the parliament were elected via PR with a 5 per cent threshold, and elections to the remaining 150 seats were governed by a plurality rule in SMDs. In 1999 the size of the parliament was reduced to 131 seats, 56 elected through PR and 75 in SMDs.

Those states that moved toward greater proportionality at a later stage included three that employed SMD absolute majority electoral systems for their first post-communist elections and subsequently adopted mixed systems: Albania, Macedonia, and Ukraine. Of these, Macedonia has since made a further move to full proportionality.

Albania   Albania retained its communist-era single-member absolute majority electoral system for the elections of 1991, before moving to a two-vote mixed compensatory system in 1992. According to this system, 40 of the 140 seats in parliament were filled via PR according to the SMD vote choices, with a 4 per cent threshold. This system was retained – though with various changes in the relative weight of the two components of the system – for the elections of 1996 and 1997. The threshold was decreased in 1997 to 2 per cent. Prior to the elections of 2001, a two-vote compensatory system was introduced with a 2.5 per cent threshold.

Macedonia   Macedonia retained its communist-era single-member absolute majority electoral system for both the republican elections of 1990 and the first post-independence elections of 1994. For the elections of 1998, 35 of the 120 seats in the parliament were elected by PR, and the remainder by absolute majority in SMDs. A period of ethnic unrest shook Macedonia in the spring and summer of 2001. The conflict was eventually resolved in an agreement reached at Ohrid in 2001. The Ohrid accords included, among other things, the provision for a fully proportional electoral system, which had been one of the ethnic Albanian side's main demands during the conflict. The elections of 2002 were thus conducted under regional PR in six electoral districts of 20 seats each, with no threshold.

Ukraine   Ukraine retained its Soviet-era single-member absolute majority electoral system with few changes through its first post-independence elections in 1994. Prior to the 1998 elections it adopted a system similar in most respects to that of Russia, with 225 seats filled in single-member districts by plurality, and the remaining 225 filled through a nationwide list. The main difference between the Russian and the Ukrainian systems was that the threshold in the latter was set at 4 per cent rather than 5 per cent.

Bulgaria, Croatia, and Yugoslavia started with mixed systems and subsequently moved to full PR.

Bulgaria   Bulgaria was the first state to adopt a mixed parallel system, and also the first to abandon this principle. The mixed system was employed only once, at the time of the Constituent Assembly elections of 1990 (and it in fact remains the legal electoral system for any future constituent assembly elections). In addition to writing a new constitution for Bulgaria, this body also functioned as a parliament, but opted for future parliamentary elections to be held under PR rules. One of the peculiarities of the Bulgarian electoral system is that although the country is divided up into 31 districts, this division is only relevant in as far as it is used to determine which members of given lists are elected; the allocation of seats among parties is conducted at the national level, with a threshold of 4 per cent.

Croatia   Like Macedonia, Croatia employed a single-member absolute majority electoral system for the republic election of 1990, before moving to a mixed system for the 1992 and 1995 elections. Though the relative proportion of seats filled by the two components of the system was altered, the 1992 and 1995 electoral systems were both parallel systems in which the single-member seats were filled by absolute majority; the nationwide PR district employed a threshold of 3 per cent in 1992 and 5 per cent in 1995. Prior to the 2000 election, Croatia adopted a fully proportional electoral system in 10 regional districts, each of which elects 14 members. Since 1992 there have been, in addition, seats reserved for ethnic minorities and also for members of the Croatian diaspora.

Yugoslavia   In 1992 the rump Yugoslav state – comprised of Serbia and Montenegro – adopted a mixed electoral system for the elections of that year. This system was subsequently abandoned in favour of regional PR, which was retained through 2000 with several revisions in district size. A 5 per cent district-level threshold was also introduced for the first PR elections in 1993.

On the measurement of electoral systems

Most of the measures used to operationalize the concepts employed in this study are straightforward. Nevertheless, there are some choices of indicator that require elaboration. The variables in question can be divided for the sake of analysis into independent and dependent categories.

Independent variables

The common division of electoral systems into single-member district, proportional representation and mixed systems will guide the investigation, though in most of the statistical analyses it will make sense to use the more nuanced measure of the proportion of PR seats in the system. In some cases explanatory leverage can be gained by establishing separate categories for the three types of system. This is because mixed systems are in certain respects 'more than the sum of their parts'. Mixed electoral systems, in which each voter is represented in the assembly by two representatives elected through different mechanisms, are a heterogeneous category. Virtually all of them employ some combination of single-member plurality/majority and proportional representation, but there are substantial variations in the details of the separate parts and also in the way in which they are combined. Many scholars are for this reason unwilling to classify mixed systems as a distinct type. Lijphart (1994), Cox (1997), and Katz (1997) place them in the category of multi-tier or multi-stage systems alongside PR formulae with upper tiers for pooled remainder votes.[6] But from the point of view of party and voter strategies, this is only a satisfactory classification if voters have one vote and the distribution of second-tier seats is calculated according to the proportional distribution of votes for SMD candidates. Where voters have two votes, mixed systems establish fundamentally different incentive structures for both voters and candidates. For this reason it will in some cases be useful to consider mixed systems as a distinctive type.

More fine-grained indicators for electoral system type will be avoided partly because of the endogeneity problems discussed above, and partly due to the difficulty associated with 'transporting' some of the most common measures from the study of established democracies to the democratizing context. This is true, for example, with the 'effective threshold' measure developed by Arend Lijphart (1994; and related to Taagepera and Shugart's (1989) 'effective magnitude'). The difficulty with this measure in the post-communist context is that it requires rather arbitrary assumptions about typical patterns of electoral outcomes in SMD electoral systems, especially those of the plurality variety. In single-member systems the threshold works at the district level; when this is translated into a national-level constraint, the threshold in a SMD governed by absolute majority rule is $.5/N$, where N is the number of seats in the parliament. In a system governed by plurality the threshold is smaller still. Yet in practice effective thresholds in plurality and majority systems tends to be higher, due to the similarities of electoral patterns across districts. Though there is no logical reason why this must be so, Cox has demonstrated that in established democracies we do observe a fair degree of consistency in electoral outcomes across districts (Cox, 1997). It is for this reason that Lijphart is able to estimate notional thresholds for absolute majority and plurality systems respectively. But this move relies on assumptions that are not met in all post-communist systems. Candidates in Russian and Ukrainian elections have managed to win seats on less than 10 per cent of the district vote. This means that elections in single-member districts can be won on miniscule percentages of the national vote. For example, the Common Cause movement in Russia won a seat in 1995 on the basis of only 0.24 per cent of the national vote, and this was not an isolated case; nine of the 21 parties that won single-member seats in this election won them on less than 1 per cent of the national vote. This suggests that the plurality systems operative in these states impose a highly variable national threshold (though in the Central European states the effective threshold may be closer to the norm in established democracies). Under these conditions it is not possible to assume any particular threshold, and therefore using the 'effective threshold' as a common measure across both list PR and SMD systems makes little sense. The two systems operate according to different principles and their constraints must be differently conceptualized.

Dependent variables

There is often held to be a trade-off between efficiency and representation. The two variables that are most frequently linked with these constructs are the effective number of parties (the assumption being that when there are too many parties the system is not efficient) and proportionality. Whatever we may think of this trade-off, it is worth examining the tools we use to measure these two aspects of electoral systems. Two of the most common ways of gauging the relationship between electoral systems and their outcomes is to examine deviation from proportionality between vote and seat shares and the 'effective number of parties'. These concepts will be discussed in turn, together with possible alternatives.

There has been considerable debate as to the adequacy of different measures of proportionality and disproportionality (a debate which has produced a variety of measures; see Lijphart, 1994 for an overview and discussion of their respective merits), yet there has been little examination of the assumptions behind the concept itself. Deviation from proportionality may be thought to be of intrinsic interest to democrats, as a proportionate outcome might be held to be in itself fair and representative. But the logic behind this argument is conditional on the assumption that parties are coherent entities with links to distinct sectors of the population; 'fairness to parties' can only have meaning if it is linked to 'fairness to voters', who are surely the real subjects of equality in a democracy. If, for example, a group of politicians form a successful electoral alliance but then go separate ways once they are elected to parliament, the concept of 'fairness to parties' loses its meaning. In as much as this is a common occurrence in states with emergent party systems, one should be wary of assuming that proportionality is necessarily relevant to the quality of representation or that it carries the same meaning in all contexts.

A more general objection to the concept of proportionality is that, even in those contexts where it could arguably be held to be meaningful from a normative point of view, it is still not clear how it can be accurately measured, and it is unlikely that any of the measures currently employed get at what we really want to know. If one is interested in the relationship between popular preferences and electoral outcomes, one must be able to measure popular preferences. All existing measures of proportionality take vote choice as a proxy for popular preferences, but inasmuch as voters vote strategically, the preferences they express at the ballot box will deviate from their 'real' preferences in ways that co-vary systematically with electoral system type. The standard indicators based on expressed preferences will most likely be downwardly biased, and extent of bias will depend on the degree to which the electoral system in question encourages tactical voting. Given that it is impossible to disentangle the 'mechanical' and the 'psychological' components of any given measure of (dis)proportionality, the concept is of limited interpretive value.

A final objection to the concept of proportionality relates not to the difficulties involved in measuring or interpreting it, but to the assumption it implies as to the exogeneity of preference formation. There are a number of reasons to believe that 'what people want' might be a function of the electoral system itself. We conventionally assume that people want their chosen party to win as many seats as possible. Yet it is unlikely that this will be true across all electoral system and party system types. In states with weak or heavily personalized party systems (especially where people vote for individuals in SMDs), the outcome desired by voters may simply be that a given individual is elected, regardless of the partisan composition of parliament. At the other extreme, in a two-party system with strong party discipline, vote choice may be conditioned mainly by considerations of which party will be in a position to form a government (voters will be 'office-maximizers', not 'seat-maximizers'). The implicit object of the vote is thus not exogenous to the electoral system or to the party system that is shaped by that electoral system. For all these reasons, the proportionality of seat shares to vote shares is an unsatisfactory means of gauging the impact of electoral systems on the quality of representation.

In all systems it can be assumed that if people vote, they want to be represented. A more satisfactory measure of the degree to which electoral systems deliver representation is therefore the simple proportion of the vote that contributes to the election of members of parliament. This measure is both more conceptually coherent than deviation from proportionality and more closely tied to the concerns of the present investigation.

The second commonly used measure of electoral system effects is the 'effective number of parties' (Laakso and Taagepera, 1979). One of the most important ways in which electoral laws are held to influence political outcomes is through the effect they have on the size of the party system. Duverger's famous 'law' holds that plurality electoral systems tend to constrain the party system to a two-party format. Duverger also hypothesized that proportional representation systems allow political parties to proliferate, resulting in multi-party systems (Duverger, 1959; Riker, 1982). The substantive political impact of this relationship is generally held to be that two-party systems enable single-party government, whereas multi-party systems necessitate coalitions. Given that the structure of parliament has been of significant concern in the post-communist context, the size of party systems is a useful measure. However, the absolute number of parties can be expected to be a relatively poor indicator of the 'real' party system size, because large parties are accorded the same weight as minor organizations that receive very little support. It is therefore preferable to have a measure of the number of parties that 'count'. Such a measure is provided by the effective number of parties, which has two variants, the effective number of elective parties and the effective number of parliamentary parties. The effective number of elective parties is calculated as the inverse of the sum of squares of the proportional vote share of each party, whereas the effective number of parties employs the same calculation but substitutes the proportional seat shares. This measure will be useful in the analyses that follow in Chapter 5 but a number of problems specific to the post-communist context remain.

In the post-communist states counting parties in any manner raises thorny issues. It is not always clear what constitutes a 'party'. For the purposes of this analysis, however, 'parties' will be deemed to be the objects of vote choice. If a political grouping is listed separately (at least as one component) on the ballot, then it will be counted as a 'party'. This makes sense if we are interested in the strategic considerations that influence the choice over political options, and it also makes sense inasmuch as we are interested in the ways in which the 'goods' of elections – campaign funds and seats – are distributed. The problem with the effective number of parties is that, though it gives a good indication of the overall size of the party configuration generated by an election, it tells us less about the 'shape' of that system. An example will help to illustrate this point: the effective number of parliamentary parties in the Romanian elections of 1990 was 2.20, very similar to the figure of 2.21, which obtained in the Hungarian election of 2002 (see Table 5.2). Yet the distribution of support differed considerably in the two cases; the National Salvation Front won 66.41 per cent of the 1990 vote in Romania, with the remainder divided among a string of small parties, none of which won more than 7.32 per cent. In Hungary, on the other hand, the two largest parties in 2002 were more or less evenly balanced, Fidesz–MMP winning 48.70 per cent of the seats and the Hungarian Socialist Party gaining 46.11. The substantive interpretation of the two party configurations is clearly quite different; in Romania a single party won two-thirds of the seats in parliament, resulting in a dominant party system, whereas in Hungary no party was able to form a majority on its own, yet the party system was more clearly of the two-party type suggested by the figure of 2.21.

It is thus useful to have information not only about the 'size' of the party system, but also about its 'shape'. For this reason, the effective number of parties will be supplemented in the analyses that follow by the seat share of the largest party, as well as the difference between the seat share of the largest party and that of the second largest. In this way it will be possible to assess the extent of single-party dominance, as well as the degree of balance in the party system.

A note on the statistical methods used in this book

Every effort has been made to ensure that the main arguments presented in this study are comprehensible to a wide audience. In many cases it is possible to provide compelling evidence for hypothesized relationships by means of tables of numbers or percentages. But great gains in precision and confidence can be made through the use of multivariate statistical analysis. Multivariate analysis also makes it possible to appreciate the ways in which different factors interact as they impact on the phenomena under investigation.

The data we will be examining include statistics from 69 elections in our set of 20 states. In some contexts we will examine trends over time by means of cross-sectional analyses, comparing the impact of a given effect in the first post-communist election in each country with its impact in the second, third, or subsequent elections. Mostly we will be interested in examining overall differences across countries by taking averages across time for each country and comparing these averages (the so-called 'between transformation' on pooled data). Though the data have a quasi-pooled format, pooling for the sake of increasing the number of cases is not a suitable option for the purposes of this study. Not only is the number of time periods too short for most conventional methods of analysing pooled data to be useful, but also the relatively restricted number of cases precludes the use of necessary controls for unit effects (due to a shortage of degrees of freedom). The upshot of this is that most of the analyses presented here will be based on approximately 20 cases. The usual caveats that apply to moderately small N investigations are therefore worth bearing in mind: not all existing relationships may be brought to light through multivariate analysis, and the findings of this study will be strengthened by confirmation on larger datasets.

Part II
Electoral Systems and Voters

3
Electoral Participation

The aggregation of electoral preferences begins with the act of voting; the decision whether or not to vote thus makes a logical starting point for the analysis of the impact of electoral institutions on political outcomes. Before delving into the empirical evaluation of electoral participation, it is worthwhile pausing to consider the normative interpretation of aggregate voting levels. Electoral participation is generally understood as being relevant to the study of democracy and democratization for two principal reasons. First, voting is often seen as an indicator of the strength of democracy in that it provides a gauge of the extent to which the citizenry is actively involved in representative politics. In this sense electoral participation may be seen as one of the most readily measurable indices of the propensity of citizens to include themselves in the political life. If democracy is a matter of rule of the people, the more people who participate in a political system, the more democratic it may be held to be (provided that participation has a meaningful impact on democratic outcomes). In this sense a high level of mass participation can be seen as a necessary – if not sufficient – condition for full democracy. Even if democracy is understood, following Schumpeter, only in terms of holding rulers to account, mass participation by different groups in society can be seen as a necessary check on the exercise of power. It is for this reason that most composite indices of democracy include the level of electoral participation as one of their components (Inkeles, 1991), and there is a consensus in most normative democratic theory on the importance of maintaining widespread participation if the health of democracy is not to suffer; the *quantity* of electoral participation is seen as an integral aspect of the *quality* of democracy, as well as being a convenient proxy (Powell, 1982; Lijphart, 1999: 284–6). Thus electoral participation has a direct normative relationship to democracy.

Participation may be especially important in the context of democratization when a new political order is struggling to legitimize itself, as very low voting rates may prevent democracy from becoming consolidated. If citizens opt not to vote, they will be incompletely socialized into politics, and they may choose other forms of protest that are less democratic. Lack of electoral participation and widespread 'alternative' participation can be expected to be destabilizing and potentially debilitating for a new democracy.

This chapter will examine patterns in electoral participation in the post-communist setting. The main goal will be threefold: to determine the extent to which these patterns are conditioned by the design of electoral institutions, to ascertain which aspects of electoral systems have the greatest impact on turnout, and to discover how important institutional factors are in comparison to other determinants of rates of participation. First it is necessary to set the scene for the examination of institutional effects by examining general patterns in rates of participation over time and across states in the region.

Trends in electoral participation in post-communist Europe

There are in theory three ways in which popular participation in political decision-making could be undermined: by restricting the suffrage, by restricting the impact of elections, and by 'self-exclusion' on the part of voters. The first and most obvious way to prevent people from participating in democratic politics is to limit the suffrage to a small sector of the electorate, or indeed to do away with elections altogether and employ an alternative method for choosing leaders. The advent of representative democracy as we understand it today was closely linked to the introduction of universal manhood suffrage at the turn of the last century, and franchise reform was the terrain on which battles over electoral institution design were fought during this so-called 'first wave' of democratization. By contrast, suffrage limitations did *not* characterize developed state socialism in Central and Eastern Europe. The Soviet Union practised universal suffrage from the 1930s onward, and the post-war communist states all prided themselves on their extremely high levels of electoral inclusion (though Yugoslavia held indirect national elections after 1974).

Not only did virtually everyone on the electoral rolls of most communist states vote, but strenuous efforts were also made to enable voters to exercise their franchise wherever they might be. Mobile ballot boxes were transported to the infirm, polling stations were set up on ships and trains, and liberal use was made in many states of district transfer to accommodate voters who planned to be away on voting day. Though the latter mechanism was often employed by voters to remove themselves from the electoral process altogether (as their names would be taken off their home register when they applied for a 'certificate to vote' away from home, but they would not be added to any other register), the lengths gone to by the communist states to ensure near universal participation was testimony to these states' ability to mobilize their populations.[1]

From the socialist perspective such mobilization was indicative of the high level of democracy in the Eastern European regimes. Yet Western theorists tended to see in full mobilization the definition of totalitarianism. This is because electoral participation does not in and of itself entail democracy; it is only a democratic tool when the elections involve real choice and when the body elected has real power. Thus in contradistinction to the first wave of democratization, the third wave democratizations in Eastern Europe involved removing restrictions on the political impact of the electoral process. Voters voted under communism, but the choices they made were limited. Even when they did have a selection of candidates – as in Poland and Hungary – those options were generally not truly political in character, and the bodies elected exercised a limited policy-making role (Furtak, 1990). Overturning this system involved not fighting for the vote as such, but fighting for the vote to be meaningful. At the same time, it involved fighting for people to be able to exercise the option of not voting. Though compulsory voting was not formalized in any of the communist states, the considerable pressure put on citizens to perform their electoral duty amounted to coercive force which was in most cases more efficacious than compulsory voting. It is therefore not surprising that democratization should have been accompanied by substantial reductions in numeric levels of electoral participation at the same time as it involved dramatic increases in the meaningfulness of that act.

There are also more general reasons to expect a fall in turnout following transition. Some students of democratization have found that turnout in elections held directly after a regime change tends to be unusually high (O'Donnell and Schmitter, 1986; Turner, 1993), though analysis on a large number of cases has shown that participation in 'founding' elections is just as likely to be especially low (IDEA, 1997: 26). The longer term rates of turnout in democratizing countries tend to be rather lower than those in established democracies, probably due to lower degrees of party identification and a lack of a habit of voting in competitive multiparty elections (IDEA, 2002; Norris, 2002). It takes time for successive generations of voters to be socialized into voting in democratic elections.

Nevertheless, the situation in post-communist states differs in some respects from that witnessed in other democratizing contexts, due to the peculiar circumstances of communism and the events which followed its collapse. Commenting on the 1989 elections to the Soviet Congress of People's Deputies, a group of Soviet geographers remarked that '[In Western democracies] the proportion of the electorate which takes part in elections is the traditional indicator of the level of social activity [of the citizenry]. Here the reverse is true. The more active the population of a region, the lower the degree of participation of electors in elections and the higher the level of absenteeism' (Berezkin *et al.*, 1989: 618; cf. Berezkin *et al.*, 1990: 107). Likewise, Soviet-era research found that non-voting in the USSR was associated with levels of political interest similar to those of voters in Western countries; non-voting was also correlated with critical attitudes toward the regime (Friedgut, 1979: 113; Karklins, 1986; cf. Brunner, 1990: 38). Voters were an older, more feminized, less educated, and more blue-collar section of the voting-age population (Karklins, 1986: 455–7); in other words, the Western patterns of involvement were reversed under communism: voters closely resembled those found to be *least* critical of the regime and those *least* involved in other forms of political activity. Voting was a sign of political acquiescence, not activism. This helps to explain why there was a decline in levels of electoral participation when the coercive forces were relaxed and eventually removed.

As noted above, the right to vote in meaningful elections also implied the right not to vote, and after the collapse of communism, many citizens chose to exercise the latter right rather than the former. In some cases rising abstention rates have been attributed to disenchantment with the new order due to lingering remnants of the old political style (McGrath, 1995), but the phenomenon of falling turnout is universal enough even among those post-communist publics that are relatively satisfied with their new democratic systems to suggest that it is an effect of decommunization itself. In the mid-1990s, Poles appear to have been among the most satisfied with the new regime in their country (Rose *et al.*, 1998: 106), yet it is in Poland that turnout figures have been the lowest.

Turnout in the 'founding' elections ranged from a high of 98.92 per cent in Albania, where the elections of 1991 retained some 'communist' features (Szajkowski, 1992; Loloci, 1994), to a low of 54.32 per cent in the turbulent Russian elections of 1993, following President Yeltsin's forcible dissolution of the parliament. The degree of subsequent change has been nothing short of dramatic. Average turnout across the region declined 29.79 per cent between the last pre-transition election and the most recent elections at the close of 2002 (see Table 3.1 for details of trends in individual states). Yet it is clear from the data presented in Table 3.1 that this decline was not uniform, and what concerns us in the present chapter is the factors that have led to turnout being lower in some states than in others.

Table 3.1 provides turnout figures for each of the 20 post-communist states, starting with the last national-level election during the communist period. The figures displayed are total vote (including invalid votes) as a proportion of the registered electorate.[2] After a dozen years of electoral competition, average turnout in the Central and Eastern European states considered here was, at 63.72, slightly below the 75.8 per cent average in 15 Western European states in the mid-1990s.[3] Turnout fell in almost all cases between the first and second post-communist parliamentary elections (the exceptions being Estonia, Hungary, Poland and Russia). The average decline was 6.34 per cent, followed by a further drop of 3.67 per cent between the second and third electoral events. Beyond that the picture is less clear, because only about half the states in our sample have held fourth elections and only three states have held five parliamentary polls since the transition. Nevertheless, the data available indicate that the decrease in participation rates has continued in most cases, and even states where turnout had appeared to level off or rise after the second or third election experienced further declines down the road (e.g. Albania, the Czech Republic, Romania). The pattern of continuous decline from election to election is observed in eleven of the 20 states under investigation. In other cases steep initial declines were followed by apparently random fluctuation at a lower level (Poland, Slovakia, possibly Croatia, Lithuania, and Russia), whereas in Bulgaria a gradual decline was followed by a considerable rise in the 2001 parliamentary elections. Only in Hungary did the last election in this series (2002) have a higher rate of electoral participation than the first.

A final noteworthy feature of Table 3.1 is the exceptionally low figures for Poland. Poland was the only case in which turnout did not approach universality during the late communist period; only about four in five voters came to the polls in the elections of 1985. The reasons for the unusually low turnout in Poland undoubtedly have to do with the lesser degree of communist penetration into Polish society and the higher level of ongoing protest this allowed. The wave of dissent that eventually brought down communist rule began in Poland as early as 1981

Table 3.1 Turnout in parliamentary elections (%)

Year	Albania	Armenia	Bosnia & Herzegovina	Bulgaria	Croatia	Czech Rep.	Estonia
1985		~99	N/A		~95		~99
1986						99.39*	
1987	~99			99.92			
1988							
1989		71.9					87.1
1990		60.4	80	90.79	84.47	96.79	78.2
1991	98.92			83.87			
1992	91.50				75.61	85.08	67.84
1993							
1994				75.23			
1995		56.00			68.80		68.91
1996	(89.08)		82.62			76.29	
1997	72.56			58.87			
1998			70.0			73.86	
1999		51.72					57.43
2000			64.4		69.30		
2001	52.98			66.77			
2002			55.44			58.00	
Average for post-communist elections (bold)	81.00	53.86	68.12	75.10	71.24	78.00	64.73
Decline since the last communist-era elections	47.01	8.68	24.56	33.15	25.7	41.39	42.47

Year	Georgia	Hungary	Latvia	Lithuania	Macedonia	Moldova	Poland
1985	~99	93.9	~99	~99		~99	78.86
1986					~90		
1987							
1988							
1989	97.0		86.9	82.5		90.5	62.11
1990	N/A	65.09	81.3	71.72	77.15	83.4	
1991							43.20
1992	74.77			75.29			
1993			91.18				52.08
1994		68.92			77.29	79.31	
1995	68.18		72.65				
1996					52.92		
1997							47.93
1998		56.26	71.99		72.88	69.12	
1999	67.60						
2000				58.63			
2001						67.52	46.18
2002		70.52	72.49		71.86		
Average for post-communist elections (bold)	70.18	65.20	78.28	62.28	75.09	71.98	47.35

Table 3.1 (Continued)

Year	Albania	Armenia	Bosnia & Herzegovina	Bulgaria	Croatia	Czech Rep.	Estonia
Decline since the last communist-era elections	N/A	23.38	27.91	41.27	~17	32.38	32.68

Year	Romania	Russia	Slovakia	Slovenia	Ukraine	Yugoslavia
1985	99.9	~99			~99	
1986			99.39*	~90		N/A
1987						
1988						
1989		87.0			93.4	
1990	86.19	77.0	95.41	83.50	84.7	71.5 (Serbia) 75.76 (Monte negro)
1991						
1992	76.29		84.21	85.90		(67.6 (Dec.))
1993		54.32				
1994			75.65		75.81	
1995		64.37				
1996	76.01			73.67		(60.69)
1997						
1998			84.15		70.78	
1999		61.68				
2000	65.31			70.36		71.29
2001						
2002			70.06		69.26	
Average for post-communist elections (bold)	75.95	60.12	84.86	76.64	71.95	66.60
Decline since the last communist-era elections	34.59	38.22	15.24	~20	30.64	N/A

* For Czechoslovakia as a whole

Notes

(1) Figures in bold are those included in the statistical analyses and reported in the text.
(2) All figures are percentages of the total vote (including invalid votes). In mixed systems there are sometimes two reported figures for turnout, one for participation in the single-member district voting and one for participation in the list voting. The difference between the two is in all cases very slight, and it is highly unlikely that any substantively interesting political significance can be attached to these differences. In cases where two different numbers are reported in official results, they have been averaged to produce the figures reported here.
(3) Pre-1993 figures for the Czech Republic and Slovakia represent turnout in the Czech Lands and Slovakia respectively in elections for the Chamber of the People in the Federal Assembly.
(4) 1989 figures in brackets for Armenia, Estonia, Georgia, Latvia, Lithuania, Moldova, Russia, and Ukraine represent turnout in those republics in the elections to the all-Union Congress of People's Deputies.

Sources: In addition to the sources listed in Appendix B; the following were consulted: Bosnia and Herzegovina, 1990: Burg and Shoup, 1999: 51; Hungary pre-1990: Barany, 1990: 81; Poland pre-1990: Raina, 1990: 107; Yugoslav republics pre-1990: Höpken, 1990; USSR republics, 1989: *Izvestiya* 5 April 1989, p. 1; Moldova, Russia, and Ukraine, 1990: Slider, 1990; Estonia, Latvia, and Lithuania, 1990: Taagepera, 1990; *Chronicle of Parliamentary Elections and Developments*, 19 (1984–85) and 20 (1985–86).

with the formation of the Solidarity trade union, which was linked to support for electoral abstention (Raina, 1990). What is interesting from the post-communist perspective is that these communist-era trends have persisted and even been magnified since 1989, making Poland the only state in the region that has regularly experienced turnout levels below the fifty per cent mark (the turnout of 52.08 in 1993 being an exception).[4] As will be seen below, Polish exceptionalism cannot be accounted for by the other institutional, political, or socio-economic factors that shape turnout in the region and must be treated as a distinct historical factor (much in the same way as the exceptionally low turnout in the United States and Switzerland are generally held to be accounted for by idiosyncratic factors). But once we control for the lower communist-era turnout, the Polish figures lose their distinctiveness; the average decline between the last post-communist elections and the most recent elections (as of 2002) was 32.68 per cent in Poland – only slightly more than the 29.79 regional average.

One of the most striking findings to emerge from studies of turnout in established democracies is that there is far more variation in turnout levels among states than between them (Crewe, 1981: 238–9; Franklin, 1996: 218). This is true in two senses; it is true in that aggregate state turnout levels are determined to a far greater extent by country-level than by individual-level factors (Franklin, 1996), and also in that turnout varies far more across states at any one point of time than within a given state at successive points of time. In our Central and Eastern European states there have been variations over time due to the specific features of the post-communist transition and adjustment-related processes. Yet the standard deviations in average turnout across countries fell somewhat following the first elections, suggesting that transition-related factors loomed larger at the outset, whereas the features common to the post-communist context led turnout to converge somewhat in subsequent parliamentary contests (see Table 3.2).

It is clear from the foregoing discussion that the most prominent feature of these data is the gradual drop in turnout over time. The first or 'founding' parliamentary elections were accompanied by generally high rates of electoral participation, averaging 77.18 per cent. What accounts for this fall? We would expect some decline following dramatic electoral events such as transitional 'founding' elections, but the overall pattern of steady decrease suggests an alternative interpretation. One might be tempted to point to the similar drops experienced in Western Europe during the 1990s and to formulate an answer in terms of general trends in democratic countries, but the falls in electoral participation are far

Table 3.2 Average turnout by election

Election	N	Average turnout	Average change in turnout since previous election	Standard deviation in turnout across countries
First election	20	77.18		14.81
Second election	19	70.84	−6.34	10.87
Third election	18	67.17	−3.67	7.96
Fourth election	9	64.42	−2.75	12.03
Fifth election	3	64.94	0.52	6.23
All elections		70.63		12.20

Source: See Table 3.1.

steeper and more universal in the East than in the West. The answer must lie elsewhere.

Electoral system design and electoral participation

The factors which influence the likelihood that any voter will go to the polls in a given election can be divided for the sake of convenience into polity-level, district-level, and individual-level categories.[5] The first category will be the primary concern of the present section, but it is worth saying a few words about the other two types of influence.

The individual-level determinants of turnout have received extensive treatment in the comparative literature on electoral behaviour in competitive party systems. The most important factors have been found to be those associated with personal resources and capacities: socio-economic level and integration into society (though the relative importance of these variables differs from country to country). There is a tendency in many countries for those with more education and those in occupations with higher status to exercise their franchise with greater frequency (Verba and Nie, 1972; Verba *et al.*, 1978). This can be interpreted as a propensity for those who are more 'cognitively mobilized' to be more politically mobilized as well. But affluence is only one path to political mobilization; the second principal route is institutional affiliation. Membership in political parties and secondary organizations have been found to affect the likelihood with which a person will turn out (Campbell *et al.*, 1960: 99–100; Crewe *et al.*, 1977; Verba *et al.*, 1978; Powell, 1980; Crewe, 1981). Several recent studies of turnout have also pointed to mobilizing agents in society as being primary movers of turnout in established democracies (Uhlander, 1989; Rosenstone and Hansen, 1993; Verba *et al.*, 1995; Gray and Caul, 2000).

At the individual level Eastern European citizens appear to be similar to their Western counterparts in that they tend to vote with greater frequency when they are older (Duch, 1998: 217),[6] yet the political context in which they are voting differs considerably from that of established democracies. Party identification – one of the factors found in established democracies to be most closely linked to turnout (Powell, 1980, 1982; Crewe, 1981; Jackman, 1986) – is considerably lower in post-communist Europe than it is in the West (Rose and Mishler, 1994; Rose, 1995; Wyman *et al.*, 1995), In Richard Rose's term, post-communist citizens tend to be 'de-mobilized'; they are generally suspicious, cynical, and many have little faith in the democratic process. Surveys during the immediate post-communist years found there to be lack of trust in the institutions of representative politics and low perceptions of political efficacy in these societies (Haerpfer and Rose, 1994; Hibbing and Patterson, 1994; Mishler and Rose, 1997).

In order for the institution of representation to function effectively, populations need to believe in its potential to cater to their needs. Faith in the possibility of collective action of any sort was largely destroyed among large sectors of the communist populations, making them doubtful of the efficacy of even the simplest forms of political participation, such as voting. It is likely that the history of coerced mobilization has two contradictory impacts on propensity to vote during the post-communist period; on the one hand socialization into the voting process can be expected to have had a lingering effect; on the other hand, the backlash against communism has led to 'de-mobilization' as people exercise their right not to vote and newly formed political parties fail in their mobilizational efforts. The two countervailing forces of socialization and demobilization may well account for the fact that turnout levels in the post-communist states are lower than in Western democracies, but not as low as in many other democratizing states (IDEA, 2002).

In the Latin American context, party mobilization has been found to be strongly linked to turnout (Pérez-Liñán, 2001), suggesting that this is a particularly important factor in newly democratic polities. The parties of the post-communist region are frequently found to have a strong elite orientation and to have little interest in grass-roots inclusion or mobilization, save at election time. As Paul Lewis argues, '[t]hroughout Eastern Europe, it seemed, questions of inter-party democracy were not just ignored but were rarely perceived to be an issue at all. Post-communist politics and the practice of liberal democracy were understood to operate at the national levels and within the narrow confines of a political elite' (2000: 104). It is not surprising, therefore, that parties' sporadic efforts to draw popular support should not bear fruit as regularly as the efforts of more assiduous political organizations.

It may also matter which parties are strongest. It is well known that left-wing parties in established democracies are better at mobilizing their supporters in many states than their right-wing counterparts (Crewe, 1981), so where and when the left is strong, turnout ought in theory to be higher. A final political factor is competitiveness, understood in terms of how close the race is; voters are more likely to think voting will make a difference if the electoral contest is closely fought. The heightened excitement surrounding a close election may have the effect of generating interest which then translates into an increased propensity to go to the polls on election day. This has been found to be the case both in individual country and cross-national studies (Powell, 1980; Crewe, 1981; Jackman, 1986; Blais and Carty, 1990; Jackman and Miller, 1995).

At the polity level the aggregate impact of lower level influences plays a role in shaping average turnout patterns in states, but a small one (Franklin, 1996). The main factors that shape aggregate differences in turnout among countries are polity-level variables, including the institutional, political, and socio-structural attributes of a state at the time of a given election. Modernization has long been known to be the principal socio-structural determinant of electoral participation at the level of the polity. A state's overall degree of development (variously measured in terms of per capita GDP, literacy, the proportion of the working population employed in non-agricultural jobs) has been found to be linked to aggregate turnout levels, partly, one may conjecture, due to the aggregate effects of individual-level factors such as education and socio-economic status, but also due to the fact that states with more developed infrastructures tend to have secular cultures in which beliefs in political efficacy are prominent (Powell, 1980, 1982; Radcliffe, 1992; Blais, 2000; IDEA, 2002; Norris, 2002). In this connection the dramatic declines in economic growth during the immediate post-communist period are plausible factors that might account for commensurate declines in electoral participation (though we would have expected this trend to reverse when growth rates started to pick up again, and in most cases this has not happened).

Several studies have also found correlations between the size of the population and average turnout levels; turnout tends, all else being equal, to be higher in smaller countries (Blais and Carty, 1990; Blais,

2000). It may be that the benefit voters perceive they may derive from voting is greater where their vote is likely to be decisive, and decisiveness is clearly correlated with the number of people who vote. Similarly, it is generally believed that smaller communities are more cohesive and engender a greater sense of belonging among their citizens which encourages them to vote. Population density has also been found to be linked to turnout levels (Blais, 2000), presumably for similar reasons.

To these factors we might link political legacy. Both the experience of communism and the process of transition vary considerably across the Central and Eastern European region. As noted above, turnout varies most at the start of the transition, suggesting that transition-related factors were important in shaping electoral participation especially at this stage. It therefore makes sense to include in the analysis variables that control for the main political sub-regions in our set of cases: the Soviet successor states (FSU), and their former Yugoslav counterparts (FYU).

Most relevant from the point of view of the object of this investigation is the impact of the structure of the electoral system on the elector's choice of whether or not to vote. Several studies have found turnouts to be higher when elections are held under more proportional rules (Crewe, 1981; Jackman, 1986; Blais and Carty, 1990; Jackman and Miller, 1995; Franklin, 1996; Blais, 2000: 28; Norris, 2002). There are a number of explanations given for this finding, the most compelling of which pertain to the greater competitiveness and fairness of elections under proportional representation (Powell, 1980, 1982; Crewe, 1981; Jackman, 1986; Blais and Carty, 1990; Jackman and Miller, 1995; Lijphart, 1996; Franklin, 1996; Blais, 2000: 26). This is largely attributable to the fact that elections held under systems of proportional representation are more likely to be competitive at the district level than SMD races. In SMDs, the likely winner is often known from the outset, whereas if a larger number of seats are up for grabs, it is more difficult to predict how those offices will be divided among the parties. Not only does this mean that voters have greater reason to be interested in the race; it also means the parties have a greater incentive to mobilize support in a larger number of districts.[7]

It may also be that voters perceive proportional systems to be inherently fairer and are more motivated to take part in the electoral process for this reason. More proportional electoral systems may also influence turnout indirectly by increasing the number of parties among which voters can choose as well as the tightness of the links between party and voter and the inclusiveness of the outcome, all of which can be expected to increase turnout.[8]

Various other aspects of the electoral architecture of a state have also been found in cross-national studies to be related to turnout. Most obvious perhaps is compulsory voting, but as none of the post-communist states require their citizens to vote, it is not possible to examine the effects of this variable in the sample we are examining. Instead of (or in addition to) the 'stick', many of the post-communist states employ 'carrots' to induce people to the polls, and these can also impact on rates of participation by making voting convenient for people. Mechanisms used to this end include communist-era practices such as mobile ballot boxes to bring voting to the infirm, and allowing voters to transfer their vote to another district should they be away from their place of residence on polling day. It is also possible to establish polling stations in diplomatic missions abroad for people who are out of the country on the day of the election. Postal and proxy voting are further measures that can in theory be used to enable people to vote in absentia.

From a logistical point of view, these techniques are easier to implement in some contexts than others, and all require a certain level of state administrative capacity that cannot be universally assumed in the post-communist context. Ballots in the 1991 Albanian election were hand-written by polling officials due to a lack of more sophisticated means of reproduction (Szajkowski, 1992: 159), and a shortage of staples loomed large in deliberations over ballot format in post-transitional Romania (Birch *et al.*, 2002). When such basic implements are lacking, more sophisticated vote-enabling devices such as postal voting and mobile ballot boxes may be a low priority.

Other devices require little additional administrative capacity. Voting can be held on a rest day rather than a work day, the polls can be open for more than one day, and/or they can be open long hours. Some comparative analysis have found that postal voting, rest-day voting, number of voting days (Franklin, 1996) all increase turnout significantly, though a recent study on a larger sample found that the only device to have this effect was the use of special polling booths (Norris, 2002: 78–9).

Some of these variables are impossible to test in the post-communist context for the simple reason that, like compulsory voting, they do not vary. Common features across all the post-communist countries are that all vote on rest days, all enable people living in special institutions (hospitals, schools, etc.) to vote, and none allows proxy voting. Of the institutional arrangements on which there is variation in our sample, the most common in post-communist Europe are legacies from the communist period: district transfer, mobile ballot boxes for the infirm and the establishment of polling stations in diplomatic missions. Postal voting is practised extensively only in the Baltic republics, and only Estonia uses advance in-person voting as its principal means of making voting possible for those who plan to be away on the day of the election. Full details of vote-facilitating mechanisms are presented in Table 3.3. Thirteen out of 20 states make some provisions for absent voting by those within the country on election day; 14 enable those abroad on the day of voting to exercise their franchise, and 11 countries employ mobile ballot boxes. The length of time polling stations are open ranges from ten hours in Albania in 2001 to 24 hours (two 12-hour days) in Latvia, with an average of about 14 hours over the 69 electoral events examined here.

A third aspect of electoral system design that can be expected to be linked to electoral participation is the propensity of a set of electoral institutions to facilitate mobilization activity by parties and civil society groups. As mentioned above, political parties and other civil society organizations are weaker in post-communist societies than is the case in the established democracies of the West. Nevertheless, there are a number of factors that we might expect to facilitate mobilizational activities. The first of these is electoral incentives to cultivate a personal vote. Though electoral systems provide this incentive to different degrees and in different ways (Carey and Shugart, 1995), the most obvious incentive is the availability of personal choices on the ballot. A personal choice can take the form of a vote for an individual candidate in a plurality or absolute majority election (either in SMDs as in Albania 1991, Ukraine 1994, Macedonia 1994, or any of the mixed systems), or in multi-member districts as in Estonia and Slovenia. The second primary means of enabling personal choice is through open lists – party lists on which voters can select one or more individuals from their slate of choice. Approximately half the states that have experienced pure PR systems have allowed preferential voting of this type in some form (see Table 2.1). If voters vote for individuals, this means that candidates have a greater incentive to campaign actively, because successful campaigning will increase not only the collective chances of their party, but also their personal chances. Open lists are thus a way for weak parties to overcome internal collective action problems (though they may also mean that candidates are less beholden to their party and are therefore more independent, which can further weaken political organizations (Ishiyama, 1998, 2000)).

Finally, several aspects of finance regulation can be expected to have consequences for mobilization. Campaign activities typically cost money. It therefore follows that the larger the absolute amount of campaign funds available to electoral competitors, the greater the collective mobilizational capacity of the candidate corpus as a whole, and in

Table 3.3   Provisions to facilitate voting

	Albania	Armenia	Bosnia & Herze-govina	Bulgaria	Croatia	Czech Rep.	Estonia
Postal voting	No	No	From 1998: out of country voters	No	No	No	For voters residing abroad
Advance in-person, in-country voting	No	No	No	No	No	No	Yes
District transfer	1991–97: Elect. Commission members only; 2001: no	No	Yes	Prior to 2001: only for those directly involved in the election; 2001: on demand	No	Yes	No
Mobile ballot boxes	No	No	No	No	Yes	No	Yes
Voting in diplomatic missions	No	Yes	From 1998: polling stations in Yugoslavia and Croatia for Bosnian citizens resident there	Yes	Yes	No	Yes
No. of hours polling stations open	1992: 11; '96, '97: 13; '01: 10	12	12	1990: 11; 1991–2001: 13	12	15	11

Table 3.3   (Continued)

	Georgia	Hungary	Latvia	Lithuania	Macedonia	Moldova	Poland
Postal voting	No	No	From 1995	Yes	No	No	No
Advance in-person voting	No	No	No	No	No	No	No
District or polling station transfer	Yes	Yes	No	No	1994, 1998: no; 02: spec. inst., including camps for internally-displaced people	Yes	No
Polling stations in diplomatic missions	Yes	No	Yes	Yes	No	Yes	Yes
Mobile ballot boxes	Yes	Yes	No	No	No	Yes	No
No. of hours polling stations open	13	12	24	1992: 15; then 14	12	1994: 13; 1998: 14	1991: 12; 1993–2001: 14

	Romania	Russia	Slovakia	Slovenia	Ukraine	Yugoslavia
Postal voting	No	No	No	1992: spec. inst. only, from 1996; spec. inst. and abroad	No	Yes
Advance in-person voting	No	1995: yes; 1999: only in remote areas	No	Yes	1994: only for voters who have	No

Table 3.3   (Continued)

	Romania	Russia	Slovakia	Slovenia	Ukraine	Yugoslavia
					changed residence; 1998, 2002: no	
District or polling station transfer	Yes	1995: no; 1999: yes	Yes	No	No	No
Polling stations in diplomatic missions	Yes	Yes	No	1992: no; 1996, 2000: yes	Yes	No
Mobile ballot boxes	Yes	Yes	Yes	Yes	Yes	Yes
No. of hours polling stations	1990: 17; 1992–2001: 15	1995: 14; 1999: 12	15	12	1994: 13; 1998: 15; 2002: 12	13

Sources: See Appendix B.

theory the higher the turnout should be. Given that as state financing of parties or candidates increases the overall amount of campaign money in circulation, it should work to boost electoral participation. A counter-hypothesis would hold that in weakening links between parties and citizens generally, state funding depletes the very resources on which parties might be able to draw at election time. Though parties may seek to use their allocation of state funds to mobilize electoral support, such tactics may be ineffective when used only once every four or five years.

The probable role of campaign spending limits is perhaps easier to discern. Limits on campaign spending should have a depressant effect on turnout if mobilizational theories hold in the post-communist setting. This effect will obviously be most prominent if limits are observed, but even if they are not observed, spending caps might serve to keep voters away from the polls. If political competitors are obviously violating the law through their lavish (and typically visible) spending, potential voters might become disillusioned with the electoral process and choose to stay home on election day.

The degree of interest aroused by parliamentary elections of the kind investigated here can also be expected to be influenced by the relative importance of the institution of the legislative chamber in relation to other institutions. This line of explanation again touches on the decisiveness of the race and the relative interest it is likely to generate among voters: in a unicameral parliamentary system where quadrennial or quinquennial elections are virtually the only opportunity voters have to influence major political outcomes, they can be expected to be more interested in voting than would be the case for legislative elections in systems with other directly elected bodies of political significance, such as upper chambers, directly elected presidents, or federal sub-units that are elected non-concurrently. In the latter type of state, voters can be expected to vote with less frequency in elections for the lower house of parliament both due to the lesser relative importance of that body in the political process and because frequent calls to the polls may engender voter fatigue.[9] Thus some authors have tested these variables individually and have found that unicameral systems have higher turnout than do bicameral states (Jackman, 1986; Jackman and Miller, 1995); a more common approach is to combine the variables into a summary measure of the 'salience' or 'decisiveness' of (lower-house) parliamentary elections in relation to other institutions (a measure that also provides a proxy for the frequency of national elections); such measures have been found to be significantly related to turnout in some cross-national settings (Franklin, 1996; Blais, 2000: 28).

The operationalization of most of these variables is straightforward. Summary measures of the opportunities for domestic absent voting, foreign absent voting, and the use of mobile ballot boxes were coded by means of dummy variables, while the total number of hours polling stations are open (on one or two days) was entered into the analysis in interval form. Overall electoral system architecture is coded in terms of the proportion of SMD seats. Federalism, unicameralism, and a directly elected president are all counted as relevant when elections to these institutions were non-concurrent with legislative elections. Given that the three factors are expected to have similar effects for similar reasons, we follow Franklin (1976) and Blais (2000) in compiling a composite index of their impact. In the present analysis one point is awarded for each type of institution, creating an index that runs from zero for unicameral, unitary, parliamentary systems (such as Hungary) to three for bicameral federal systems with a non-concurrently, directly elected executive president (such as Russia). Ex-Soviet and ex-Yugoslav republics are represented by dummy variables. The closeness of the race is measured in terms of the actual electoral outcome as the vote share of the largest party minus the vote share of the second-largest party at national level;[10] the vote share of the largest party and that of left parties are also taken from the final national outcome. Population (logged) and population density were both measured in terms of the size of the registered electorate, while per capita GDP (logged) was measured in terms of the entire population. Finally, A dummy variable was added to account for the exceptionally low turnout in Poland. The only variables that it was not possible to include in the analysis were the strength of party identification and party–voter linkage, due to lack of adequate cross-national data for all our cases.

In order to gauge the overall impact of electoral institutions on participation rates across states, country turnout averages are regressed on averages of the variables discussed; the results are presented as Table 3.4. In order to maximize degrees of freedom, only statistically significant variables are included in the models reported here. The evidence in Table 3.4 confirms the findings of previous research that more proportional electoral systems are associated with higher average turnout levels than systems with fewer PR seats.[11] Having a fully proportional electoral system is associated with an 8 per cent higher turnout rate than would be the case under a pure single-member system, all other things being equal. This suggests that the processes at work in the post-communist world are not so different – in this respect at least – from those found in established democracies. Proportionality is clearly and strongly related to electoral participation.

Interestingly, none of the institutional variables hypothesized to be associated with elite mobilizational capacity proved significant.[12]

Table 3.4   OLS model of turnout (country averages)

Variable	B
Proportion PR seats	8.415 (3.635)**
Location in the FSU	−8.097 (2.555)***
Poland	−30.072 (5.896)***
Constant	69.004 (2.796)

Entries are unstandardized regression coefficients (standard errors).

$N = 20$

Adjusted $R^2 = 0.605$

* $p < 0.10$;

** $p < 0.05$;

*** $p < 0.01$.

The availability of an individual vote had no discernable impact on participation levels, suggesting that individual candidates were largely unsuccessful in mobilizing would-be voters, despite the incentive to do so provided by the electoral system. It is unclear from these findings whether the problem lay with the candidates, who did not have the skills, the resources, or the inclination to try to get the vote out in their favour, or if it was voters who were unreceptive to efforts to bring them out. Vote-facilitating mechanisms also failed to have a statistically significant impact; voting was evidently easy enough for post-communist voters that institutions designed to enhance vote convenience played little role in shaping overall participation levels. Neither were other specifically political variables, including the regulation of campaign money, significantly associated with aggregate turnout rates. We might conjecture that formal limits and disclosure requirements were ineffective because they were not observed in practice (and voters either did not notice or did not mind the overspend). There is considerable evidence that caps on fund-raising and spending have been routinely violated in many of the post-communist states (see the discussion of campaign finance in Chapter 2).

What we can say from these results is that there is no strong evidence that mechanisms which might be expected to enable or inhibit popular mobilization by élites did in fact have the effects posited. This finding supports Duch's (1998) conclusion that at the individual level group membership was not linked to propensity to vote in five Central and Eastern European cases. Also interesting is the fact that none of the socio-structural or political variables posited to influence turnout had an impact. The lack of relevance of socio-structural variations across the post-communist region can most likely be explained by the fact that they differ considerably less than they do in larger, more diverse cross-sections in which they have been found to matter.

The only other variable to be significantly associated with turnout (in addition to the Poland dummy) is location in the former Soviet Union; ex-Soviet voters were considerably less likely to exercise their franchise than their Central European counterparts. A control for level of democratization (which proved insignificant) reveals that this influence is not a function of democratic under-development *per se*. As we shall see in later chapters, electoral patterns in the former Soviet states are distinctive in many ways, even when institutional and socio-economic factors are taken into consideration. We shall have more to say about the possible reasons for this in the Conclusion.

Separate cross-sectional models for the first, second and third elections (not shown here) indicate little change in these effects over time.

Though turnout has fallen, the role of electoral institutions in shaping differences across states has remained relatively stable, suggesting that this is a factor that will continue to influence regional variations in rates of electoral participation into the future.

Conclusion

Many post-communist voters are opting out of politics, and élites are either incapable of or unwilling to bring them back in through mobilizational tactics. Despite the unusual – unique? – conditions of 'demobilized' voters in post-communist Europe, we find that electoral systems affect participation levels in this part of the world in ways that differ little from their effects in established democracies. Proportional list voting has a positive impact on rates of electoral participation, even controlling for other relevant factors. Jackman and Miller (1995: 474–5) found that turnout in the newly democratic states of Southern Europe responded to the same variables as established democracies. This chapter has shown that the same is by and large true for the post-communist states, except that in this case institutional factors loom far larger than other determinants of electoral participation.[13] This may be because many of the socio-structural differences evident in larger samples of countries vary too little in the post-communist context for them to reach statistical significance in the relatively small sample analysed here. The context of high uncertainty and low levels of party identification in the post-communist states undoubtedly account for the fact that political variables known to be important in the comparative context – such as the closeness of the race or support for left parties – do not have the same measurable influence on electoral participation as elsewhere. It may be that in the rapidly changing political context of post-communism, the measurable importance of institutional variables is greater than it might otherwise be.

Set in a wider frame, this analysis suggests that regional contextual factors may be as important as universal or country-level influences on electoral participation, especially in democratizing countries. A recent analysis of the determinants of turnout in Latin America has also identified institutional factors as being of central importance in affecting rates of electoral participation, but the relevant institutions are entirely different from those that are important in the post-communist setting. By contrast with post-communist Europe where no state has adopted compulsory voting, mandatory electoral participation is widespread in Latin America. At the same time, the state's capacity to register the eligible population varies considerably (as is not the case in Central and Eastern Europe, where registration is relatively efficient). Compulsory voting and the proportion of the eligible population that the state manages to register are found to be among the most important determinants of turnout in Latin America (Pérez-Liñán, 2001). These differences suggest that families of democratizing states may be 'unhappy in different ways'.

Inasmuch as turning out to vote in parliamentary elections is a necessary prerequisite to representational inclusion, significant sectors of post-communist citizens appear to have excluded themselves from representation due to the institutional choices made by their leaders at the time of transition. In Chapter 4 we will examine whether electoral system design also had a direct influence on how many of those who made it to the polls saw their votes go toward the election of a parliamentary representative.

4
Representation Inclusion

We have seen that electoral institutions are clearly associated with variations in electoral participation across the post-communist region. Yet voting is but the first stage in the representational process. In order to have an input into decision-making, citizens also need to ensure that their vote counts. This chapter will evaluate the effect of various aspects of electoral system design on the representational inclusion, understood as the proportion of voters whose choices are reflected in the composition of the assembly. *How* voters are represented will be the subject of Chapters 5 and 6; the present analysis will be concerned with *whether* they are represented, from both the collective (national-level) and the dyadic (district-level) perspectives.

Electoral inclusion is of inherent normative interest in any polity. Votes that do not contribute to the election of parliamentary representatives leave those who cast them outside the collective decision-making process. Yet in the context of established democracies even high levels of exclusion may not pose a threat to the system, as both parties and voters generally have sufficient information about overall patterns of electoral support for self-exclusion to be a conscious choice. Strongly committed adherents of minor political streams may opt to preserve their ideological purity by contesting elections that they know they have no chance of winning; likewise voters may vote 'expressively' for no-hope political options, either out of ideological commitment or as a form of protest. In most democratic systems, activity of this kind is of relatively minor significance and represents little more than a legitimate, if marginal, alternative to the parliamentary party system.

The same cannot necessarily be said of democratizing states, in which high levels of electoral exclusion may call the democratic legitimacy of the political system into question. When half the votes in the PR component of the ballot were 'wasted' in the Russian elections of 1995, there was considerable concern that democratic institutions were failing to function in the manner expected by the electorate (White *et al.*, 1997: Chap. 11). In this context, representational inclusion is of interest not only because of its inherent normative importance, but also because of what it tells us about the ability of the electoral process to integrate the electorate of a newly democratic state. Inclusion can be expected to be particularly relevant immediately following a transition to competitive multi-party politics, for those voters excluded from representation may become disillusioned with democracy in consequence.

A third reason why the study of inclusion is of interest is that it tells us about the willingness and ability of political actors to engage in strategic behaviour. High levels of exclusion can be interpreted in terms of co-ordination failure. In discussing the Russian election of 1995, White *et al.* argue that Russian parties were 'irrational' in their failure to join together in coalitions that would have stood a better chance of surmounting the 5 per cent threshold (1997: 198–204). Though this interpretation has been disputed by Moser (2001a: 38–9), most scholars agree that inclusion provides a useful means of gauging strategic behaviour. We shall have more to say in Chapter 5 about co-ordination (and non-co-ordination) by parties. We will be mainly concerned in this chapter with strategic behaviour by voters.

There may be good reasons why voters may want to 'waste' their votes. But we would expect that much vote wastage would be unintentional during the immediate post-tradition period. With levels of uncertainty about the prospects of electoral options high and electorates that have little experience with their electoral systems, vote wastage may result from failure to judge with sufficient accuracy the relative chances of different electoral options. As voters gain knowledge about the relative popularity of different parties, as parties develop regularized patterns of competition, and as voters 'learn' their electoral system, we should observe a decrease in exclusion over time.

Whatever the role of strategic decision-making, it is also important to consider the political context in which such decisions are being made. This context is one in which legacies of the communist past can be expected to play an important role in shaping perceptions of the strategic situation inherent in the vote decision. Voters will respond to the electoral situation, at least in part, according to what they believe elections mean (Pammet and DeBardeleben, 1996).

Electoral inclusion and communism

Though the rhetoric of communism was one of inclusion, voters were in practice excluded from political decision-making. The communist ideology was predicated on the assumption that voters ought to be integrated into the political process in a variety of ways – through their contribution to the policy process, as well as through participation in various aspects of public administration. Electoral inclusion was generally understood according to the Soviet model in terms of descriptive representation (Carson, 1956; Pravda, 1978; Friedgut, 1979; Hill, 1980; Barany, 1990; Brunner, 1990; Höpken, 1990; Raina, 1990). In practice this amounted to attempts to co-opt various groups by giving them representation at various levels. Workers were included in decision-making through their incorporation in legislative and party decision-making bodies. The same was true of peasants, women, and members of different ethnic groups. In those states where satellite parties were allowed to operate, such groups were often included via the parties that notionally represented them (e.g. the peasant parties in Bulgaria and Poland). Though the principle of direct proportionality was never applied, there were informal quotas for the representation of members of different groups in most communist states.

The success of this strategy of co-optation varied considerably from state to state, from group to group, and from time period to time period. There is evidence that in some states large sectors of society did feel that they were represented by their communist institutions (Millar, 1987). At the same time, there were many who were frustrated by the fact that formal inclusion meant little real power. Mimetic or 'mirror' representation did not lead to a genuine reflection of interests, given that those chosen to speak for the groups in question tended to be politically unrepresentative of the bulk of the members of those groups. The loyal were chosen, and during the course of their terms in office they typically became socialized into the élite (Friedgut, 1979).

In Central and Eastern Europe democratization was above all else, an effort to transform the system from one of mimetic representation to genuine interest aggregation. This involved two sorts of shift; on the one hand it involved a shift from a largely quantitative to a qualitative understanding of the representative process, understood in terms of responsiveness and accountability. On the other, it involved a change in the common understanding of democratic input from descriptive to partisan representation. People were to be represented by those who thought like them, not by those who shared their socio-demographic attributes; in other words, they were to be represented on a political rather than a social basis, and this meant that they were to be represented by political parties.

Whatever laments might have been voiced at the time about the decline in numbers of women in the parliaments of post-communist Europe, or the virtual exclusion of members of the working classes from representative institutions, and whatever disillusionment there was with the performance of parties, in practice, the principle of multi-party representation was one that was barely challenged during the post-communist period. Where it was challenged, objections were not based on alternative principles of representation as such, but on the view that strong individuals (such as directly elected presidents) were better positioned to make decisions; in others words, these were challenges to the principle of representation as a form of rule, and they were typically linked to criticism of representative institutions such as parliaments. There was little appetite during the post-communist period for a return to an entirely different principle of governance. From 1990 onwards, representation meant parties for the majority of the citizens and the élites alike. The partial exceptions to this general rule – Russia and Ukraine – will be discussed more fully in the Conclusion, but even in these states parties (however weak and ephemeral) have come to be the primary means through which political power is aggregated.[1] There was a strong feeling among large numbers of post-communist citizens that descriptive representation was valuable, but it was held to be secondary.[2] For this reason this study will focus principally on partisan representation and will assess electoral inclusion from the point of view of the election of party representatives to parliament.

Expectations about representational inclusion

Electoral systems exclude votes through the seat allocation process. Even the most proportional electoral system is unlikely to award seats to all contestants if the number of contestants is large and the number of seats is finite. This suggests that the size of the legislative chamber may influence inclusion (Taagepera and Shugart, 1989). Lower (or only) houses of parliaments in post-communist Europe varied greatly from the 42-seat Bosnian assembly to the 450-seat chambers of Russia and Ukraine. A larger number of seats can be expected to be positively related to inclusion, in that it allows small parties a greater chance of being represented.

In addition, all electoral systems impose representational thresholds of some kind. These thresholds can be the formal barriers to representation employed in many in PR systems, or the natural thresholds created by small district size, especially in SMDs. The greater the threshold, the higher is likely to be the level of exclusion, especially when large numbers of parties compete. We can thus expect three distinct factors to have 'mechanical' impacts on vote wastage: the number of contestants, the size of the parliamentary chamber, and the effective threshold. As mentioned in Chapter 1, a composite measure of the effective threshold is not possible given the typical range of vote distribution in SMD systems in post-communist Europe, but it can be hypothesized that, all else being equal, SMD systems will impose a higher threshold than their PR counterparts. Within PR systems, we can expect the formal threshold of representation to have an impact on vote wastage as well.[3] In fact, there was found to be no correlation between average inclusion rates across states and the thresholds they have introduced into their PR systems. In view of this, as well as the interpretive difficulties associated with employing dependent variables that have been manipulated by the very politicians who have benefited from them, this variable will not be explored further. The principal difference we should expect to find is that between the relatively 'wasteful' SMD systems and the more 'efficient' PR systems (controlling, of course, for the number of parties). Finally, a word about mixed systems is in order. Mixed two-vote electoral systems can be expected to exhibit high levels of inclusion, in that they allow for two separate channels of representation. If different types of party are successful in the two components of the ballot, a mixed system will afford voters with two 'shots' at the electoral target, and their chances of picking a winner are therefore greater than is the case with one vote.

In addition to these 'mechanical' effects on vote wasting, Duverger recognized that electoral systems have a number of 'psychological' effects that to some extent counteract the tendency of electoral systems to discard votes. These psychological effects, studied in detail by Cox (1997), are derived from the strategic incentives that are embedded in different electoral systems. These effects are both more complex than their mechanical counterparts, and also potentially more interesting from the point of view of the study of politics, so it pays to dwell on them at some length.

As Blais and Carty (1990) recognize, it is often difficult to disentangle the effects of strategic behaviour by parties from that of strategic behaviour by voters, but the two are at least distinct at the conceptual level.

If voters want to avoid 'wasting' their votes, they will opt for parties or coalitions that have a reasonable chance of winning seats. Office-seeking politicians, for their part, have an incentive to group together into electoral formations that have the best chance of promoting them to positions of power. Duverger's main thesis – which has been validated empirically on numerous occasions since – was that a high threshold of success would generate consolidation in the party system, as only relatively large parties would be electorally viable, and voters would adjust their behaviour accordingly. According to Cox's well-known 'M + 1' rule, the number of candidates that stand in a given district can be expected to be equal to the district magnitude plus one when the electoral system is in equilibrium. Strategic voters will tend to gravitate toward the most successful candidates, leaving very few votes excluded from representation.

The ability of voters to act strategically – assuming that is their aim – is conditioned by two factors: (1) the degree of precision of their knowledge of the likely outcome of the election (in terms of party vote shares), and (2) the extent to which they understand the incentives inherent in the electoral system. There are reasons to believe that during the early days of the post-communist transition both of these conditions would be problematic.

Scholars who have studied strategic voting have often predicted that the high levels of uncertainty that typically surround elections in emergent democracies make the transition context unfavourable to successful strategic co-ordination (Cox, 1997: 85, 159). There are several aspects to this. Firstly, in as much as stable patterns of party identification represent a co-ordination mechanism, lack thereof will make the co-ordination problem greater. (If party identification is 'too' strong, however, committed partisans of minor political organizations may well be unwilling to abandon their favoured party in order to vote strategically.) Secondly, high uncertainty may be generated by poor information – or voters' distrust of information – about the likely outcome of the contest, which will decrease co-ordination capacity.

Prior to the first or 'founding' elections there was little accurate knowledge of likely electoral outcomes in the post-communist states, and voters had in most cases had virtually no experience with the electoral system they were about to use. These are problems that can be expected to affect many transition settings. There are a number of further factors specific to the post-communist context. Initially, post-communist opinion polling was slow to develop the quality and reliability of Western polls (see Miller *et al.*, 1993). This was firstly due to the technical learning process of the pollsters themselves, secondly due to the suspicion of many post-communist citizens and their reluctance to answer polls accurately. Inaccurate polls increase uncertainty, and thereby make co-ordination more difficult. There is also evidence to suggest that many post-communist voters have made their vote decisions relatively close to the date of the election, generating large numbers of 'don't knows' in many poll results (White *et al.*, 1997: 230). Inasmuch as the 'don't knows' eventually plump disproportionately for one option or another, the polls give a misleading picture of the races prior to the day. Several notable 'failures' of opinion pollsters to predict the outcome with accuracy suggest that high numbers of last-minute decisions can be decisive in determining outcomes (as in Russia, 1995 and in Hungary, 2002). If strategic voting is a matter of co-ordination among voters, voters must have means of signalling their intentions to other members of the electorate. When too many voters wait too long, co-ordination does not occur, and voters do not have the wherewithal to engage in strategic behaviour. Similarly, when publication of poll results is not permitted in the immediate run-up to the election, as is the case in a number of states in the region, voters will have less information about the likely decisions of their fellows and thus less ability to cast a successful strategic vote.

Such co-ordination failures can also result from misunderstandings of the incentives built into the electoral system, or lack of knowledge of the details of how electoral results are determined. Voters can perhaps be forgiven for ignorance of all the details of the electoral law, but we would expect that over time they would come to respond to those aspects of electoral institutions that impose the greatest constraint on results.

The number of electoral contestants can also be expected to affect the ability of voters to make strategic calculations. Large numbers of parties represent choice, but they may also confuse voters. Faced with a ballot that took the form of a booklet many pages long, the average Romanian voter in 1990 was likely to be bewildered to say the least. Under these circumstances, we can expect information-economizing measures to be particularly useful. The question is, what such measures were available to the post-communist voter? The traditional information-economizing device employed by voters in established democracies is party identification (Downs, 1957; Fiorina, 1981), yet party identification has been weak in most of the post-communist states examined here. Moreover, as we shall see in Chapter 6, there has been considerable turbulence in the party system at the élite level, such that voters' parties could well disappear entirely from one election to the next, leaving them to seek information elsewhere. In the absence of effective information-economizing mechanisms, we can anticipate large numbers of competitors to hinder the ability of voters to gauge which parties will be successful. This can be expected to make them more likely to cast an unintentional wasted vote. It is possible on the basis of this discussion to conjecture that strategic voting will be relatively unlikely during the first post-transitions elections, but that it may well increase over time as the party system stabilizes and voters come to have a better understanding of the incentives built into electoral institutions. Voters should also develop party loyalties which can serve to guide them in accessing and processing information. If trust in and allegiance to specific parties grows over time, voters can be expected to tap into party information resources that may well be richer than those they would have access to through other channels (though of course parties may also have an interest in convincing their supporters that their political organization is stronger than is actually the case). In short, the dual forces of institutionalization and socialization ought to facilitate strategic co-ordination and decision-making among voters, making it more likely that voters will seek to engage in strategic behaviour, making it easier for them to do so, and increasing the chances that they will be successful.

What institutional factors, might we predict, will impact on the extent to which voters consciously seek to avoid wasting their votes? In addition to the design variables mentioned above, three aspects of the electoral system can be expected to influence rates of vote wastage: the availability of a personal vote, state finance, and the regulations governing the dissemination of opinion poll results.

If individual candidates are successful in mobilizing voters to their cause, the votes cast as a result of this process will in all probability not reflect strategic considerations. Personal loyalty and character evaluation are likely to blur perceptions of electoral chances, and they may well override rational decision-making. A secondary effect of SMD systems may thus be that they fragment the vote by promoting ties between voters and individual politicians. If this is the case, it would reinforce the depressant effect we expect SMD systems to have on inclusion due to their 'mechanical' impact.

If successful in promoting the campaign capacity of existing parliamentary parties, the provision of state finance (allocated as it typically is on the basis of previous electoral success) ought to have the effect of 'freezing out' newcomers by providing existing parliamentary parties with the means of mobilizing votes and preventing them from being dispersed among a large number of small electoral competitors. This accords with the notion that the post-communist electoral systems are becoming 'cartelized'. If it is true that cartelization increases the inclusiveness of the system, then this may be one of the positive effects of a process that is generally described in pejorative terms. All in all, we should expect to see a positive association between the provision of state resources and representational inclusion. Furthermore, spending limits ought to reinforce this effect, in as much as such limits benefit incumbents by restricting the ability of outsiders to establish an electoral foothold. It is less clear what impact – if any – we should expect to see from finance disclosure requirements. On the one hand they may encourage parties to moderate their spending (in the absence of limits); on the other, voters may become cynical about parties' electoral success if they are provided with evidence of how it was 'bought'.

A final institutional effect we can expect to observe is the impact of pre-election opinion poll bans (a dummy variable designating a ban on polls at least seven days prior to the elections was employed to test this hypothesis). Though certain canny polling organizations have managed to get round such restrictions by dressing the results of their surveys up as 'prognoses', bans have generally been fairly well enforced in most post-communist countries, and they represent a real impediment to strategic calculation.[4]

In addition to institutions, we might also expect the political context of the election to have an impact on the decision calculus of the voter. If the election is a close race between large parties, the voter has a greater incentive not only to turn out, but also to vote strategically, because he or she has a greater chance of influencing the outcome. Though the chances of any one vote being decisive in even a moderately large polity are miniscule, the perceptual impact of the competitive situation may well influence whether a voter will be prepared to 'throw away' his or her vote by choosing a no-hope option. We can therefore expect closer races to be associated with greater inclusiveness.

These 'mechanical' and 'psychological' effects can be tested through multivariate analysis, but first it will be necessary to define more precisely what we mean by inclusion and how it is to be measured.

Measuring inclusion

Representational inclusion can be conceptualized and measured in two senses, in terms of whether an individual vote contributes to the election of a representative, or whether the voter's favoured party is represented in the resulting legislature. There are reasons for believing that both methods are worthy of analysis; if a voter makes an electoral choice on the basis of party – which can with some reservations be assumed in systems of proportional list representation – they can be held to be represented by any member of their party who enters parliament, regardless of whether that person comes from their district. By extension, the voter can be thought of as being represented by the parliamentary faction of their party as a whole. This is collective representation. But if a voter does not vote exclusively on the basis of a candidate's party affiliation (or, in the case of independent candidates, does not vote on that basis at all – except perhaps in a negative sense of preferring a candidate with no party ties), then it makes more sense to think in terms of 'dyadic' representation, in terms of whether the person or persons for whom the voter actually voted have entered parliament (Weissberg, 1978; cf. Dalton, 1996).[5]

Ideally we would want to choose the measure that corresponds most accurately to the way voters themselves understand representation and the way they view their own vote choices. Unfortunately raw vote totals do not reveal this information, and survey evidence that might shed light on the matter is sparse. What evidence there is suggests, not surprisingly, that voters differ in their views of voting (partly, one might imagine, depending on the electoral system in force in their country). Some see voting largely in partisan terms, whereas for others it is the personal characteristics of the voters that are most important (Pammet and DeBardeleben, 1996; Birch, 2000). It thus makes most sense to measure inclusion both collectively at the national level and dyadically at the district level.

Mixed two-vote systems present additional difficulties, both from a conceptual and a measurement point of view. If voters vote twice, then it makes sense to measure their inclusion in two separate ways. In theory it would be desirable to know how many voters were represented (both dyadically and collectively) by at least one of their votes, and how many were represented by both their votes. Regrettably, the construction of such indicators would require individual-level vote data, which we do not possess for the range of the countries under consideration here. The best solution is to consider inclusion in terms of the two separate figures, and to measure national-level inclusion as a weighted average of vote percentages for all parties that win seats through either mechanism at the national level.[6]

For the purposes of assessing the overall impact of party systems on voters, we will pay greatest attention to national-level inclusion rates. This is true for three reasons: (1) this is most likely to be the focus of attention in national debates, as electoral districts are in many cases territories with little substantive meaning to voters, and voters are not likely to identify to any great extent with their district unless it coincides with other regional or administrative boundaries; (2) many voters are unaware of the identity of the member(s) of parliament from their district, and are thus unable to hold them personally to account; in many cases district-level results have not been widely publicized; (3) the perennial problem of data availability imposes restrictions on the range of elections it would be possible to analyse in detail on the basis of district-level results.

Analysis

Table 4.1 contains both national- and district-level inclusion scores (where available) as well as mean scores for each election. The highest national-level inclusion was 97.48, achieved in the Bosnian elections of 2002, and the lowest was the 38.50 score that resulted from the Georgian PR elections of 1995. The mean score for the entire dataset is 86.46 and the mean of country means is virtually identical – 84.08. These data provide us with a number of clues as to the impact of electoral system design (in the narrow sense) on inclusion at both national and district levels. Inclusion levels were generally higher in PR than in SMD systems (though with six instances of the opposite in mixed systems – Albania 2001, Armenia 1999, Lithuania 1996 and 2000, Russia 1995, and Ukraine 2002). Inclusion is by construction higher at national than at the district level, but the difference between the two is far greater in SMD than in PR systems; the mean difference between the two types of inclusion is a mere 6.41 per cent under PR (where data are available for both measures), whereas it is 36.44 per cent in the SMD systems for which we have data.

Contrary to what we might expect from theories of strategic voting, there is no clear pattern of change over time in PR systems. There is some evidence of an increase in inclusion in SMD systems (which would point to strategic behaviour), though data are difficult to interpret because missing observations and changes in electoral system make comparisons from one election to the next difficult at the aggregate level. At the level of individual countries, we find that there was a noteworthy increase in national-level PR inclusion in Estonia, Georgia, and Slovenia, a decline in Moldova and Romania, and no marked trend one way or the other in the remaining cases. The most common pattern is a decline in the second elections from initially high levels of inclusion that preceded the fragmentation of the party systems, and a subsequently slow rise; this

Table 4.1 Inclusion rates in post-communist Europe (%)

Country	National-level PR	District-level PR	National-level SMD	District level SMD	National-level mixed system inclusion*
Albania 1991	—	—	95.89	66.53	—
Albania 1992	—	(92.19)	98.20	65.35	—
Albania 1997	—	(94.46)	96.00	N/A	—
Albania 2001	53.27	53.27	82.98	50.86	95.55
Armenia 1995	84.72	N/A	N/A	N/A	N/A
Armenia 1999	80.02	80.02	84.19	N/A	82.37
Bosnia & H. 1996	90.12	90.12	—	—	—
Bosnia & H. 1998	87.3	N/A	—	—	—
Bosnia & H. 2000	98.4	N/A	—	—	—
Bosnia & H. 2002	97.48	67.77	—	—	—
Bulgaria 1990	97.41	N/A	N/A	N/A	N/A
Bulgaria 1991	75.04	73.57	—	—	—
Bulgaria 1994	84.40	78.25	—	—	—
Bulgaria 1997	92.33	85.32	—	—	—
Bulgaria 2001	85.52	82.61	—	—	—
Croatia 1992	87.18	87.18	58.81	N/A	86.60
Croatia 1995	89.00	89.00	87.41	N/A	88.60
Croatia 2000	86.75	84.86	—	—	—
Czech Rep. 1990	81.19	N/A	—	—	—
Czech Rep. 1992	80.88	N/A	—	—	—
Czech Rep. 1996	88.84	87.49	—	—	—
Czech Rep. 1998	88.68	88.68	—	—	—
Czech Rep. 2002	87.47	87.25	—	—	—
Estonia 1992	80.38	70.90	—	—	—
Estonia 1995	87.31	77.95	—	—	—
Estonia 1999	91.61	84.23	—	—	—
Georgia 1992	N/A	N/A	N/A	N/A	N/A
Georgia 1995	38.50	N/A	N/A	N/A	N/A
Georgia 1999	75.30	75.30	N/A	N/A	N/A
Hungary 1990	84.16	73.89	82.64	27.97	84.03
Hungary 1994	87.34	76.85	79.74	31.31	88.36
Hungary 1998	89.85	82.54	82.59	30.53	90.46
Hungary 2002	88.70	85.68	80.42	44.42	88.01
Latvia 1993	89.31	N/A	—	—	—
Latvia 1995	87.97	N/A	—	—	—
Latvia 1998	88.61	88.32	—	—	—
Latvia 2002	84.01	84.01	—	—	—
Lithuania 1992	83.81	83.81	77.64	42.22	95.00
Lithuania 1996	67.37	67.37	87.70	28.65	88.39
Lithuania 2000	76.59	76.59	89.60	29.65	93.54
Macedonia 1994	—	—	50.22	36.71	—
Macedonia 1998	90.23	90.23	55.26	50.20	87.42
Macedonia 2002	88.52	84.15	—	—	—
Moldova 1994	81.92	N/A	—	—	—
Moldova 1998	76.43	76.43	—	—	—
Moldova 2001	71.67	71.67	—	—	—

Table 4.1 (Continued)

Country	National-level PR	District-level PR	National-level SMD	District level SMD	National-level mixed system inclusion*
Poland 1991	92.46	79.14	—	—	—
Poland 1993	64.86	57.55	—	—	—
Poland 1997	87.20	32.13	—	—	—
Poland 2001	90.63	31.73	—	—	—
Romania 1990	94.46	85.95	—	—	—
Romania 1992	80.03	73.92	—	—	—
Romania 1996	80.08	75.97	—	—	—
Romania 2000	76.81	73.69	—	—	—
Russia 1993**	90.90	90.90	61.92	35.38	88.62
Russia 1995**	51.91	51.91	52.63	32.52	71.00
Russia 1999**	84.14	84.14	64.50	38.18	77.96
Slovakia 1990	92.40	N/A	—	—	—
Slovakia 1992	76.20	N/A	—	—	—
Slovakia 1994	86.98	N/A	—	—	—
Slovakia 1998	94.21	94.21	—	—	—
Slovakia 2002	81.79	81.79	—	—	—
Slovenia 1992	82.31	N/A	—	—	—
Slovenia 1996	88.71	N/A	—	—	—
Slovenia 2000	96.25	N/A	—	—	—
Ukraine 1994	—	—	44.39	26.45	—
Ukraine 1998**	69.48	69.48	67.19	34.17	79.53
Ukraine 2002**	80.79	80.79	89.09	38.54	84.94
Yugoslavia 2000	94.88	N/A	—	—	—
Mean: 1st election	87.98 ($N = 16$)	82.74 ($N = 8$)	67.36 ($N = 7$)	39.21 ($N = 6$)	88.56 ($N = 4$)
Mean: 2nd election	76.59 ($N = 18$)	73.69 ($N = 12$)	76.54 ($N = 8$)	40.37 ($N = 6$)	82.86) ($N = 6$
Mean: 3rd election	85.65 ($N = 17$)	77.60 ($N = 14$)	84.36 ($N = 5$)	34.23 ($N = 4$)	87.32 ($N = 3$)
Mean: 4th election	85.12 ($N = 9$)	73.82 ($N = 9$)	81.70 ($N = 2$)	47.64 ($N = 2$)	91.78 ($N = 2$)
Mean: 5th election	84.93 ($N = 3$)	83.88 ($N = 3$)	—	—	—
Overall mean	83.54 ($N = 63$)	77.14 ($N = 46$)	75.86 ($N = 22$)	39.42 ($N = 18$)	86.46 ($N = 15$)

* These figures are weighted averages of vote percentages for all parties that won seats at the national level through either the PR or the SMD components of the system.

** Russian and Ukrainian figures are adjusted to account for 'against all' votes; the vote percentages on which these data are based are recalculated on the basis of a denominator which includes only votes cast for given electoral options.

Notes: In two-round systems inclusion rates are for the first round only. Croatian and Slovenian totals exclude separately elected minority seats. In calculating the Polish and Romanian inclusion rates, parties that are excluded from the formal threshold were also excluded from the totals reported here.

pattern is in evidence in Bosnia, Poland, Russia, and until 2001 in Bulgaria and Slovakia. There is also a moderate trend of this type in the ordinal averages.

At the level of PR districts, we find a similar picture, though with some variation at the country level; there were gradual rises in district level inclusion in Bulgaria, Estonia, and Hungary, falls in Poland and Romania, and a decline followed by a rise in Russia. The relative paucity of SMD data (due both to missing data and to the fact that fewer SMD elections were held) make it more difficult to generalize. The overall means paint a picture somewhat at variance with that evident in the data for inclusion in PR systems; SMD elections in Hungary have exhibited a gradual rise at the district level but no evident pattern at the national level; in Ukraine there was a substantial rise in inclusion at both levels over time. In Lithuania, there has been a decrease at the national level but an increase (following an initial fall) at the district level, generating a gradual widening of the gap between the two figures. In Russia the national-level SMD pattern is similar to the pattern for PR elections: a decline followed by a rise; at the SMD district level, however, there is little evidence of change. In Albania there was an apparent decrease at both levels in the 2001 elections. With the exception of the most recent Albanian election, then, inclusion increased over time at the district level in all SMD systems for which data are available and which exhibit a clear trend.

In order to control for the effects of a wider range of variables, multivariate regression is needed. Table 4.2 presents the results of an OLS regression based on country averages. As can be seen, SMD systems exhibit significantly lower rates of inclusion than the baseline PR system. In confirmation of the analysis presented above, these results show that mixed systems are the most inclusive of electoral system types; this is because in multiplying channels for inclusion, they allow different types of parties to achieve representation. It is for this reason that the continuous variable used in Chapter 3 to designate electoral system type is not significant here: the effect of electoral systems on inclusion is not a continuous one. This finding belies the common view of mixed systems as a moderate compromise between PR and SMD; in terms of inclusion the mixed system delivers more than the sum of its parts.

Contrary to expectations, the state financing of electoral campaigns appears to have had a marked negative impact on representational inclusion. Rather than helping to consolidate the electoral system, the provision of state money for campaign purposes seems to be associated with a dispersal of the vote, resulting in a rise in vote wastage. It is

Table 4.2   OLS model of representational inclusion (country averages)

Variable	B
SMD system	−21.283 (11.959)*
Mixed system	10.885 (3.720)***
State financing	−9.171 (3.492)**
Number of contestants	−0.378 (0.119)***
Location in the FSU	−13.025 (2.742)***
Constant	104.215 (4.071)

Entries are unstandardized regression coefficients (standard errors).

$N = 19$

Adjusted $R^2 = 0.663$

* $p < 0.10$; ** $p < 0.05$; *** $p < 0.01$

Notes: This model excludes Croatia due to lack of complete data on the number of contestants. When this variable is excluded from the model and Croatia is included in the equation, the signs and magnitudes of the remaining variables remain substantially unaltered. The Georgian election of 1992 is omitted entirely due to lack of data.

The dependent variable for the mixed elections held in Bulgaria 1990, Armenia 1995, Georgia 1995, and Georgia 1999 is the inclusion rate for the PR component of the ballot only, due to lack of complete data for the SMD races. These cases are coded as PR elections for the purposes of this analysis.

unclear why this might be the case, but we may conjecture that the provision of public money has in many cases enabled those parties in receipt of it to perform better than anticipated at elections, leading to co-ordination difficulties among voters, whose expectations prove inaccurate. Alternatively, it may be that voters resent the cosy relationship that large parties build with the state via financing provision and cast protest votes in consequence, opting for parties that they know have little chance of success.

As anticipated, the number of contestants exerted a negative influence on inclusion, though this effect is small. Once these institutional variables are controlled, regional factors are still important determinants of variations in the extent to which post-communist elections succeed in drawing electorates into the representational process. Inclusion rates are significantly lower in the Soviet successor states. This may be due to the fact that many of these states have witnessed higher levels of political turbulence (though a control for level of democratization was not significant). Whatever the explanation for these effects, the legacy of the past does appear to exert an impact above and beyond that of institutions.

Also noteworthy are the variables that were not significant in this equation. Neither the size of the chamber,[7] opinion poll bans, the personal vote, or competitiveness appeared to influence inclusion in this sample. This suggests that the mobilizational (and demobilizational) effects associated with these variables were not strong determinants of vote choice, and that strategic behaviour was rare.

Because it is based on country averages, the above equation combines early elections where little strategic behaviour can be expected with later ones in which we might have anticipated tactical voting to have been deployed with greater frequency and success. In order to probe the relevance of strategic decision, it therefore makes sense to conduct separate cross-sectional analyses of the first three elections held in each state. Table 4.3 presents the result of a series of cross-sectional models of vote inclusion at the time of the first, second, and third post-communist elections.

It was argued above that strategic voting would lead to an increase over time in the institutional variables hypothesized to be associated with it. Evidence in the equations presented here of an increase in the strength of the electoral system variable over time is weak. At the time of the first post-communist election the only variable that appears to have had a discernable impact on national inclusion rates was the presence or absence of an SMD system. As suggested in the data presented in Table 4.1 above, SMD depressed inclusion significantly and substantially. (After the first elections there were no pure single-member systems, making comparability across time somewhat problematic.) The magnitude of the coefficient for mixed systems actually decreases

Table 4.3 OLS models of inclusion at the first, second, and third elections

Variable	Election		
	1	*2*	*3*
SMD system	−24.988 (6.928)***		
Mixed system		12.511 (4.990)**	10.402 (2.312)***
Size of chamber		−0.045 (.018)**	−0.016 (.008)*
State financing			−10.876 (2.547)***
Location in the FSU		−8.353 (4.879)*	−9.574 (1.906)***
Constant	88.488 (2.753)	88.018 (4.972)	99.828 (2.182)

Entries are unstandardized regression coefficients (standard errors).

N:	19	19	18
Adjusted R^2	0.400	0.337	0.740

* $p < 0.10$; ** $p < 0.05$; *** $p < 0.01$

Note: See the notes to Table 4.2.

between the second and the third elections. All in all, evidence of strategic voting in post-communist elections is rather limited. Yet in their survey-based study of Hungary, Duch and Palmer (2002) found that 13.6 per cent of voters were willing to cast a tactical vote in 1997 (prior to the third post-transition election). The question arises as to whether we may have missed some important aspects of strategic behaviour through the analyses conducted here, or whether Duch and Palmer's survey respondents were largely acquiescing to the suggestion of the interviewer that they might have reason to cast a strategic vote. Duch and Palmer claim to have observed the effects of actual strategic voting in Hungarian electoral results. They note that the effective number of parties had gradually declined over successive elections between 1990 and 1998, which they take as indicative of 'how quickly Hungarian voters co-ordinated on a small number of parties' (2002: 70). Yet there are problems with this inference. The number of effective parties is unlikely to be proof of an increase in strategic voting for two reasons. First, this decline can be attributed at least in part to co-ordination at the elite level, including the formation of coalitions and a drop in the number of overall contestants (noted by Duch and Palmer, 2002: 71). Second, voter 'co-ordination' around a small number of parties has in all probability resulted at least as much from change in actual party preferences as it has from strategic choices. The 13.6 per cent of voters evidently willing to vote strategically is far too low a figure to account for the shifts in vote choice over time in Hungarian elections. This suggests that much of the 'co-ordination' evident in the decline in the effective number of parties has been the result of changing preferences, not strategic behaviour.

A better measure of strategic behaviour (though a measure also not without its faults) is ticket splitting in mixed systems, operationalized as is the sum total of differences in the electoral results of each party on the two components of the ballot. Duch and Palmer asked their survey respondents a general question about 'which party [they] would vote for', but in fact Hungarian voters have two votes, so they can, if they wish, vote for two different parties. If they are strategic, they may well choose to split their tickets in this way. The different components of mixed electoral systems dictate different strategies to voters; a voter whose first option is a relatively small party may decide to vote for that organization on the PR component of the ballot but select a larger party in the SMD race. At the time of the first election, voters have little way of knowing for sure what constitutes a 'large' party and what might be a party best avoided in the SMD vote. Over time, however, the relative strength of different parties ought to become evident, and if voters are learning to vote strategically we should expect to see a rise in the difference between vote totals in the two parts of the system. Ideally we would want to examine change over time in all the mixed systems in our dataset, but Hungary and Russia are the only countries for which this is truly feasible. Albanian, Bulgaria, and Macedonia (have) had two-vote systems for too short a period for over-time analysis to be possible at all, and too few data points are available for Armenia, Croatia, Georgia, and Ukraine. Lithuania, for its part, moved prior to the 2000 elections from an absolute majority to a plurality rule in its SMDs, which may well have had the effect of blurring incentive structures. Though Hungary raised its threshold from 4–5 per cent following the 1990 elections, we have not discerned any impact of formal thresholds on strategic vote choice, and this change is in any case minor enough that voters ought to have been able to adjust their calculations to account for it.

Table 4.4 presents changes over time in the summed differences between vote shares in the SMD and PR races for the full set of post-communist elections in Hungary and Russia.

Contrary to what we might expect to observe on the basis of a strategic voting hypotheses, the differences between the two parts of the system have not increased over time. The high figure for Hungary 1998 may well be due to the complex SMD-level coalition structure in this race, but if we exclude this as an anomaly, the difference in success rates in the two parts of the system has actually declined over time. In Russia, on the other hand, ticket splitting appears to be ubiquitous (probably due to the role of local notables and independents at the district level), but there is no evident trend in either direction. If anything the evidence here also points away from an increase in strategic behaviour on the part of voters.

Table 4.4 Summed differences between party vote shares in SMD and PR contests

Election	Hungary	Russia
Election 1	12.28	58.36
Election 2	7.40	54.61
Election 3	20.40*	55.07
Election 4	6.15	

* Fidesz–MDF joint candidates were counted together with Fidesz votes; MDF–Fidesz joint candidates were counted together with MDF votes.

Voters do not appear to be responding to strategic incentives inherent in the electoral system, but they do appear to be willing to cast strategic votes, as Duch and Palmer show. What are we to make of this conflicting evidence? It seems that voters are beginning to think strategically, but that they are not responding to the incentives of the electoral system as such. Instead they seem to be taking their cue from the overall political situation. The 1998 Hungarian elections that took place six months after Duch and Palmer conducted their survey were extremely closely fought, with the Fidesz–MDF coalition ultimately winning 148 seats to the Socialists' 134. It may be that at this juncture Hungarians were particularly aware of the impact their vote might have on the electoral outcome and were open to the idea that they might increase their chance of having a decisive vote by opting for one of the large parties. There is little evidence, however, that the electoral system itself was playing a major role in shaping strategic behaviour among voters.

Conclusion

This chapter has demonstrated that representational inclusion has been influenced by various aspects of electoral system design during the years of post-communist transition. The SMD electoral systems that persisted in some of the countries in the region were least conducive to including the electorate in parliamentary representation, whether understood in terms of district-level or national-level inclusion. Of the other two types of electoral system design dominant in the region, the mixed system is best suited to inclusion at the national level, in that it maximizes channels of access to parliament. There is rather limited evidence of strategic voting in the post-communist states, and it does not seem to be clearly linked to electoral institutions as such. Sub-regional factors are far more important in influencing the extent to which electoral outcomes represent people.

At its starkest, we can phrase the significance of electoral inclusion thus: to be represented or not to be represented is to exist politically or to be marginalized from the political process. Democratic transitions are perhaps the point at which inclusion matters most. At the same time, those who design political systems cannot guarantee inclusion once they move away from quota representation on sociological grounds, for partisan representation through elections depends also on the actions of voters. Though electoral institutions shape the extent to which voters' expressions of preferences are translated into broadly representative outcomes, it will never be possible to include all strands of political life in a parliament of finite size. Moreover, the inclusion of large numbers of small parties in parliament may have a detrimental impact on the ability of that institution to perform its job. This is where the third part of this book takes us from the realm of the individual voter to that of collective representation and party politics, shifting the level of analysis from the individual vote decision and strategies of voters to the decisions and strategies of parties.

Part III
Electoral Systems and Parties

5
Party System Size and Shape

In the last two chapters we considered the institutional factors that influence the inclusion of voters into the political process in post-communist Europe. In this part of the book we turn to an examination of the effects of electoral institutions on party configurations, examined in this chapter from a static perspective in terms of the size and shape of party systems, and in the next chapter with reference to the dynamics of party system stability and change over time. Investigating the quantitative dimension of parliamentary representation, and specifically the number of parties represented in parliament, we are entering the terrain most commonly trodden by students of electoral systems. It is fair to say that there have been more studies of the impact of electoral systems on the size of party systems than on all other variables combined. Our aim will be both to test the findings of previous research and to explore previously untested hypotheses.

Transition and the institutionalization of party systems

Most scholars agree that the development of stable, coherent representative parties that can shape and channel popular preferences is crucial to successful democratization in the wake of political transition. In the early days of political reform in Central and Eastern Europe, politicians and citizens alike were often sceptical of the efficacy of parties in contributing to representation, given the experience of one-party rule. But in all cases the need for parties soon became apparent to a large majority of the political class, and subsequent efforts by politicians have been directed at attracting votes to their fledgling political organizations. At the same time, parties have begun to establish working relations and patterns of alliance within national legislatures. These dual processes have been influenced by numerous contextual factors, including the pre-communist experience, the legacy of the old regime, the pace of socio-economic change, institutional choices, and the attributes of specific countries.[1]

Some (e.g. Mair, 1997) have argued that many of the post-communist states do not possess party systems at all, due to the lack of regularized patterns of competition exhibited by the constellations of parties that contest elections. Yet in the absence of clear criteria for determining the 'systematicity' of party configurations, the term 'party system' will be used here to refer to the sum total of parties that are electorally active in a given country at a given time. Rather than jettisoning the term 'party system' altogether, it makes more sense in the post-communist context to talk of institutionalized as opposed to uninstitutionalized party systems. (It is necessary in this connection to distinguish between *party* institutionalization and *party system* institutionalization (cf. Randall and Svasand, 2002); the main focus in this study is party system institutionalization, which is more susceptible to measurement and comparison across a relatively large number of cases.)

In order to be institutionalized, democratic party systems must be competitive (not dominated by one actor) yet at the same time small enough to enable the development of stable patterns of alliance and competition. Party systems may be considered uninstitutionalized if they are (1) highly fragmented, or (2) highly regionalized, such that different parties contest and win elections in different parts of the country. Party system institutionalization can thus be understood of being a combination of consolidation, regularization, and nationalization (as well as autonomy from the state). Consolidation and nationalization are primarily synchronic concepts; regularization refers to patterns of continuity over time (Rokkan, 1970; Sartori, 1976; Mair, 1997).

Before we consider the factors that are likely to influence party system institutionalization, it is necessary to say a few words about how these concepts may be operationalized. The discussion in Chapters 1 and 2 provided justification for our choice of dependent variables. Not only will we be interested in examining the overall size of party systems, we will also be interested in their shape. The size of party systems can be conveniently measured by means of the effective number of parties (though we shall also consider the absolute number; see Table 5.1). The 'shape' of party systems can be understood in terms of the distribution of party support among parties. Relevant aspects of this distribution include the vote share of the largest party, which can tell us whether there is a 'dominant' party that overshadows all the rest. A related measure is the difference in

Table 5.1 Absolute number of parties

Country	Contestants			Winners		
	PR	SMD	All	PR	SMD	All
Albania 1991	—	11	11	—	4	4
Albania 1992	—	11	11	3	5	5
Albania 1997	—	23	23	8	9	12
Albania 2001	38	27	38	6	2	7
Armenia 1995	13	N/A	13	5	6	8
Armenia 1999	21	35	35	6	9	9
Bosnia & H. 1996	21	—	21	6	—	6
Bosnia & H. 1998	33	—	33	10	—	10
Bosnia & H. 2000	17	—	17	13	—	13
Bosnia & H. 2002	33	—	33	11	—	11
Bulgaria 1990	40	N/A	41	4	6	7
Bulgaria 1991	38	—	38	3	—	3
Bulgaria 1994	48	—	48	5	—	5
Bulgaria 1997	39	—	39	5	—	5
Bulgaria 2001	54	—	54	4	—	4
Croatia 1992	17	N/A	N/A	7	3	7
Croatia 1995	15	N/A	N/A	5	7	8
Croatia 2000	N/A	—	N/A	5	—	5
Czech Rep. 1990	13	—	13	4	—	4
Czech Rep. 1992	19	—	19	8	—	8
Czech Rep. 1996	20	—	20	6	—	6
Czech Rep. 1998	18	—	18	5	—	5
Czech Rep. 2002	29	—	29	4	—	4
Estonia 1992	17	—	17	9	—	9
Estonia 1995	16	—	16	7	—	7
Estonia 1999	12	—	12	7	—	7
Georgia 1992	N/A	N/A	36	24	N/A	24
Georgia 1995	54	N/A	54	3	11	11
Georgia 1999	33	N/A	N/A	3	4	4
Hungary 1990	19	28	28	6	7	7
Hungary 1994	19	35	35	6	6	6
Hungary 1998	15	26	26	5	5	8
Hungary 2002	13	20	20	3	3	3
Latvia 1993	23	—	23	8	—	8
Latvia 1995	19	—	19	9	—	9
Latvia 1998	21	—	21	6	—	6
Latvia 2002	20	—	20	5	—	5
Lithuania 1992	17	26	26	5	8	8
Lithuania 1996	24	28	28	5	13	13
Lithuania 2000	15	28	28	4	13	13
Macedonia 1994	—	40	40	—	11	11
Macedonia 1998	17	22	23	5	8	8
Macedonia 2002	38	—	38	7	—	7

Table 5.1 (Continued)

Country	Contestants			Winners		
	PR	SMD	All	PR	SMD	All
Moldova 1994	13	—	13	4	—	4
Moldova 1998	15	—	15	4	—	4
Moldova 2001	16	—	16	3	—	3
Poland 1991	111	—	111	29	—	29
Poland 1993	35	—	35	8	—	8
Poland 1997	21	—	21	6	—	6
Poland 2001	14	—	14	7	—	7
Romania 1990	54	—	54	16	—	16
Romania 1992	62	—	62	7	—	7
Romania 1996	33	—	33	6	—	6
Romania 2000	35	—	35	5	—	5
Russia 1993	13	13	13	8	12	12
Russia 1995	43	43	43	4	23	23
Russia 1999	26	27	27	6	13	14
Slovakia 1990	23	—	23	5	—	5
Slovakia 1992	16	—	16	5	—	5
Slovakia 1994	17	—	17	7	—	7
Slovakia 1998	17	—	17	6	—	6
Slovakia 2002	26	—	26	7	—	7
Slovenia 1992	25	—	25	8	—	8
Slovenia 1996	24	—	24	7	—	7
Slovenia 2000	16	—	16	8	—	8
Ukraine 1994	—	32	32	—	17	17
Ukraine 1998	30	35	35	8	19	20
Ukraine 2002	33	30	36	6	9	10
Yugoslavia 2000	8	—	8	6	—	6
Mean: 1st election	26.69	25.00	28.84	8.13	8.22	10.00
Mean: 2nd election	27.78	29.86	30.06	6.11	11.25	9.00
Mean: 3rd election	23.81	26.80	24.94	6.35	9.80	7.78
Mean: 4th election	25.22	23.50	26.00	5.89	2.50	6.00
Mean: 5th election	36.33	—	36.33	5.00	—	5.00
Overall mean	26.52	27.00	28.17	6.60	9.08	8.41

Notes: These figures do not include independent candidates. 'Parties' are counted according to separate candidacy on the ballot; they thus include partisan groupings of any kind and coalitions for which voters vote as a unit. In some mixed-systems parties contest elections separately in one part of the system (and are thus counted separately) and in coalition in the other part (and are therefore counted as a single unit).

When two parties present joint candidates in some districts but separate candidates in other districts, they are counted as two parties.

Minority candidates in Croatia, Romania, and Slovenia are excluded.

vote share between the largest and the second largest party, which we have already encountered in our analysis of turnout. In the context of the present discussion, 'closeness' can be understood as a measure of competitiveness (and the two terms will be used interchangeably), though the way the variable is operationalized means that a higher figure corresponds to a less competitive situation.

The *seat* share of the largest party provides an indication of the potential for single-party governments. Government formation *per se* will not be examined here because other elements of constitutional design complicate this process. In the presidential systems of Russia and Ukraine, governments have not generally been party-based, and parliamentary majorities have played a blocking rather than a facilitating role. In Central Europe, by contrast, party governments have been the rule. Given these two very different contexts, we shall content ourselves with an examination of the *potential* for the formation of parliamentary majorities, bearing in mind that this potential will be put to different uses depending on the constitutional and political contexts that obtain in a given state at a given point in time.

Expectations about electoral system effects on party system size and shape

There is particular reason to believe that single-member district electoral systems and the single-member components of mixed systems will have characteristic results in Eastern Europe that differ considerably from those they have in established democracies. In his famous analysis of the effects of electoral laws on party systems, Duverger (1959) predicted that SMD systems would have a reductive effect. But it is well known that Duverger's 'law' does not hold under conditions of regional fragmentation, as it applies primarily to the district level. When there is lack of party system nationalization and districts are heterogeneous in terms of party support, the aggregation of results from across districts will generate a highly heterogeneous parliament (Duverger, 1959: 223; for detailed discussions see Leyes, 1959; Wildavski, 1959; Sartori, 1968; Rae, 1971; Kim and Ohn, 1992; Cox, 1997). In the post-communist context this has been found to be the case in those states with weakly integrated party systems (Moser, 1997, 1999, 2001a). Certainly it does seem that SMD systems have had a reductive effect in established post-communist states, but they appear to have had a fragmenting effect in many of the newly formed states, especially those of the former Soviet Union. We may therefore expect to see an interaction between electoral system effects and sub-region.

Proportional representation, on the other hand, encourages the formation of national parties, which will tend to homogenize party competition across regions. Furthermore, the three to eight per cent thresholds incorporated into the PR formulae used in the post-communist countries represent strong constraining factors that can be expected to have not only a reductive effect on the number of parties, but also a powerful 'freezing' effect on party systems.

In addition, to these 'mechanical' effects, we may also observe 'psychological' electoral system effects, particularly effects that pertain to party strategy. The electoral conditions typical of post-transitional Central and Eastern Europe create strategic incentives for large numbers of contestants to enter the electoral race. Though White *et al.* (1997) have seen the proliferation of electoral contestants in Russia as indication of the 'irrationality' of parties, parties may actually have rational reasons for contesting a race when the outcome is difficult to predict. With high levels of uncertainty, parties will have an incentive to form in order to test the electoral waters in the hopes that, in a very large field, they will be able to establish an electoral niche on the basis of a relatively modest share of the vote (Cox, 1997: 159).

The impact of mixed systems is potentially more complex. Most scholars hold that mixed electoral systems generate moderately sized party systems, somewhere in between the small systems typical of SMD rules and large PR systems (Reynolds and Reilly, 1997; Moser, 2001a; Nishikawa and Herron, 2001; Kostadinova, 2002). Yet in the last chapter we saw that mixed electoral systems are 'more than the sum of their parts' in that they generate greater inclusiveness than either PR or SMD variants. The same may also be true of party system size. List systems encourage electoral alliances to overcome formal thresholds, whereas single-member district races encourage alliances to overcome effective thresholds and achieve the necessary majority for victory. The complication arises when the two sets of alliances differ, as they will tend to do in mixed systems with strong regional variations in electoral support bases. Varying patterns of alliance formation in mixed systems may lead to a fragmentation of the party system as a whole.

A second set of theoretical expectations revolves around the ways in which the two component parts of a mixed electoral system interact. The interaction is in some cases formalized at the level of seat distribution through compensatory mechanisms (Hungary and Albania are the only cases in post-communist Europe), but observers have noted a number of other types of interaction that affect parallel systems as well. Though some early work treated mixed electoral systems as laboratories in which to assess the effects of seat distribution formulae on party system change, others have since recognized that the two component parts of mixed systems tend to influence each other, even when there is no formal link between them (Farrell, 1997: 99–100; Moser, 1997, 1999, 2001a; Gabel, 1995; Montgomery, 1999; Nishikawa and Herron, 2001; Kostadinova, 2002). SMD elections encourage candidates who have local support bases but not necessarily strong party affiliation, whereas party list voting puts priority on parties as organizational mechanisms and encourages loyalty on the part of party members. We thus expect that different sorts of candidates will contest the two types of election, as has found to be the case in Hungary (Benoit, 1996, 1999) and Russia (Moser, 1995). The question is whether there will be 'spill-over' effects either way, in other words, will the personalization of the electoral contest encouraged by the SM elections weaken party coherence, or will the 'partification' of electoral competition promoted by the PR elections serve to consolidate party allegiance among SMD candidates and representatives? There are reasons for believing that both of these effects may be found. A party with little chance of clearing the threshold may put forward a list so as to gain visibility for its single-member district candidates (and possibly also to gain resources via the state financing of electoral campaigns). This can explain a number of the highly personalized lists in recent Russian elections (see Moser, 1997: 293; 2001a).[2] Evidence of the opposite tendency has been found in the Hungarian context by Kathleen Montgomery, who shows that SMD candidates were considerably more eager to bind themselves to a party and to serve the party's interest when they realized that party seats were 'safer' when it came to re-election than were SMD seats (Montgomery, 1999).

Following the analyses in Chapters 1 and 4, we can expect the availability of an individual vote to have a fragmenting effect on the party system, given that it institutionalizes personal ties between voters and candidates and thereby shifts the basis of decision-making from the national level to the level of character evaluations. Character evaluations are idiosyncratic, so they should work against co-ordinating devices that might be expected to consolidate the party system.

The provision of state financing, by contrast, should have a consolidating influence (though there was little evidence of this in the last chapter). If indeed the post-communist party systems have become 'cartelized' as some would have us believe, the allocation of state funds on the basis of previous electoral success ought in theory to have a freezing effect on the party system, squeezing out newcomers and gradually magnifying the support of existing political organizations. It is less clear what effects we should observe from spending limits and disclosure requirements. They had no evident impact on inclusion, and though spending limits appear in established democracies to benefit incumbents (see Chapter 1 above), they may work differently in an emergent democracy, preventing leading parties from gathering too many votes and allowing those votes to go to smaller political groups. Disclosure requirements may inhibit the accumulation of excessive amounts of wealth in established democracies, but in the post-communist setting they may lead to a cynical backlash among the electorate, who are either shocked at how much has been spent trying to woo them or disbelieving of the figures. In either case, such cynicism could lead voters to cast votes for new entrants into the electoral arena, thereby fragmenting the system further.

Finally, the institution of the presidency may, where it is found, fragment the vote by providing an incentive for would-be presidential candidates to create parties as launching pads for the presidential race. If many politicians attempt this but no one individual is successful in building a strong political organization on this basis, such activity will generate a plethora of small splinter parties. If, on the other hand, a successful presidential candidate is able to establish a powerful political base sufficient to win him or her enough votes to become president, this party is likely to be relatively large, which should prompt rivals to come together in opposition (Shugart and Carey, 1992; Jones, 1995; Moser, 2001a: chap. 6).

Analysis

The most intuitively obvious means of assessing the extent to which a party system has consolidated is the absolute number of parties that appear in tables of electoral results. Two figures are noteworthy in this context: the number of partisan groupings that contest elections, and the number that win seats in parliament. Table 5.1 presents data on the absolute number of parties that have contested and won post-communist elections between 1990 and 2002. Several comments are in order. The total number of contestants ranges from a low of eight in the Yugoslav elections of 2000 to a high of 111 in Poland in 1991. The next highest figures are found in Romania, which, like Poland, started out in the 1990 elections with no threshold. Though the large number of parties in Romania is due in part to the incentives created by the allocation of ethnic minority seats, these figures exclude parties that might have benefited from this rule, yet they are still among the highest in the dataset.

And unlike in Poland, their number actually increased at the time of the introduction of a threshold in 1992, remaining high in 1996 despite an increase of the threshold to five per cent.

We would expect partisan electoral contestants to be numerous initially, due to the degree of uncertainty surrounding the first competitive multi-party elections. We should expect their number to fall off subsequently as parties are initiated into the painful truths of electoral competition and the system 'shakes down'. This pattern is found in several states; elsewhere the 'explosion' in parties occurred after the first elections, in some cases due to the break-up of the transition-era anti-communist front movements, and perhaps also because electoral hopefuls sought to imitate the successful strategies of other organizations (either in their own country or in neighbouring states). The incentives built into the electoral system ought, however, to 'kick in' not too long after the electoral system comes into use. There is evidence of a limited 'shakedown' effect over time as 'rational' small parties unite or exit from the system. Yet even by the end of the period there were large numbers of unsuccessful organizations fielding candidates. The average ratio of winners to losers remained at about 1 : 2 through the first three elections (the events for which we have full data).

As far the decision to enter the race is concerned, there is no evident difference between PR and SMD systems. This may be because most of the SMD systems listed here are actually components of mixed systems, and if parties decide to field candidates in one part of a mixed systems they are likely also to contest the other part. Yet this is not true for all the individual mixed systems, despite the fact that the overall averages for the number of contestants in each system type are virtually identical.

There is a clear difference between the two types of system in the numbers of winning parties they generate; PR systems have notably *fewer* successful parties overall than their SMD counterparts. This finding runs counter to the general wisdom that PR has a proliferative effect on the party system (though as we shall see later the picture is different when we measure the effective number of parties). It is also worth noting that this difference is not evident in the first elections, where the numbers of winners in the two system types were, on average, similar. The effect began to come into relief at the time of the second elections, perhaps because of a general increase in PR thresholds at around this point. Finally, this table provides evidence that in terms of the number of parties active in politics, mixed systems are again 'more than the sum of their parts', just as we found in the last chapter with regard to inclusion. However, this tendency is only evident at the level of electoral contestation; when it comes to the number of winners, mixed systems appear to be 'moderate' systems, generating typical parliamentary party systems in between those with SMD and PR rules. The measure of the effective number of parties developed by Laakso and Taagepera (1979) is likely to provide a better indicator of the 'real' party system size, as it weighs each party by its strength. Table 5.2 presents data on the effective number of elective and parliamentary parties for the 20 countries. As with the absolute number of parties, the average effective number of elective parties is approximately equal in PR and SMD systems. (Here there is no indication that mixed systems are 'more than the sum of their parts', for the simple reason that the figure for mixed systems is the weighted mean of the figures for the two parts of the system.) When we turn to the effective number of parliamentary parties, we see a reverse pattern from that observed in the preceding table. Though SMD systems allow a large number of parties to enter parliament, most of these are relatively minor organizations, and the average effective size of the parliamentary party systems elected in SMDs is smaller than those elected through PR. In conformity with the results of previous research, the effective number of parties in mixed systems tends to fall between that generated by the single-member part of the system and that resulting from the proportional seat distribution.

In addition to the size of the party system, we are also interested in its 'shape', that is, the way parties tend to cluster at different points in the spectrum. There are many aspects to the shape of the party system that could in theory be mentioned; we could analyse its 'tail' – the number of small parties that persist in contesting seats and perhaps even winning them. Or we could look at how many parties are in theory necessary to form a majority in parliament. But for the purposes of the present investigation it makes sense to concentrate on the 'head'. The ability of elections to generate compact coalitions or single-party governments may be linked to the long-term stability of emerging democracies. If, on the other hand, one party dominates the system and no other organization stands a chance of dislodging it from power, the situation can be said to be uncompetitive, which may also be detrimental to the consolidation of democracy. Table 5.3 presents vote and seat shares of the largest party and the two largest parties (from which the difference between the two top contestants can be derived).

It is clear from a cursory examination of these data that majorities of any kind have been relatively unusual in the post-communist region, and that most of them have been manufactured. Earned majorities

Table 5.2   Effective number of parties

Country	Effective number of elective parties			Effective number of parliamentary parties		
	PR	SMD	All	PR	SMD	All
Albania 1991	—	2.15	2.15	—	1.83	1.83
Albania 1992	—	2.19	2.19	1.50	1.59	1.97
Albania 1997	—	2.86 (.01)	2.86 (.01)	2.61	1.93	2.07
Albania 2001	3.19	2.93	3.00	3.04	1.68	2.60
Armenia 1995	4.24 (.02)	N/A	N/A	3.09	1.12	1.47
Armenia 1999	4.77	5.22	5.03	3.14	2.56	2.60
Bosnia & H. 1996	4.36	—	4.36	3.40	—	3.40
Bosnia & H. 1998	5.92	—	5.92	4.59	—	4.59
Bosnia & H. 2000	7.70	—	7.70	7.29	—	7.29
Bosnia & H. 2002	8.88	—	8.88	7.95	—	7.95
Bulgaria 1990	2.75	N/A	N/A	2.59	2.19	2.40
Bulgaria 1991	4.17	—	4.17	2.41	—	2.41
Bulgaria 1994	3.85	—	3.85	2.73	—	2.73
Bulgaria 1997	3.03	—	3.03	2.52	—	2.52
Bulgaria 2001	3.95	—	3.95	2.92	—	2.92
Croatia 1992	4.23 (0.01)	5.22 (0.04)	4.79 (0.02)	3.09	1.23	1.93
Croatia 1995	3.78 (0.04)	2.63	3.48	3.12	1.73	2.70
Croatia 2000	3.89 (0.05)	—	3.89 (0.05)	2.71	—	2.71
Czech Rep. 1990	3.50	—	3.50	2.22	—	2.22
Czech Rep. 1992	7.31	—	7.31	4.80	—	4.80
Czech Rep. 1996	5.33	—	5.33	4.15	—	4.15
Czech Rep. 1998	4.76	—	4.76	3.70	—	3.70
Czech Rep. 2002	4.82	—	4.82	3.67	—	3.67
Estonia 1992	8.12	—	8.12	5.90	—	5.90
Estonia 1995	5.92	—	5.92	4.15	—	4.15
Estonia 1999	6.68	—	6.68	5.50	—	5.50
Georgia 1992	10.06 (0.28)*	N/A	N/A	11.22	17.57	13.93
Georgia 1995	12.50	N/A	N/A	2.20	4.51	2.64
Georgia 1999	3.98	N/A	N/A	2.25	1.44	2.06
Hungary 1990	8.54	6.71	7.70	—	2.15	3.78
Hungary 1994	5.50	6.22	5.83	—	1.38	2.90
Hungary 1998	4.46	5.80	5.08	—	2.70	4.00
Hungary 2002	2.84	3.05	2.94	—	2.05	2.21
Latvia 1993	6.21	—	6.21	5.05	—	5.05
Latvia 1995	9.71	—	9.71	7.59	—	7.59
Latvia 1998	6.92	—	6.92	5.49	—	5.49
Latvia 2002	6.81	—	6.81	5.04	—	5.04

Table 5.2 (Continued)

Country	Effective number of elective parties			Effective number of parliamentary parties		
	PR	SMD	All	PR	SMD	All
Lithuania 1992	3.83	6.09	4.96	2.86	2.78	3.28
Lithuania 1996	7.16	7.31	7.24	3.40	2.74	3.14
Lithuania 2000	5.59	10.10	7.85	3.43	6.35	6.23
Macedonia 1994	—	5.63	5.63	—	1.66	1.66
Macedonia 1998	5.04	4.95	5.00	4.02	3.81	3.95
Macedonia 2002	4.14	—	4.14	2.88	—	2.88
Moldova 1994	3.76	—	3.76	2.62	—	2.62
Moldova 1998	5.19	—	5.19	3.43	—	3.43
Moldova 2001	3.57	—	3.57	1.85	—	1.85
Poland 1991	13.87	—	13.87	10.89	—	10.89
Poland 1993	9.80	—	9.80	3.88	—	3.88
Poland 1997	4.59	—	4.59	2.95	—	2.95
Poland 2001	4.50	—	4.50	3.60	—	3.60
Romania 1990	2.21	—	2.21	2.20	—	2.20
Romania 1992	7.08	—	7.08	4.78	—	4.78
Romania 1996	6.09	—	6.09	3.94	—	3.94
Romania 2000	5.26	—	5.26	3.57	—	3.57
Russia 1993	7.58	8.91	8.25	6.49	6.17	7.21
Russia 1995	10.06	10.99	10.53	3.31	5.11	4.23
Russia 1999	6.10	6.33	6.22	4.57	3.62	4.67
Slovakia 1990	5.80	—	5.80	4.99	—	4.99
Slovakia 1992	5.35	—	5.35	3.19	—	3.19
Slovakia 1994	5.81	—	5.81	6.97	—	6.97
Slovakia 1998	5.33	—	5.33	4.76	—	4.76
Slovakia 2002	8.86	—	8.86	6.12	—	6.12
Slovenia 1992	8.53	—	8.53	6.32	—	6.32
Slovenia 1996	6.38	—	6.38	5.29	—	5.29
Slovenia 2000	5.14 (.02)	—	5.14 (.02)	4.55	—	4.55
Ukraine 1994	—	5.17	5.17	—	3.37	3.37
Ukraine 1998	10.73	8.70	9.72	4.96	6.02	5.49
Ukraine 2002	7.87	5.56	6.72	4.67	2.75	4.43
Yugoslavia 2000	N/A	—	N/A	3.12	—	3.12
Mean: 1st election	6.10	5.70	5.90	4.86	4.01	4.38
Mean: 2nd election	7.02	6.03	6.76	3.88	3.27	3.88
Mean: 3rd election	5.39	6.13	5.36	4.06	3.13	4.14
Mean: 4th election	4.96	2.99	4.94	4.39	1.87	3.99
Mean: 5th election	5.88	—	5.88	4.24	—	4.24

Table 5.2   (Continued)

Country	Effective number of elective parties			Effective number of parliamentary parties		
	PR	SMD	All	PR	SMD	All
Overall mean	5.60	5.67	5.87	4.25	3.41	4.12

* This figure is based on first-preference votes.

Notes: These figures do not include independent candidates. Party vote and seat totals were recalculated on the basis of denominators from which independents were excluded. The figures also exclude ethnic representatives of minority, regional, and overseas groups elected according to different rules and/or through separate processes.

In mixed systems, the effective number of elective parties is calculated as the weighted average of the effective number of parties in the two votes.

Figures in brackets are margins of error. Where data were incomplete, Taagepera's method of bounds was used to perform the calculations. According to this method the logical maximum and minimum are calculated on the basis of the available data, and the estimate reported is the mean of these two figures (Taagepera, 1997). The estimates reported here have margins of error ranging from 0.01 to 0.05. The precise margins for each figure are indicated in the table in brackets where they are 0.01 or greater.

Table 5.3   Party vote and seat shares

Country	Vote shares (%)		Seat shares (%)	
	Largest party	Largest two parties	Largest party	Largest two parties
Albania 1991	56.17	94.88	67.60	97.60
Albania 1992	62.29	87.86	65.71	92.85
Albania 1997	52.75	78.45	66.45	85.53
Albania 2001	SM: 43.89	SM: 81.96	*SM: 73.00*	SM: 100
	PR: 41.51	PR: 78.32	*PR: 52.50*	PR: 68.00
Armenia 1995	SM: N/A	SM: N/A	*SM: 94.29*	SM: 96.19
	PR: 42.66	PR: 59.54	*(66.00)**	(67.33)
			PR: 50.00	PR: 70.00
Armenia 1999	SM: 37.46	SM: 52.08	*SM: 60.53*	SM: 71.05
	(20.64)	(28.70)	*(30.67)*	(36.00)
	PR: 41.67	PR: 53.77	*PR: 51.79*	PR: 66.07
Bosnia & H. 1996	37.92	52.02	45.24	66.54
Bosnia & H. 1998	33.97	46.46	40.48	54.77
Bosnia & H. 2000	18.76	36.76	21.43	40.48
Bosnia & H. 2002	21.92	35.96	23.81	38.10

Table 5.3   (Continued)

Country	Vote shares (%)		Seat shares (%)	
	Largest party	Largest two parties	Largest party	Largest two parties
Bulgaria 1990	SM: N/A	SM: N/A	*SM: 57.58*	SM: 92.43
	PR: 47.15	PR: 83.36	*PR: 48.50***	PR: 86.00
Bulgaria 1991	34.36	67.50	45.83	90.00
Bulgaria 1994	43.50	67.73	*52.08*	80.83
Bulgaria 1997	52.02	73.99	*57.08*	81.24
Bulgaria 2001	42.74	60.92	50.00	71.25
Croatia 1992	SM: 38.30	SM: 51.97	*SM: 90.00*	SM: 91.67
	PR: 43.72	PR: 61.05	*PR: 51.67*	PR: 71.67
Croatia 1995	SM: N/A	SM: N/A	*SM: 60.00*	SM: 71.43
	PR: 45.2	PR: 63.5	*PR: 52.50***	PR: 72.50
Croatia 2000	39.38	66.51	*50.71*	79.28
Czech Rep. 1990	53.15	66.63	*67.32*	82.17
Czech Rep. 1992	33.90	48.16	48.50	67.70
Czech Rep. 1996	29.62	56.06	34.00	64.50
Czech Rep. 1998	32.31	60.05	37.00	68.50
Czech Rep. 2002	30.20	54.67	35.00	64.00
Estonia 1992	22.00	35.60	28.71	45.54
Estonia 1995	32.23	48.42	40.59	59.40
Estonia 1999	23.41	39.50	27.72	45.54
Georgia 1992	SM: N/A	SM: N/A	SM: 8.75	SM: 17.50
	PR: 22.7	PR: 34.8	PR: 15.22	PR: 24.35
Georgia 1995	SM: N/A	SM: N/A	*SM: 42.00*	SM: 56.00
	PR: 23.71	PR: 31.66	*(27.27)*	(36.36)
			PR: 61.64	PR: 82.87
Georgia 1999	SM: N/A	SM: N/A	*SM: 82.46*	SM: 94.74
	PR: 41.75	PR: 66.93	*(64.38)*	(73.97)
			PR: 56.67	PR: 90.67
Hungary 1990	SM: 23.93	SM: 45.66	SM: 64.77	SM: 84.66
	PR: 24.73	PR: 46.12	PR: 27.14	PR: 50.95
Hungary 1994	SM: 31.27	SM: 49.89	*SM: 84.66*	SM: 93.75
	PR: 32.99	PR: 52.73	*PR: 28.57*	PR: 53.81
Hungary 1998	SM: 29.82	SM: 42.68	SM: 31.25	SM: 61.93
	PR: 32.92	PR: 62.40	PR: 38.10	PR: 65.72
Hungary 2002	SM: 40.50	SM: 79.93	SM: 53.98	SM: 98.39
	PR: 42.05	PR: 83.12	PR: 47.62	PR: 91.91
Latvia 1993	32.41	45.76	36.00	51.00
Latvia 1995	15.22	30.19	18.00	35.00
Latvia 1998	21.30	39.45	24.00	45.00
Latvia 2002	23.93	42.87	26.00	50.00

Table 5.3   (Continued)

Country	Vote Shares (%)		Seat shares (%)	
	Largest party	Largest two parties	Largest party	Largest two parties
Lithuania 1992	SM: 34.98	SM: 49.24	*SM: 52.11*	SM: 70.42
	PR: 43.98	PR: 65.15	*PR: 51.43*	PR: 75.72
Lithuania 1996	SM: 28.65	SM: 41.89	SM: 55.22	SM: 62.68
	PR: 31.34	PR: 41.77	PR: 31.34	PR: 41.77
Lithuania 2000	SM: 15.65	SM: 31.06	SM: 32.39	SM: 57.74
	PR: 31.08	PR: 50.72	PR: 31.08	PR: 50.72
Macedonia 1994	29.49	43.79	*72.50*	80.83
Macedonia 1998	SM: 33.05	SM: 57.98	SM: 54.12	SM: 74.17
	PR: 28.10	PR: 53.24	PR: 31.43	PR: 60.00
Macedonia 2002	40.46	64.87	50.00	77.50
Moldova 1994	43.18	65.18	*53.85*	80.77
Moldova 1998	30.01	49.43	39.60	65.34
Moldova 2001	50.07	63.43	*70.30*	89.11
Poland 1991	12.32	24.34	13.47	26.51
Poland 1993	20.41	35.81	37.17	65.86
Poland 1997	33.83	60.96	43.69	79.34
Poland 2001	41.04	53.72	46.96	61.09
Romania 1990	66.31	73.54	**66.41**	73.73
Romania 1992	27.72	47.73	35.67	60.67
Romania 1996	30.17	51.69	35.57	62.10
Romania 2000	36.61	56.09	44.93	69.28
Russia 1993	SM: 19.55	SM: 35.16	SM: 38.46	SM: 58.97
	(8.08)	(14.53)	(13.70)	(21.01)
	PR: 23.93	PR: 40.12	PR: 26.22	PR: 44.00
Russia 1995	SM: 18.53	SM: 27.33	SM: 39.19	SM: 52.70
	(8.02)	(11.83)	(26.66)	(35.54)
	PR: 22.92	PR: 34.41	PR: 44.00	PR: 66.22
Russia 1999	SM: 30.50	SM: 49.98	SM: 41.96	SM: 67.84
	(15.56)	(25.50)	(20.98)	(33.92)
	PR: 25.02	PR: 48.31	PR: 29.77	PR: 58.21
Slovakia 1990	29.35	48.56	32.00	52.67
Slovakia 1992	37.26	51.96	49.33	68.66
Slovakia 1994	34.97	45.39	30.50	42.50
Slovakia 1998	27.00	53.33	28.67	56.67
Slovakia 2002	24.00	42.67	19.50	34.59
Slovenia 1992	23.46	37.97	25.00	42.05
Slovenia 1996	27.01	46.39	28.41	50.00
Slovenia 2000	36.23	52.03	38.64	54.55

114   *Electoral Systems and Political Transformation*

Table 5.3   (Continued)

Country	Vote shares (%)		Seat shares (%)	
	Largest party	Largest two parties	Largest party	Largest two parties
Ukraine 1994	37.91 (12.72)	53.26 (17.87)	35.83 (25.44)	44.17 (31.36)
Ukraine 1998	SM: 26.88	SM: 38.48	SM: 34.86	SM: 47.71
	(14.69)	(21.03)	(16.44)	(22.67)
	PR: 24.65	PR: 34.05	PR: 37.33	PR: 51.55
Ukraine 2002	SM: 27.98	SM: 52.81	SM: 50.77	SM: 82.31
	(16.36)	(30.88)	(29.33)	(47.55)
	PR: 23.57	PR: 43.55	PR: 31.11	PR: 57.33
Yugoslavia 2000	43.86	76.81	42.03	73.91
Mean: 1st election	36.36	54.63	45.20	63.41
Mean: 2nd election	31.25	48.68	44.18	64.68
Mean: 3rd election	33.59	54.52	41.88	66.08
Mean: 4th election	35.39	59.66	42.29	67.61
Mean: 5th election	32.31	52.75	34.83	56.61
Overall mean	33.93	53.54	43.22	64.71

* Single-member district vote totals are not available; it seems probable that this was an earned majority of those seats won by parties but a manufactured majority overall.
** Single-member district vote totals are not available, but it seems probable that these were manufactured majorities.
Notes: Earned single-party majorities are in bold; manufactured single-party majorities are in bold italics.
For two-round systems, all calculations are based on first-round votes.
All estimations are for the party (coalition) share of the total vote. Independent candidates are excluded and totals are recalculated on the basis of denominators that include only partisan contestants. In most cases this adjustment has little impact on the overall percentages, but in the Armenian, Georgian (1995 and 1999), Russian and Ukrainian single-member district contests the differences are substantial, as independents have won between one-fifth and two-thirds of these seats in each election held in these countries. The figures for the totals including independents are therefore included in brackets after the party totals.

(indicated in the table in plain bold font) were generated by the Albanian elections of 1991, 1992, and 1997, Armenia 1995, Bulgaria 1997, the Czech Republic 1990, Moldova 2001, and Romania 1990. Only in the case of Romania 1990 was the majority large enough that the party in question could be described as 'dominant' (if it were not for the fact that it failed to remain in power). If we add in manufactured majorities (noted in bold italics), we find that parliamentary majorities have been possible regularly in Albanian and Croatia, usually in Armenia, Bulgaria, Georgia, and Moldova, once and nearly twice in Macedonia, and once each (mostly at the first election) in the Czech Republic, Hungary, Lithuania, and Romania.

Interestingly, there has been relatively little variation over time in either the vote or the seat share of the top parties. Given that we have observed consolidation in party system size, we can conclude that most of the changes have been taking place in party system 'tails' rather than their 'heads'.

These data provide some confirmation of our hypotheses vis-à-vis the overall electoral system architecture. Multivariate analysis will enable us to establish more complex effects. Regression models were constructed on the basis of the effective number of elective and parliamentary parties in order to examine the effects of institutional factors on the size of the party system. Separate models were then built to test the impact of these factors on the shape of party systems, understood in terms of the seat distribution among the most successful entrants.

Table 5.4 presents models for the effective number of elective and parliamentary parties (based on country averages). Electoral system type by itself does not appear to have a significant impact on the effective number of elective parties. Neither dummy variables for discrete electoral system type nor the proportion of PR districts is significant. Duverger's 'psychological effect' does not appear to have been strong in these transitional elections, possibly because voters have too little reliable information to act strategically in the post-communist setting. As we expected, the overall size of party systems is demonstrably larger in the former Soviet states, but there is no evident interaction effect between location in the former Soviet Union (FSU) and electoral system type.

The option of voting for an individual does, however, have the expected effect of dispersing the vote among parties. This indicates that it is not district design *per se* that is the most important institutional determinant of vote decisions, but the personalization of vote choice engendered by the option of selecting individual candidates, be it in the context of SMD elections or preference voting on PR lists.

116   *Electoral Systems and Political Transformation*

Table 5.4   OLS models of the effective number of parties (country averages)

Variable	Effective number of elective parties	Effective number of parliamentary parties
Proportion PR seats		3.350 (1.282)**
Vote for an individual	1.965 (0.962)*	1.605 (0.673)**
Location in the FSU	1.421 (0.668)**	3.338 (1.245)**
Interaction between proportion of PR seats and FSU		−3.123 (1.632)*
Constant	3.707 (0.856)	0.182 (1.230)

Entries are unstandardized regression coefficients (standard errors).
$N =$ 19   20
Adjusted R^2 =0.303, 0.352
* $p < 0.10$; ** $p < 0.05$

Note: Yugoslavia is excluded due to lack of complete data. The dependent variable for the mixed elections held in Bulgaria 1990, Armenia 1995, Georgia 1995, and Georgia 1999 is the effective number of elective parties for the PR component of the ballot only, due to lack of complete data for the SMD races. These cases are coded as PR elections for the purposes of this analysis.

If parties are mobilizing voters, they appear to be doing so primarily via personal links, for none of the campaign finance variables was significant here. The 'cartelization' hypothesis thus receives little support from these results. Existing parliamentary parties may be attempting to restrict the number of parties in the system and concentrate the vote around incumbent players by introducing campaign finance measures, but there is little evidence that they have been effective in shaping vote choice through this mechanism.

In the final columns of Table 5.4 we can observe the effects of these variables on the effective number of parliamentary parties. The impact of the traditional electoral system indicators is in evidence at this level; as was clear from the data in Table 5.2, systems with greater numbers of PR seats are associated with significantly larger parliamentary party systems. In this model we also find the expected interaction between electoral system type and location in the FSU. As predicted, SMD electoral systems have a different effect on the process of aggregating votes into seats in regionally fragmented party systems from that found in more nationally homogeneous contexts. Once we take the interaction term into account, the effect of SMDs is only a slightly reductive one in the FSU, whereas the proportion of SMDs has a marked consolidating effect in Central Europe. There is scant evidence, however, that mixed systems are distinctive in their reductive impact on parliamentary party systems; a model (not reported here) in which the system types were entered as separate

Table 5.5 OLS model of closeness of the race (difference between the vote shares of the two largest parties) (country averages)

Variable	B
Proportion PR seats	−5.674 (2.917)*
Location in the FSU	−5.273 (2.068)**
Constant	25.574 (2.307)

Entries are unstandardized regression coefficients (standard errors).
$N = 20$
Adjusted $R^2 = 0.308$
* $p < 0.10$; ** $p < 0.05$

dummy variables reveals that mixed and pure SMD systems operate in similar ways.

Again the variables designating campaign finance regulations failed to achieve statistical significance, as did controls for presidentialism, socioeconomic level, and level of democratic development. The principal influences on party system size appear to be those associated with electoral institutions and sub-regional location.

Turning now to the 'shape' of the party system, Table 5.5 displays a model for closeness of the race, measured in terms of the difference between the vote share of the largest party and that of the second-largest. It is necessary to bear in mind when interpreting the coefficients in this model that, because the dependent variable is operationalized as the distance between the two largest parties, it is actually a measure of *un*competitiveness. The results of this analysis suggest that PR seats enhance competitiveness, most likely because the seat share of the largest party is not magnified under PR rules to nearly the same extent as occurs in SMD contests. Once this variable is entered into the equation, none of the other institutional indicators comes even close to achieving significance. The only other factor to be significantly associated with competitiveness is once again location in the FSU. Interestingly, elections in the former Soviet states appear to be more competitive than those elsewhere, once we take the electoral system into account.

Conclusion

Existing theories of electoral system design predict that districting and vote-to-seat conversion formulae will be linked to the size of party systems. The findings of this chapter confirm this to be the case in post-communist Europe. But they also add some new twists; they show that the effect of SMD elections is heavily dependent on the political context in which they occur. Where party systems are nationalized, SMD rules have a restrictive impact on both the effective number of elective parties and the effective number of parties that succeed in winning places in parliament. However, where the party system exhibits high levels of regional fragmentation, as is the case in the former Soviet states, SMD systems have little or no such effect, and in many cases they actually generate substantially more fragmented parliamentary party systems.

A second valuable insight to come out of this analysis is that the overall electoral system architecture is not the only factor to influence party system size; the availability of a personal vote also has significant impacts on parliamentary party system size. This is an aspect of electoral systems that has not been extensively studied in previous empirical work, and our findings suggest that the relative influence of this variable could be profitably tested in the context of established democracies as well.

The institution of the directly elected president did not have any discernable impact on either the size or the shape of the parliamentary party system. This may either be because post-communist presidents have tended to shun party politics and to build political support on the basis of personal characteristics, or it may be that the effect was simply not strong enough to be evident in the small dataset employed here. Whatever the reason, it is attributes of the electoral system itself which appear to have the strongest impact on party system dimensions.

These findings suggest that electoral engineers can employ a number of tools to encourage party system institutionalization. Not only can they alter the overall architecture of the electoral system (with attention to the regional distribution of partisan support); if the party system is deemed too large they can also consider ridding the electoral law of elements of personal voting. Yet the impact of electoral institutions is strongly conditioned by the socio-political context of the state in question; where national integration of the party system has not taken place, electoral systems 'behave' differently. What this chapter has not told us is how the electoral system affects the over-time stability of the party system. As we have argued, institutionalization involves both the generation of moderately sized competitive party systems and the creation of relatively stable patterns over time. The temporal dimension of this process is the subject of Chapter 6.

6
Party System Stability and Change

This chapter will examine the impact of electoral systems on party system stability, understood in terms of electoral volatility and the ability of new entrants into the electoral arena to penetrate the support bases of existing political organizations. Stability and change in party systems have long fascinated political scientists, but the nature of the research questions they have asked has been conditioned by the cases they have taken as their objects of study. When we turn our attention to areas of the world that have not been subject to such intense scholarly investigation as the established democracies of the 'West', we may need to re-think the conceptual tools we use in interpreting and explaining changes in the configuration of electoral contenders. The specific aim of this chapter is to formulate new ways of understanding party system change and to assess how electoral institutions have affected recent party system developments in post-communist Europe. The focus of the analysis will be on two distinct aspects of party system dynamics: volatility and replacement. Volatility, a concept already well developed in the literature, refers to changes over successive elections in the balance of party support. Yet volatility understood in this sense fails adequately to capture the numerous party foundations, splits, mergers, and name changes characteristic of post-communist politics. In this context it is also desirable to deploy the complementary concept of party replacement – the extent to which new political formations are successful in drawing electoral support.[1]

Mobility in the party system has both advantages and disadvantages. As Bartolini and Mair (1990) argue, variations in electoral support are the main basis on which party leaders plan strategies. Likewise, rises and falls in partisan strength may be taken to indicate that the party system is responsive to the changing preferences of voters (Budge, 1982). In the context of rapid socio-economic change such as that experienced during the period of post-communist economic restructuring, adaptability may be a good thing. But turbulence in the party system cannot necessarily be attributed to variations in electoral preferences alone. On the contrary, there is much research indicating that the basic political proclivities of post-communist electorates have remained relatively stable over the past 10 years and that most of the change in post-communist party systems has been driven instead by élite-level fluidity (e.g. Markowski, 1997; Miller *et al.*, 1998; Birch, 2000b; King, 2000; Rose *et al.*, 2001). A consistently high level of party system instability has four main consequences that can be expected to be detrimental to democratic consolidation.

1. It reduces accountability – voters cannot 'throw the rascals out' if the rascals no longer exist as a unified group. In the absence of mechanisms that ensure accountability, voters may become disillusioned with democracy itself.
2. It impedes party institutionalization by decreasing the level of long-term commitment which politicians, activists, and voters have to 'their' party.
3. It significantly increases uncertainty, hampering the ability of politicians and voters to engage in strategically-driven co-ordination which, as we have argued, can play an important role in shaping the impact of electoral institutions.
4. It raises the stakes of the electoral game. This may have the consequence of weakening the democratic commitment of politicians, who could then seek other ways of feathering their beds so as to insure themselves against possible political loss at the next election.

The successful consolidation of democracy requires enough uncertainty to keep losers in the political game, but not so much that elections become a lottery. Despite the potential benefits of flexibility in the party system, excessive instability undermines the basis for political representation; it is likely to be associated with general political and social instability which has the potential to generate an authoritarian backlash.[2] The conceptualization and measurement of party system change is thus key to an adequate understanding of post-communist political transformation. This analysis will necessarily build on valuable previous work that has been conducted on post-communist party system development. Yet it will also challenge some of the generalizations that have been made about party systems in the region on the basis of a more limited range of cases.

Conceptualizing and measuring party system instability

The concept of electoral volatility was long understood to explain change *in electoral preferences* over time as a result of secular transformations in values and social structure.[3] Yet the way in which the concept is measured confounds mass level variation in preferences and élite-driven variation in the objects of choice on offer. Measured in terms of the sum of change in support for individual parties between one election and the next, electoral volatility is a 'multi-layered and multi-dimensional concept' (Crewe, 1985: 8). The overall or aggregate volatility between election t and election $t+1$ is the result of a combination of three factors: (1) changes in party support on the part of individual voters who vote at both election t and election $t+1$; (2) change in the composition of the electorate as a result of exits, entries, and variations in abstentionism; (3) changes in the range of parties on offer due to party entries, exits, alterations in the composition of coalitions, and non-contestation. Most studies of volatility in established democracies have been primarily concerned with voter behaviour, so they have been mainly interested in the first and possibly the second of these factors. They have generally assumed that third – the turnover of electoral contenders – is small enough that the standard measures of volatility are a good proxy for changing voter behaviour. In other words, the assumption in much of the literature has been that élite-level change in the supply of parties reflects and is prompted by changes in the demands made by the electorate.[4]

Whether or not this market model is an accurate reflection of party system development in existing democracies, it is not an apt characterization of party system change in many democratizing states. Whereas in most established democracies there is a high degree of continuity in the range of political options on offer from one election to the next, emergent party systems in post-transition countries are often considerably less stable. Most countries in the Eastern European region have followed a far more 'command economy' style development in which the supply of parties has been based primarily on the whim of élites with little reference to the demands, desires, or preferences of the electorate. As has already been noted, most of the emerging party systems of Central and Eastern Europe have been characterized by fluidity, splits, mergers, and weak links with their corresponding electorates. In this context the turnover of parties – or *party replacement* – is of substantive interest in its own right, especially when it is thought to form a large component of overall party system instability. A high level of 'churn' in the range of parties contesting elections can be expected to generate voter disorientation and hamper party institutionalization. Thus when dealing with systems that experience much inter-electoral change in the identities of parties, it is desirable to disentangle volatility within the existing system from the emergence of new parties. Not only will this give greater conceptual clarity to the measure of volatility, but it will also make it easier to trace the impact of institutional design on electoral outcomes.

Unfortunately a number of difficulties arise in attempting to develop two separate measures for volatility and replacement. Some of these difficulties are inherent in any measure based on aggregate electoral results alone. The impossibility of ever measuring individual-level volatility on the basis of aggregate results is well known, and though aggregate and individual-level volatility have been found to co-vary in established Western democracies (Crewe and Denver, 1985; Bartolini and Mair, 1990), we cannot assume that this will be the case in other contexts. Furthermore, a voter who votes for party A at election t may not have had any change in party preference at election $t + 1$, but they will nevertheless be required to change their expressed preference and vote for party B (or C, or some other party) if party A is no longer on the ballot. But the voter might equally have switched their preference and would have voted for party B even if party A had still been available. It is therefore impossible ever to capture the true amount of switching – forced or voluntary – without recourse to specially designed comparative surveys (which do not exist for most of the states under consideration here), nor is it ever possible to know how much aggregate change is due to true variations in party preference or changes in the choice of parties on offer. Fortunately we can develop approximations of both volatility among existing parties and party replacement by examining trends in the electoral support for different types of party.

Volatility among existing parties can be estimated by calculating the amount of change observed within the set of parties (or other groupings that present themselves to voters) that contest two consecutive elections. For this purpose we exclude all those parties that did not contest both elections and sum the differences in the vote shares of the remaining political organizations. This corresponds to the standard procedure used to construct the 'Pedersen index' of volatility. But to obtain the 'true' volatility score, it is necessary to divide not by 2 as with the Pedersen index, but by the sum of the fractional shares of the total vote at each election of the parties which are included in the calculations.[5]

More formally, volatility is defined as:

$$V = \frac{\Sigma \left| c_{i,t+1} - c_{i,t} \right|}{\Sigma c_{i,t+1} + \Sigma c_{i,t}}$$

where V is volatility, $c_{i,t}$ is the vote share of continuous party i at the first election (t) and $c_{i,t+1}$ is the vote share of continuous party i at the second election ($t + 1$).

If volatility thus defined is a measure of changes in the electoral fortunes of existing players in the political game, party replacement can be understood as the degree of penetration of new players into the party system. It can be measured as the proportion of the electorate attracted to new political formations, or the sum of the vote shares won by electoral contenders at election $t + 1$ that had not contested election t.

It is worth noting that though volatility and replacement both vary from 0 to 100, they are not directly comparable, given that they are measured in different ways and from different vote totals. In order to enhance the comparability of the two figures, it is useful to supplement the volatility score as defined above with the conventional (Pedersen) score using 2 as a denominator. This second measure provides an approximation of the proportion of the *total electorate* that switched votes among existing parties (see Table 6.1).

These measures are straightforward in theory, but in practice it is necessary to decide what constitutes the 'same' electoral contender. The formation of entirely new parties presents no problems, nor does the electoral extinction of an existing party. The problems arise when parties split, merge, form or leave coalitions, and/or change their names from one election to the next. As noted above, such changes have been very common in post-communist Europe, so it makes sense to deal with this problem systematically rather than making *ad hoc* assumptions about the continuity of party identities. From the point of view of the research questions addressed in this analysis, the crucial criterion is that of *institutional continuity*, which involves such factors as continuity of organizational resources from one election to the next as well as aspects of party identity, most importantly the degree to which voters are aware of the changes of identity that 'their' party has undergone and are willing to follow 'their' party under its new guise. Again this is something that we can not know for certain without detailed (and non-existent) individual-level data. But we can make some educated assumptions as to which parties and coalitions satisfy criteria of

Table 6.1   Volatility scores

Country	First–second election	Second–third election	Third–fourth election
Central Europe			
Albania – SMD	29.39 (27.83)	18.18 (13.01)	13.03 (12.21)
Bosnia & H.	18.63 (16.10)	24.25 (17.13)	13.29 (12.57)
Bulgaria – PR	10.94 (9.68)	20.92 (9.95)	25.10 (21.98)
Croatia – PR	10.13 (9.64)	24.77 (23.77)	
Croatia – SMD	17.46 (15.28)		
Czech Republic	19.56 (6.91)	19.11 (16.11)	8.56 (7.62)
Hungary – PR	24.98 (23.87)	30.69 (29.39)	20.20 (19.05)
Hungary – SMD	26.79 (25.10)	23.43 (22.30)	26.22 (23.47)
Macedonia – PR		16.46 (11.97)	
Macedonia – SMD	22.03 (17.73)		
Poland	24.26 (17.86)	13.21 (12.26)	38.38 (30.01)
Romania	56.52 (43.83)	16.34 (13.99)	30.88 (16.59)
Slovakia	16.17 (8.55)	14.21 (12.77)	17.13 (9.42)
Slovenia	22.93 (17.39)	19.82 (17.03)	
Mean CE*	*23.48 (18.30)*	*19.81 (15.85)*	*21.47 (16.59)*
FSU			
Armenia – PR	36.77 (12.64)		
Estonia	23.14 (13.20)	23.74 (12.08)	
Georgia – PR	28.99 (16.23)**	32.68 (21.65)	
Latvia	41.71 (25.67)	48.58 (22.99)	N/A
Lithuania – PR	41.49 (20.36)	42.72 (36.74)	
Lithuania – SMD	36.14 (24.35)	35.77 (28.16)	
Moldova	78.17 (32.06)	33.98 (22.45)	
Russia – PR	35.86 (24.51)	24.00 (12.77)	
Russia – SMD	30.22 (19.45)	30.79 (16.57)	
Ukraine – PR		12.73 (16.89)	
Ukraine – SMD	19.71 (16.83)	18.61 (10.65)	
Mean FSU*	*37.55 (20.12)*	*31.61 (20.24)*	
Mean*	29.40 (19.83)	24.40 (17.56)	21.47 (16.59)

* Figures for mixed systems are averaged so that each state is counted once.
** These figures are estimates based on incomplete data for first preferences only. The margins of error are 5.7 and 2.6 respectively.

Note: Numbers in parentheses are the Pedersen volatility score (employing a denominator of 2).

Sources: See Appendices B and C.

institutional continuity and which do not. The details of the criteria used to classify parties and other political groupings into continuous and non-continuous are laid out in Appendix C, together with assumptions made about data from individual countries.

Explaining party system change in post-communist Europe

The majority of Eastern European states have what Peter Mair describes as 'open' party systems in which patterns of competition are not well established and parties do not have stable support bases (Mair, 1997). A number of scholars have noted the high volatility levels in post-communist Europe in comparison with average rates in Western European countries (Cotta, 1996; Mair, 1997; Olson, 1998; Rose *et al.*, 1998: 118–19; Lewis, 2000). In a survey of party system development in Western Europe between 1885 and 1985, Bartolini and Mair find that the average volatility over this period was 9.1 (Bartolini and Mair, 1990: 148). The highest scores were 32.1 in Germany between 1919 and 1920, followed by 31.1 in France 1902–06 (1990: Appendix 2). In post-communist Europe the average volatility in the 13 years following the communist collapse was 18.76 – measured in terms of the total vote (using the Pedersen index). Levels of 'Pedersen' volatility have been as high as 43.8 (Romania 1990–92), and there have been four cases of scores over 30 (Romania 1990–92, Moldova 1994–98, Lithuania 1996–2000, and Poland 1997–2001). In only three cases has volatility as a proportion of the total vote been *lower* than the Western European average – the Czech Republic 1990–92 and 1996–98, and Slovakia 1990–92 (see Table 6.1). There have also been extremely high levels of electoral replacement in some countries. Second elections in both Armenia and Georgia saw nearly 80 per cent of voters opt for party lists that had not contested the first elections. In Moldova not one of the parties elected in 1994 was re-elected in 1998. And in Latvia the two largest parties in 1995 between them polled only 3.35 per cent of the vote four years later (see Table 6.2). These patterns indicate that party system change in post-communist Europe has more in common with patterns observed in other democratizing regions such as Latin America than with patterns found in the West.[6]

These high levels of instability can be explained with reference to several aspects of the post-communist transition process. First, the lack of 'usable' pre-existing party systems in most countries in the region has meant that politicians have effectively had to form partisan structures from scratch; at the same time civil society has been severely under-developed and voter identification with parties has generally been low (Wyman *et al.*, 1995: 546; Miller *et al.*, 1998: 170). Parties formed from scratch may be rather inexpertly organized and subject to the whims of a small number of leaders. Second, rapid socio-structural change has

Table 6.2   Party replacement scores

Country	First–second election	Second–third election	Third–fourth election
Central Europe			
Albania – SMD	8.03	15.50	7.09
Bosnia & H.	16.84	29.71	10.53
Bulgaria – PR	58.09	55.63	12.34
Croatia – PR	4.76	3.30	
Croatia – SMD	11.98		
Czech Republic	61.44	8.07	11.13
Hungary – PR	5.64	2.22	4.03
Hungary – SMD	7.90	4.95	5.59
Macedonia – PR		31.61	
Macedonia – SMD	10.62		
Poland	26.11	10.88	30.72
Romania	41.77	14.69	32.89
Slovakia	52.00	22.77	50.70
Slovenia	27.32	16.83	
*Mean CE**	*28.68*	*19.32*	*20.02*
FSU			
Armenia – PR	78.26		
Estonia	44.38	40.97	
Georgia – PR	79.26	27.03	
Latvia	48.77	63.44	N/A
Lithuania – PR	61.27	22.80	
Lithuania – SMD	44.48	32.81	
Moldova	91.55	36.45	
Russia – PR	45.63	57.66	
Russia – SMD	45.72	45.23	
Ukraine – PR		16.99	
Ukraine – SMD	25.70	12.40	
*Mean FSU**	*58.31*	*37.99*	
*Mean**	*41.16*	*27.18*	*20.02*

* Figures for mixed systems are averaged so that each state is counted once.

Sources: See Appendices B and C.

accompanied economic change, resulting in significant shifts in the objective interests of large sections of the electorate over the course of the past decade. If party support is based at least in part on social cleavages in the electorate as hypothesized by Lipset and Rokkan (1967), then rapid shifts in social structure will tend to generate instability in the party system. There is considerable debate as to whether the 'Lipset–Rokkan thesis' is indeed valid in the post-communist states (Cotta, 1996, 1998; Mair, 1997), but some evidence suggests that there have been elements of sociologically based vote choice in the post-communist region (Evans and Whitefield, 2000; Birch, 2000b).

Under these circumstances, institutional design can be predicted to affect levels of electoral instability, though the precise relationship may be complex. We would expect to see volatility dampened under electoral systems such as SMD with high natural thresholds of success, because voters will be wary of opting for electoral alternatives that have little chance of winning, and with fewer viable objects of choice, there ought to be less switching.[7] For the same 'psychological' reasons that SMD systems are hypothesized to restrict the size of the party system, they ought also to stabilize it over time. We might also expect to observe less volatility in any system that involves voting for individuals. In as much as individual candidates can retain the personal allegiance of voters, they may be able to bind voters to parties more effectively than parties can do through other means. Voter loyalty to candidates should tend to introduce an element of 'stickiness' into the vote calculus.

A final set of electoral institutional variables that we might anticipate would have an impact on volatility is the suite of predictors we have developed to represent campaign finance regulatory devices. If it is true that the state funding of parties 'freezes' the party system, we should expect lower levels of volatility in states that fund election campaigns. Parties that win large numbers of votes at one election will receive correspondingly large amounts of money to fight the next race. If this money is spent effectively it should create a feed-back loop which will have a multiplicative effect on the vote share of large parties (bearing in mind the inevitable ceilings implicit in the competitive situation). For the same reason, limits on spending ought to reduce vote shifts in as much as they restrict the capacity of one political contestant to poach votes from another.

Several additional aspects of electoral competition can be hypothe-sized to have discernable impacts on volatility, among them variables that have been modelled in previous chapters of this book. Bartolini and Mair (1990) found electoral participation to be positively associated with volatility in Western Europe. This makes sense if we accept that turnout shapes levels of party loyalty among the voting public. When large sectors of the population turn out to vote, they are more likely to include those who are only weakly tied to parties, whereas when voting is restricted to hard-core supporters, there is likely to be less switching. Levels of representational inclusion could also influence volatility, in as much as those excluded from representation at election t might chose to vote for a party with better prospects at election $t = 1$.

Similarly, there are reasons for believing that electoral systems should influence volatility indirectly due to the effect they have on party system size. The number of parties that compete for elections has been found to be positively associated with electoral volatility (Pedersen, 1979; Crewe, 1985; Bartolini and Mair, 1990), and we saw in the last chapter that electoral system is one of the main determinants of party system size in post-communist Europe (as elsewhere). Fewer parties in the system mean fewer alternatives that might appeal to voters at given points in the ideological spectrum, whereas a greater number of parties means more parties that are proximal to voters in ideological space, so more options that each individual voter might be attracted to (Pedersen, 1979; Crewe, 1985). We would thus expect the electoral system to influence volatility indirectly *via* the number of parties it encourages to compete (understood either in terms of the absolute or the effective number of elective parties).

A final electorally related factor we may see associated with volatility is the length of time between elections. The reasoning here is simple: over longer periods of time more voters will become disaffected with the party they voted for at the previous election and hence more likely to opt for a different choice when the election is finally held. (There is, however, relatively little variation over states in the average length of time between parliamentary elections – the lowest is 2 in Bosnia, which held such events every two years between 1996 and 2002, and the highest is 4, an average that reflects the orderly cycle of full-term parliaments in Armenia, Hungary, Lithuania, Macedonia, Slovenia, and Ukraine, as well as a slightly more erratic pattern in Croatia.)

There is reason to believe that a number of variables not directly related to the institutions of parliamentary elections may also affect volatility, including presidentialism. If parliamentary office is a lesser goal for politicians than the presidency – which it will surely be in any system with a directly elected executive presidency – then popular politicians may use political parties primarily as vehicles to launch a bid for the presidency. As noted in previous chapters, comparative research has found that two-round presidential electoral systems – which are universal among the presidential democracies of Central and Eastern Europe – have the effect of fragmenting the party system by encouraging popular politicians to form separate political organizations in their efforts to jockey for a place in the second round (Shugart and Carey, 1992; Jones, 1995).

Finally, changing economic conditions may well have a substantial impact on propensity to switch parties, as has been found in Latin

America (Roberts and Wibbels, 1999). Theories of economic voting hold that voters will support the incumbent when times are good and vote for an opposition party when times are bad. Post-communist Europe has undergone substantial economic change since the transition from communism at the start of the 1990s. During that time the economies of most states in the region experienced precipitous declines. In some cases – Slovenia, Poland, Hungary, the Czech Republic – the economic hardship was limited to a relatively brief period, whereas elsewhere – Armenia, Georgia, Ukraine, Moldova – it has been ongoing and relief came belatedly. If it is the case that vote-choice in post-communist Europe is affected by pocket-book considerations, then we should see more switching when the economy has been in decline (measured in terms of change in per capita GDP since the previous elections) and more stability when there has been growth. A slightly different hypothesis is that it is not short-term changes that voters respond to, but the general economic conditions over an extended period. It therefore also makes sense to test for the impact of differences in overall levels of wealth among states.

Previous research gives us less material with which to make predictions about what influences party replacement. But we would expect the electoral systems to have direct effects on replacement under conditions of high uncertainty such as those which exist in post-communist countries. Supporters of major parties (which will in almost all cases be in a majority) have an incentive to stick with political organizations whose seat-winning ability has been proven rather than gravitating to new or small political organizations, and the number of 'trustworthy' parties will mostly be smaller in systems with high natural thresholds (i.e. SMD). With high thresholds we would anticipate a more pronounced learning curve as parties come to appreciate their electoral strength (or lack thereof) and react accordingly by merging with other parties or dropping out of the game.

The opportunity to cast a vote for an individual candidate should also make vote choice 'stickier' and reduce the likelihood that voters will opt for new political organizations at election time. The provision of state finance to parties can be anticipated to have a similar impact. In fact, we should expect to see state financing have a greater effect on replacement than it does on volatility, as it should serve to exclude new hopefuls from electoral success by depriving them of the means of drawing votes (for as we know, state financing is typically linked to previous electoral success). Spending limits, for their part, could give the advantage to new parties, as they reduce the capacity of existing political players to deny access to newcomers. They could also, however, benefit incumbents who can rely more readily on reputational resources and are not so dependent on monetary means of financing their campaigns.

The electoral prize of the presidency may also provide an incentive for hopefuls to form new parties in order to increase their chances of success in the presidential race. A tendency toward the creation of 'presidential parties' has been particularly evident in Armenia, Georgia, Russia, and Ukraine[8] and this may be one of the reasons for the relatively high levels of party replacement in these states. Finally, electoral participation may be of relevance; we did not find much power in mobilizational theories in Chapter 3, but if there is some truth in them, new parties may succeed in mobilizing previously inactive sectors of the electorate, and we would thus expect to find an association between high turnout and high levels of party replacement.

Analysis

As can be seen from the data presented in Table 6.1, average volatility exhibits a modest decline from first to second data points. Thereafter the picture is less clear; the paucity of data on fourth and subsequent elections makes generalization difficult. Nevertheless, there is little evidence that volatility has fallen substantially since third elections, and it appears to be on the rise in a number of Central European states. Dramatic highs in volatility between third and fourth elections in states such as Poland and Romania suggest that the post-communist electoral systems are far from 'settling down'. Turbulence in party support was manifestly *not* a phenomenon characteristic of the immediate post-transition years alone, but seems to be a more general attribute of electoral patterns in the region.

There are also distinct sub-regional patterns evident in these data. Volatility has been substantially higher in the FSU states than in Central Europe. It is interesting to note that this has been the case both in states such as Russia, Ukraine, and Moldova that have little pre-communist experience of competitive multi-party politics, as well as in the Baltic states where such experience is present. This suggests that the sub-regional difference we observe here is due either to other factors that co-vary with region (factors we can test in multivariate analysis) or that it has to do with factors specific to the Soviet form of rule.

As far as institutional variations are concerned, we find that in some cases volatility is, as predicted, lower in the single-member district components of mixed systems than in their PR counterparts – Hungary 1994–98, both Lithuanian data-points, and Russia 1993–95. But the reverse was just as likely to be true; in Croatia 1992–95, Hungary 1998–2002, Russia 1995–99, and Ukraine 1998–2002 volatility levels were higher in the SMD races that they were on the PR ballot. This provides little evidence to support the theory that PR should increase volatility more than elections in single-member districts, and it suggests there may be intervening factors which only multivariate analysis can untangle.

Similar patterns are evident in the replacement data (Table 6.2). The popularity of new parties has exhibited a decline in tandem with both the number of parties in general and the volatility of support for existing parties. We expect party replacement to be linked to volatility, as more votes for new political formations will in most cases translate into fewer votes for those partisan contenders that are continuous from one election to the next. Indeed there is a correlation of 0.67 (significant at 0.002) between average volatility and replacement scores.

As with volatility, we find that party replacement is considerably (and significantly) higher in the former Soviet Union than it is in Central Europe. New parties and groupings in the former Soviet republics have attracted nearly half the vote on average during the post-1991 period, and the proportion of the vote they have won has declined only moderately over time. This pattern may be self-reinforcing as political entrepreneurs recognize the potential gains to be had in the electoral market by founding a new party. They may then leave existing parties in large enough numbers that voters have fewer familiar options to choose from and are more likely to vote for something new. This high level of replacement undoubtedly reflects the general availability of post-Soviet electorates, but it can also be taken as an indication of the extent to which politics in the former Soviet states revolves around individual politicians rather than around institutionalized parties.

The relationship between electoral institutions and party replacement is unclear. Within mixed systems, there were higher levels of party replacement in some states in the single-member district voting than in the PR component (Croatia, Hungary), in Ukraine we find the opposite, and in Lithuania and Russia the situation was mixed; in Lithuania replacement was higher on the PR ballot at the first time point and higher on the SMD ballot at the second, whereas in Russia the reverse was true. This makes it difficult to generalize as to the effects of electoral system variables on party replacement, just as it is unclear what to expect *vis-à-vis* volatility.

Interestingly, there was little indication that a high level of instability at election *t* was linked with a high level at election *t* + 1. Although there is clear continuity in some countries, overall there are no significant correlations between levels of electoral instability at successive elections. Country-specific dimensions of change were evidently of less importance in the early post-transition phase than factors linked to the transition itself. Over time we may well begin to see country-level factors become more prominent, but the limited data on fourth and fifth elections provide scant material on which to base generalizations. Rather it makes sense to analyse the relevant impact on party system change of the variables already examined. Table 6.3 presents the results of regression models of both volatility and replacement, based on country averages over time.

In both cases the electoral system had a clear, strong impact, but different aspects of electoral system design mattered. In the case of volatility, the availability of a personal vote appears to have been successful in binding candidates to parties, for average volatility scores were substantially lower where the personal vote option was in place. This finding fits with our predictions, but it is interesting to note that the proportion of PR seats is not significant once we have controlled for the availability of the personal vote. In the replacement equation the reverse is true; personal voting is not significant once we control for the proportion of PR districts, which, as expected, has a positive effect on replacement, increasing the chances for new parties to break through the electoral barrier and gain substantial shares of the vote.

The other variable to be significant in both equations is the location of a state in the former Soviet region. The significance of this variable

Table 6.3   OLS models of volatility and replacement (country averages)

Variable	Volatility	Replacement
Proportion PR seats		38.779 (9.260)***
Vote for an individual	−14.651 (5.046)**	
Location in the FSU	13.082 (3.505)***	25.458 (5.101)***
Freedom House Political Rights rating (inverted)	3.191 (1.520)*	
Change in per capita GDP (thousands of $US) since the last election		−4.581 (2.224)*
Constant	15.058 (7.062)	−4.527 (7.773)

Entries are unstandardized regression coefficients (standard errors).

$N = 19$

Adjusted R^2 =	0.543	0.729

* $p < 0.10$; ** $p < 0.05$; *** $p < 0.01$.

should not surprise us, given the obvious differences across sub-regions noted above. Nevertheless, its relevance in multivariate analysis requires comment, as it suggests that the gap between regions in both volatility and replacement levels is not due to other institutional, economic, or partisan attributes that vary across the region, but rather to factors specific to the Soviet system.

Higher levels of party replacement in the former Soviet states may well reflect the fact that the Soviet Union was more patrimonial than most of its Central European satellites. A patrimonial legacy can be expected to translate into personalistic relations between voters and politicians during the post-communist period (Kitschelt, 1995). Though personalism has been found here to be linked to party system stability, this link will only be effective if the individuals in question remain loyal to their political organization of choice. In many post-Soviet states personalism undermines the institutional continuity of parties, because support comes to be based on allegiance to or admiration for an individual rather than with the party as a representative of specific interests or a given ideology. Under these conditions individual leaders have the power to bring their supporters with them if they defect to a different party or opt to form their own political association. Thus any leader who becomes popular – or perceives that they are popular – has an incentive to 'trade up' so as to be part of a more powerful political group or to have a larger role in the group of which they are part. In a comparative study of the three Baltic states, Pettai and Kreuzer (2001) find that candidate replacement – the proportion of candidates on party lists at election $t + 1$ who were *not* candidates at election t – averaged about three quarters of the total corpus. This puts instability of electoral results in context. Average rates of electoral-level party replacement hovering around the 50 per cent mark may seem high, but the voters in this case are actually more constant than the political organizations they are voting for. As the most important measures of party strength, elections are engines of both party system consolidation and division. On the one hand they encourage existing parties to come together so as to make concerted appeals to as large a sector of the public as possible; on the other hand they also promote the emergence of new contenders on the basis of perceived changes of popularity since the previous election.

Uniquely in this study, volatility is positively associated with levels of democracy (measured here in terms of the inverted Freedom House Political Rights scale). Though volatility can be understood as one of the 'ills' of a functioning democracy, it is also indicative that elections are competitive and that voters are able to exercise genuine choice.

Economic factors were not significant in the volatility model; however, economic growth (though not the overall level of economic development) was found to have a depressant effect on party replacement, suggesting that an improvement in economic conditions encourages voters to stick with existing parties, whereas poor economic performance prompts them to take chances on outsiders. This finding is in line with our expectations, but it is worth highlighting that this is the only model in which an economic variable was found to be significant. Broad democratic and economic factors appear to affect changes over time more than they do the details of given electoral results.

Finally, it is worth pausing to consider the variables that were *not* significant in either of these equations. We had anticipated that party finance variables might play an important role in shaping volatility and replacement, especially the state financing of parties and limits on spending during electoral campaigns. No such effect was found; certainly there is no evidence of the supposed 'cartelization' of post-communist party systems as a result of the introduction of state funding. New parties are in most countries finding little difficulty in gaining large amounts of support, even without the benefit of the monies allocated to those that have won elections before. At the same time, formal limits on spending appear, on balance, to be advantaging neither newcomers nor incumbents.

Nor does party system stability seem to be strongly related to presidentialism, the number of parties, turnout, time since the previous election, or inclusion. The latter findings suggest that the political effects we have measure in this volume are to an extent discrete, and that electoral systems influence politics in a variety of different ways.[9]

Conclusion

Party system instability in post-communist Europe appears to be the effect of a combination of influences, including institutional design and specific features of sub-regions within the post-communist area. All in all, the diversity of influences on inter-electoral volatility and party replacement in post-communist Europe confirm the desirability of separating these two aspects of party system instability. Also of note is that fact that party proliferation *per se* is not a cause of volatility. The tendency of voters in post-communist states to support new or different parties is largely structured by aspects of the electoral system, by whether or not the state in question belonged to the Soviet Union, and by general political and economic conditions. Soviet voters – including those in the Baltic countries that many would classify together with Central Europe – have been far more likely to defect from their electoral choices than their counterparts in Central Europe or the former Yugoslav states.

Unlike in Western Europe, where parties are known for their ability to adapt and absorb successive generations of voters (Bartolini and Mair, 1990; Broughton and Donovan, 1999), most party systems in post-communist Europe are 'uncoupled' (Lawson, 1999) or 'floating' (Rose *et al.*, 2001). They respond more to élite-level changes in configurations of alliances than to shifts in the electoral 'base', and in many states individual politicians rather than political parties constitute the basic building blocks of politics. Yet despite the much greater degree of party system instability in the post-communist region than in the West, electoral system factors are still of relevance, and they still operate in more or less the way they have been found to do in established democracies. Electoral systems that build in thresholds to success and those that bind voters to candidates reduce the level of defection.

The findings reported here also accord in large part with studies of party system volatility in other parts of the democratizing world, notably Latin America, where Roberts and Wibbels (1999) found that institutional factors play by far the largest role in determining levels of volatility. When· more comparative analysis is done on party systems elsewhere, we may well discover that Western European party system stability is the exception rather than the rule.

7
Conclusion

The analyses undertaken in this volume have demonstrated the importance of electoral institutions in shaping political development in the crucial years following regime transition in post-communist Europe. Post-communist political transformation was accompanied by a spate of electoral reforms that did away with the communist-era single-member district absolute majority electoral systems inherited from the *anciens régimes* and installed new systems that were either based entirely on proportional representation or had a strong proportional element. At the same time, these systems typically included relatively high thresholds of representation. These seat allocation rules were accompanied by campaign finance regulations that also exhibited certain similarities; state financing of media access was universal, and in most cases there were also direct subsidies to parties, either on a regular basis or at the time of electoral campaigns.

The post-communist experience with electoral system design confirms the common view of electoral systems as 'sticky' institutions. Once adopted, there were relatively few large-scale redesigns of electoral regimes in the region. Though politicians often had erroneous opinions as to the likely impact of given electoral institutions during the initial post-transition period, this was largely due to the high degree of uncertainty surrounding the early electoral events that followed the collapse of communism and the proliferation of new political parties. Political leaders gradually learned to understand the electoral dynamics of their country and to appreciate the way their electoral institutions worked. In some respects the effects of post-communist electoral systems have been found to be similar to those in established democracies. In other respects they have been different. This conclusion will trace the links among the results obtained in the preceding chapters.

What we have learned

The bulk of this investigation has been devoted to assessing the impact of electoral systems on various aspects of the way in which voters and parties are integrated into the electoral process. In so doing we have viewed electoral systems from a variety of different angles. Now we need to put together the pieces of the puzzle in order to draw conclusions and to provide tentative guidelines for would-be electoral engineers.

It is often argued that there is a trade-off between popular inclusion in the electoral process and effective party institutionalization. Both the legitimacy engendered by inclusion and the governability made possible through party institutionalization are seen as desirable from a normative perspective, yet choices over electoral institutional design are commonly held to entail compromises in the structuring of citizen-élite linkage patterns. The evidence presented here suggests that the situation is in fact more complex than the simple notion of trade-off would suggest, for the impact of electoral institutions depends on the political context in which they are embedded, and a range of different design elements have countervailing effects.

The impact of 'electoral systems' in the narrow sense appears to be largely what we would expect on the basis of previous research, but with some important caveats. Electoral systems with more single-member districts are associated with a reduction in the size of parliamentary party systems in post-communist Europe overall, though this effect is not so clearly manifest in the former Soviet states, where single-member districts are just as likely to have a fragmenting effect. This points to the importance of considering the specific features of the political context when seeking to understand the likely impact of a proposed electoral system innovation.

As has been found elsewhere, SMD systems appear to depress inclusiveness in post-communist states. But the relationship between the proportion of SMD seats in a system and inclusiveness is not linear. Interestingly, mixed systems are actually more inclusive than their PR counterparts, and considerably more inclusive than pure SMD systems. Given that (at least in the Central European context) mixed systems also have a moderating influence on the size of parliamentary party systems, this design option may represent a useful tool for electoral engineers, allowing the achievement of relatively compact parliamentary party systems without sacrificing inclusiveness. Such an outcome is, however, contingent on the national integration of the party system, and is therefore less likely to result in highly fragmented states. In the latter context, the evident tendency of PR rules to increase turnout, make electoral contests more competitive, and strengthen political parties undoubtedly outweighs the advantages of including single-member districts in the design of an electoral system.

Also of interest is the impact of the 'politician-enabling' device of ballot formats that allow a personal vote. For electoral system designers ballot format may represent an additional trade-off. Although the personal vote appears to dampen volatility, it also tends to fragment the party system at the levels of both vote and seat distribution, suggesting again that in an already fragmented system SMD seats are best avoided. Depending on the political context in which a state finds itself, the decision whether or not to adopt a personalized voting system may thus be a difficult one. For political scientists, the independent impact of personalized voting points to the oft-neglected need to separate constituency design from ballot format when assessing electoral system effects.

The findings vis-à-vis campaign finance regulatory regimes are somewhat disappointing from a political science point of view. The state funding of electoral campaigns has the expected effect of reducing inclusiveness, but overall the measures associated with the regulation of campaign money were not found to be closely related to the outcome variables considered. There are a number of possible reasons for this. It may be that campaign finance rules are simply too poorly enforced in the post-communist world for formal mechanisms to bear strongly on electoral outcomes. The small number of cases included in this study may also account for the fact that stronger statistical associations were not in evidence.

The small number of cases may also be one of the reasons why other variables such as presidentialism, socio-economic level and extent of democratization were not found to be strongly related to most of the variables investigated. Nevertheless, the paucity of statistically significant associations between these measures and electoral variables does suggest that these factors are not key determinants of electoral outcomes. The analyses reported here lead to the conclusion that in post-communist Europe institutional variables are one of the most important factors shaping the results of the electoral process.

The findings of this study also shed light on a number of theories advanced to account for electoral behaviour and outcomes. We have uncovered patchy evidence of strategic behaviour on the part of voters, but much stronger indications that party élites are acting strategically to deploy their resources and co-ordinate in fighting electoral campaigns. The strategic incentives faced by parties in the electoral arena typically involve choices as to how best to mobilize voters. Though parties do not appear to be particularly successful at mobilizing non-voters, they seem to have greater success in building alliances among themselves. This has not, however, had the effect of substantially reducing volatility in most cases. Post-communist voters are inclined to be fickle, and personal links seem to be more important resources than money in retaining their trust.

All in all, electoral engineers have a variety of different mechanisms at their disposal should they seek to use electoral reform as a means of regulating political inclusion and party system characteristics. This variety may enable flexibility, but it also entails increased complexity, as the multiple effects of different options will need to be taken into account. The study of past electoral system reform debates in the region has revealed that most of the results found here were not considered by those in charge of designing post-communist electoral systems. With luck, the impact of these factors will gain greater visibility over time.

The investigation undertaken here points to the ways in which the historical evolution of institutions prior to and at the time of the transition conditioned their impacts. What is 'different' about the post-communist context appears to be tied not so much to culture as to the impact of previous institutions on perceptions of new ones. These include the perceptions held by leaders, many of whom favoured the adoption of proportional representation and state funding because they saw them as mechanisms for strengthening the multi-party form of competition that, having lived under a one-party system, they equated with democracy.

Past experience also appears to have conditioned the views of voters vis-à-vis electoral participation and choice. At the same time, the uncertainty inherent in the politics of transition appears to have limited voters' ability to act strategically. This has meant that the 'psychological effects' often attributed to electoral systems have been less in evidence than their 'mechanical' impacts. More relevant has been the evident ability of individual candidates to mobilize voters. In the transitional setting, the institution of the personal vote appears to be of key importance in structuring party system size and change. All in all, electoral systems have played an important role in shaping political outcomes during the post-communist years, and the nature of their effects has been conditioned by features of the transition context.

Examining the exceptions

The analyses conducted up to now have given us a general picture of overall patterns in the region. But generalizations such as these are of limited help when it comes to cases that do not conform to the trend. It therefore makes sense to examine in somewhat more detail several cases of 'outliers' in order to have a better understanding of why electoral systems operate differently in different contexts. One of the variables that was most consistently associated with electoral outcomes was location in the former Soviet Union. The former Soviet states were found to have lower turnout, less inclusive electoral results, more fragmented parliamentary party systems, higher volatility, and higher levels of party replacement, all else considered. It therefore makes sense to examine in more detail electoral trends in the most important of the ex-Soviet countries: Russia and Ukraine.[1]

Russia and Ukraine

In Russia and Ukraine the political party system covers only part of the political terrain; independent politicians play an important role in parliament as well as in the executive branch of government. Unaffiliated candidates have regularly won substantial numbers of single-member seats in these states, with limited evidence of a decrease over time. Table 7.1 presents the overall vote and seat totals for independent candidates in the three elections that have been held in each country since independence. These figures are far higher than those found in most other states in the region; elsewhere independent candidatures have generally yielded at most a handful of seats (virtually always in single-member district races), whereas in Russia and Ukraine they have at times dominated the SMD contests. In both cases there has been a slight drop in the vote shares of non-partisans, mirrored in Ukraine by a parallel decline in the number of seats independents have taken. In Russia the relative success rates of such candidates has bounced around, such that it is not possible to generalize. Whatever spin we may put on these figures, it is clear

Table 7.1   Independent vote and seat shares in Russia and Ukraine

	Votes (%)	Seats (%)
Russia 1993	58.63	64.38
Russia 1995	56.78	34.22
Russia 1999	48.97	50.00
Ukraine 1994	66.48	64.20
Ukraine 1998	45.95	51.56
Ukraine 2002	41.50	41.44

that non-partisans continue to have an important place in the political life of both countries, and that political parties are far from being the only actors in these systems. There are a number of ways of accounting for the success of independents in Russia and Ukraine. It undoubtedly has to do in part with the regional fragmentation of the party systems in both states, which can in turn be attributed to the novelty of competitive multi-party politics for the Russian and Ukrainian voters and to geographical diversity, as well as to the effects of the electoral system itself under such conditions. This is clearly a context in which single-member districts are unsuitable from the point of view of party system institutionalization.

It might also be tempting to attribute the lack of party system institutionalization in these two states to their strong presidencies. We would need to be cautious in so doing, as presidentialism did not prove a significant variable in any of the analyses undertaken here, but there are nevertheless reason to suspect that the way in which presidential power has been exercised in Russia and Ukraine has had a detrimental impact on the party systems of these states that goes well beyond the workings of the electoral law.

According to Shugart and Carey's typology, both Russia and Ukraine fall broadly into the category of the 'president-parliamentarism' (Shugart and Carey, 1992; Shugart, 1996). Both presidents are directly elected for a maximum of two consecutive five-year terms by an absolute majority of the popular vote. As is common in post-communist Europe, they cannot by law be leading members of political parties.

Not surprisingly, the main axis of opposition since the Soviet collapse has been that between presidents and parliaments rather than among parties representing competing ideological positions. This has often degenerated into 'institutional warfare' in which the each branch of government seeks to expand the reach of its powers and to block similar initiatives by the other branch. And though competition among parties has generally been secondary or subordinate, the two modes of competition have been linked, in that presidents have sought to ally themselves with parliamentary parties in order to dominate the policy process. This situation can be found in many of the states in the post-Soviet region, of which Russia is most familiar to students of comparative politics. In Russia institutional warfare became real warfare when President Yeltsin blew up the parliament in October 1993 and effectively imposed a constitutional settlement through unconstitutional means in a referendum of dubious legality. President Kuchma in Ukraine has also sought to use the referendum to by-pass parliamentary decision-making, most notably in April 2000 when he succeeded in polling the people on a number of questions that ought, according to the constitution, to have been decided first by parliament.

Inasmuch as political parties represent alternative power bases (and possible launching pads for presidential opponents), it has been in the president's interest to limit their capacity to organize. Successive Russian and Ukrainian presidents have been aided in this regard by the low status of parliament relative to the presidential administration and by the limited authority of both the Russian Duma and the Ukrainian Rada, as well as by an extremely fragmented party system. The consequences of this high degree of fragmentation are easy to work out. There have been no true partisan veto players in parliament on any other than constitutional decisions (where cohesive communist factions have at times been able to block legislation in both states, obliging presidents to resort to bullying tactics). Furthermore, governments have not generally been based on parties; few of either state's prime ministers have been party members, and partisan support has not typically been the basis for the approval of prime ministerial nominees. Finally, the large number of independents parliamentarians, most of whom have very weak ideological commitment, has facilitated the presidents' ability to generate supportive coalitions through the distribution of extra-parliamentary 'incentives'. The electoral system also has another important consequence in the Russian and Ukrainian contexts; a disproportionate number of presidential allies in parliament have been elected in single-member districts where local notables can use their powers of patronage to deliver the vote to pro-governmental forces. A highly personalistic electoral system such as this has the effect of encouraging particularistic legislation as a means of paying off electoral debts (cf. Cox and McCubbins, 2001).

This brief examination of power relations in Russia and Ukraine suggests the limits of the analysis we have undertaken here. The characteristics of individual states will always mediate between electoral system design and political outcomes. The electoral system may help to shape those outcomes, but it can not determine them. At the same time, electoral institutions can interact in important ways with other aspects of the political context, and however anomalous the case, their effects cannot be ignored if political dynamics are to be understood.

Bulgaria

At the opposite extreme from the highly fragmented party systems of Russia and Ukraine lies Bulgaria, which until the earthquake elections of

2000 had exhibited exemplary two-party alteration in power and a moderately sized party system. In the parliamentary elections of 2000, however, a completely new political formation grouped around former King Simeon II (re-styled Simeon Saxegoburggotsky) mobilized a campaign barely three months before the polling and ended up with half the seats in parliament on the basis of 42.74 per cent of the vote.

During the first decade of the post-communist transitions, the two main parties – the Bulgarian Socialist Party (BPS) and the Union of Democratic Forces (UDF) had alternated in power, and no more than five electoral contestants had won seats in any of the country's parliamentary elections since 1991. The Bulgarian transition of 1989 was an attempt by the then Bulgarian Communist Party to pre-empt the type of radical loss of power that had been experienced by communists elsewhere in the region. The nascent opposition scrambled to keep up with events, mobilizing only belatedly into the loose UDF, composed of over a dozen discrete groups. One of their first demands was for the leadership to meet with them in round-table talks, on the model of Poland and Hungary. The communists obliged, and the talks ran spasmodically between January and May 1990 (by which time the Communists had renamed themselves Socialists). The result of these meetings was a series of agreements on economic and democratic reforms, including the terms under which multi-party elections would be held in June (Kolarova and Dimitrov, 1996). The June 1990 Grand National Assembly elections were the among the few transitional elections in Eastern Europe in which ex-communists won an absolute majority of the seats. It was not till the parliamentary elections of October 1991 – held on the basis of the recently adopted constitution – that the democratic opposition finally came to power and the communists-turned-socialists were toppled. As in many post-communist countries, the BSP made a comeback in the subsequent elections, held three years later. After a disastrous term that saw the Bulgarian economy virtually collapse, the UDF once again won power in elections held in 1997. This government proved the first since the transition to serve out its full four-year term, yet the 1997–2001 period witnessed growing popular disquiet as corruption scandals rocked the country and public opinion became increasingly alienated from politicians in general. The UDF and the BSP were perceived by many as being equally corrupt, full of people who entered politics only to enrich themselves and who paid little attention to popular opinion (Ganev, 2001).

Under these circumstances, it is not surprising that former King Simeon was an appealing alternative. There appears to be a common recognition among Bulgarian politicians that the political élite had for too long been out of touch with popular opinion and unresponsive to the needs of the people. The alternation of parties led élites to believe that they were likely not to remain in power for more than one term. This undermined accountability and bred a catch-as-catch-can mentality on the part of many politicians. Given that they had no real expectation of being able to win two consecutive terms in office, they had little incentive to try to please the people. It made more sense to serve their own interests in the knowledge that they could ride back to power once again on the crest of popular dissatisfaction with the next power-holders. The de facto duopoly served the interests of both parties while maintaining the outward appearance of democratic alternation in power. The vote for the ex-King's newly formed political grouping may be interpreted as an act of desperation by an electorate that could not imagine a leadership worse than the one they had, and was therefore prepared to 'try anything'. On the other hand, the electorate also demonstrated that it was not subservient to the two main parties. The structures of patronage which the UDF and the BSP had attempted to cultivate were not strongly enough entrenched to be able to retain voters, whose independence the parties will not soon forget.

The radical destabilization of the apparently entrenched Bulgarian party system suggests that party system institutionalization involves far more than the quantitative reduction of party system size and the generation of regular parliamentary majorities; it also involves the qualitative rooting of parties in society. This is what evidently did not take place in Bulgaria, perhaps due to the lack of a personal vote in the electoral system, perhaps due to its highly proportional nature. The consequence, ironically, was widespread support for an individual, suggesting that what the electoral system does not readily supply, the public may seek out in other forms.

Topics for future research

Democratic transition and consolidation are complex processes that are only partially understood. There is a growing appreciation among scholars of the importance of institutional design in shaping the trajectory of democratization and influencing its outcome. At the same time there is enough variation among different transition contexts that it is difficult to generalize from one region of the world to another, or from time period to time period. This study has undertaken the more limited task of seeking to articulate and test a range of hypotheses as to the impact of electoral system design on political outcomes in a discrete transition context in which a number of common conditions and starting points can be assumed. Nevertheless, it is to be hoped that the findings presented here will be of interest to scholars studying other parts of the world. These findings point to a number of avenues for future research. One obvious topic of investigation would be to test the results of this study in other democratizing contexts. This would make it possible to disentangle the features specific to post-communism in Europe from the more general attributes of democratic transition. Another fruitful area of investigation would be the systematic comparative analysis of the relative importance of campaign finance regulation and the personal vote in shaping electoral outcomes in established democracies. A third area would be the exploration of additional aspects of electoral system design, such as regulation of the media during electoral campaigns, nomination requirements, and so on. Electoral system design is a rich and complex institutional structure that has only just begun to be mined for possible associations with political outcomes.

Appendix A: Summary Election Results for 20 Post-Communist States*

The tables contained in this Appendix include vote and seat totals for all parties that won seats and/or at least 5 per cent of the valid vote.

Table A1   Albania: Kuvendi Popullor

Party	1991		1992			
	Vote (%)	SMD seats	Vote (%)	SMD seats	PR seats	All seats
Workers'/ Socialist Party	56.17	169	25.57	6	32	38
Democratic Party	38.71	75	62.29	90	2	92
Omonia	0.73	5				
National Veterans	0.28	1				
Social Democratic Party			4.33	1	6	7
Human Rights Party			2.92	2	0	2
Republican Party			3.18	1	0	1
Other	4.11	0	1.71	0	0	0
All	100	250	100	100	40	140

* More detailed results can be found in the sources listed in Appendix B.

Table A1 (Continued)

Party	1997				2001				
	SMD vote (%)	SMD seats	PR seats	All seats	SMD vote (%)	SMD seats	PR vote (%)	PR seats	All seats
Socialist Party	52.75	79	22	101	43.89	73	41.51	0	73
Democratic Party/Victory	25.70	15	11	26	38.07	25	36.81	21	46
PD					2.99	0	5.09	6	6
Monarchist Party	3.20	0	2	2					
Human Rights Party	2.84	3	1	4	2.06	0	2.61	3	3
Democratic Alliance	2.72	1	1	2	1.94	0	2.55	3	3
Soc Dem	2.49	9	1	10	3.53	0	3.64	4	4
Republican Party	2.41	0	1	1					
Balli Kombatar	2.35	0	1	1					
Christian Democratic Party	0.97	1	0	1					
Agrarian	0.80	1	0	1	0.96	0	2.57	3	3
PUK	0.80	1	0	1					
United Right	N/A	2	0	2					
Independents	N/A	3	0	3	2.87	2		0	2
Other	N/A	0	0	0	3.69	0	5.22	0	0
All	100	115	40	155	100	100	100	40	140

Table A2   Armenia: Azgayin Joghov

Party	1995				1999				
	PR votes (%)	PR seats	SMD seats	All seats	PR votes (%)	PR seats	SMD votes (%)	SMD seats	All seats
Republican block	42.66	20	99	119					
Shamiram	16.88	8	0	8					
Communist Party	12.10	6	1	7	12.10	8	7.05	1	9
National Democratic Union	7.51	3	2	5	5.17	4	3.21	2	6
National Self-Determination Union	5.57	3	0	3					
Ramkavar	2.52	0	1	1					
Scientific-Industrial and Civil Union	1.29	0	1	1					
Revolutionary Party			1	1	7.83	5	8.06	3	8
Unity					41.67	29	24.63	27	56
Right and Accord					7.97	6		1	7
Law-Based State					5.28	4	1.39	2	6
National Movement					1.17	0	1.78	1	1
Mission					0.76	0	0.27	1	1
Independents	—	0	45	45	—	—	40.34	37	37
Other	11.47	0	0	0	18.05	0	13.27	0	0
All	100	40	150	190	100	56	100	75	131

Table A3   Bosnia and Herzegovina: Zastupnicki/Predstavnicki Dom

Party	1996 Vote (%)	1996 Seats	1998 Vote (%)	1998 Seats	2000 Vote (%)	2000 Seats	2002 Vote (%)	2002 Seats
Party of Democratic Action (KCD in 1998)	37.92	19	33.97	17	18.76	8	21.92	10
Serb Democratic Party	24.11	9	9.45	4	16.68	6	14.04	5
Croatian Democratic Union (Koalicija in 2002)	14.10	8	11.64	6	11.40	5	9.48	5
Joint List	4.41	2						
Party for Bosnia and H.	3.91	2			11.34	5	11.07	6
Popular Party for a Free Peace	5.67	2						
Sloga			12.49	4				
Social Democratic Party			9.30	4	18.00	9	10.43	4
Serb Radical Party			6.89	2			2.00	1
Social-Democrats of BiH			1.87	2				
New Croatian Initiative (and allies)			2.33	1	1.58	1	1.37	1
Democratic People's Union			1.25	1	1.31	1	1.39	1
Radical Party of the Republika Srpska			1.61	1				

Table A3 (Continued)

Party	1996 Vote (%)	1996 Seats	1998 Vote (%)	1998 Seats	2000 Vote (%)	2000 Seats	2002 Vote (%)	2002 Seats
Party of Democratic Progress					6.39	2	4.61	2
SNSD-DPS					5.09	1		
DPS								
Independent Social Democrats							9.80	3
Bosnian Patriotic Party					1.16	1		
Pensioner's Party					1.07	1	1.43	1
Socialist Party of the RS					2.61	1	1.91	1
Serbian Popular Union					1.89	1		
HDU Economic Block							1.33	1
BOSS							1.54	1
Other	9.88	0	9.20	0	7.22	0	7.68	0
All	100	42	100	42	100	42	100	42

Table A4   Bulgaria: Subranie

Party	1990				1991		1994	
	PR vote (%)	PR seats	SMD seats	All seats	Vote (%)	Seats	Vote (%)	Seats
Socialist Party and allies	47.15	97	114	211	33.14	106	43.50	125
Union of Democratic Forces	36.21	75	69	144	34.36	110	24.23	69
Movement for Rights and Freedoms	8.03	12	11	23	7.55	24	5.44	15
Agrarian National Union and allies	6.02	16	0	16			6.51	18
Fatherland Front			2	2				
Fatherland Party of Labour	0.60	0	1	1				
Social Democratic Party	0.72	0	1	1				
Business Block							4.73	13
Independents			2	2				
Other	1.27	0	0	0	24.95	0	15.59	0
All	100	200	200	400	100	240	100	240

	1997		2001	
	Vote (%)	Seats	Vote (%)	Seats
Socialist Party and allies	21.97	58	17.15	48
Union of Democratic Forces	52.02	137	18.18	51
Movement for Rights and Freedoms	7.57	19	7.45	21
Euroleft	5.48	14		
Business Block	4.91	12		
National Movement Simeon II			42.74	120
Other	8.05	0	14.48	0
All	100	240	100	240

Table A5 Croatia: Zastupnicki Dom*

Party	1992 PR vote (%)	PR seats	SMD vote (%)	SMD seats	All seats	1995 PR vote (%)	PR seats	SMD vote (%)	SMD seats	All seats	2000 Vote (%)	Seats
Croatian Democratic Union	43.72	31	38.30	54	85	45.2	42	59.06	21	63	27.13	40
Social Liberal Party	17.33	12	13.67	1	13	11.6	10	12.60	1	11		
Party of Rights (with Christian Democrats in '00)	6.91	5	7.46		5	5.0	4	7.09	4		5.28	5
People's Party	6.55	4	9.03		4							
Social Democrats	5.40	3	7.54		3	8.9	8	8.66	9			
Social Democrat Social Liberal coalition											39.38	71
Peasant Party	4.16	3	5.69		3							
Peasant Party-led joint list						18.3	16	12.60	4	20	14.96	24
Regional coalition	3.11	2	3.32	4	6							
Independents		0	3.52	1	1							
Other	10.61	0	11.48	0	0	11.0	0	12.59	8	8	13.25	0
All	100	60	100	60	120	100	80	100	35	115	100	140

* These data do not include seats reserved for ethnic minorities and the diaspora, as these are elected through separate mechanisms.

Table A6 The Czech Republic: Poslanecka Snemovna

Party	1990 Vote (%)	1990 Seats	1992 Vote (%)	1992 Seats	1996 Vote (%)	1996 Seats	1998 Vote (%)	1998 Seats	2002 Vote (%)	2002 Seats
Civic Forum	49.50	127								
Communist Party/Left Block	13.24	32	14.05	35	10.33	22	11.03	24	18.51	41
Movement for Self-Governing Democracy –Society for Moravia and Silesia	10.03	22	5.87	14						
Christian Democratic Union	8.42	19								
Civic Democratic Party			29.73	76	29.62	68	27.74	63	24.47	58
Party of Social Democracy			6.53	16	26.44	61	32.31	74	30.20	70
Liberal Social Union			6.52	16	8.08	18				
Christian-Democratic Union – People's Party			6.28	15	8.01	18	9.00	20		
Rally for the Republic – Republican Party			5.98	14	6.36	13				
Civic Democratic Alliance			5.93	14						
Freedom Union							8.60	19		
Coalition									14.27	31
Other	18.81	0	19.11	0	11.16	0	11.32	0	12.55	0
All	100	200	100	200	100	200	100	200	100	200

Table A7 Estonia: Riigikogu

Party	1992 Vote (%)	1992 Seats	1995 Vote (%)	1995 Seats	1999 Vote (%)	1999 Seats
Homeland	22.00	29				
Secure Home	13.60	17				
Popular Front	12.25	15				
Moderates	9.73	12	5.99	6	15.21	17
National Independence Party	8.79	10				
Independent Royalists	7.12	8				
Estonian Citizens	6.89	8				
Greens	2.62	1				
Entrepreneurs	2.39	1				
Coalition Party and Rural Union			32.23	41		
Estonian Reform Party			16.19	19	15.92	18
Estonian Centre Party			14.17	16	23.41	28
Homeland and ERSP			7.86	8		
Our Home is Estonia			5.87	6		
Right Wingers			5.00	5		
Homeland Alliance					16.09	18
Coalition Party					7.58	7
People's Party					7.27	7
United People's Party					6.13	6
Other	19.62	0	12.69	0	8.39	0
All	100	101	100	101	100	101

Table A8 Georgia: Sakartvelos

Party	1992				1995			
	PR vote (%)*	PR seats	SMD seats	All seats	PR vote (%)	PR seats	SMD seats	All seats
Peace Block	22.7	29	6	35				
11th October Block	12.1	18	3	21				
Unity Block	8.4	14	7	21				
Democratic Party	7.1	10	7	17				
National Democratic Party	9.3	12	4	16	7.95	31	3	34
Greens	5.0	11	5	16				
Union of Georgian Traditionalists	5.6	7	6	13	4.22	0	2	2
Charter 91	4.9	9	4	13				
Ilia Chavchavadze Society	3.1	7	6	13				
Merab Kostova Society	2.9	5	5	10				
Socialist Party of the Working People	N/A	4	4	8				
Party of National Independence	N/A	4	4	8				
Union of National Agreement and Revival	N/A	4	3	7				
Party of People's Friendship and Justice	N/A	2	2	4				
Union of God's Children	N/A	2	2	4				
Union of Social Justice	N/A	2	2	4				
Farmers' Union	N/A	2	2	4				
Social Democratic Party	N/A	2	2	4				
Party of State and National Integrity	N/A	1	1	2				
Constitutional Democrat Party	N/A	1	1	2				
Radical Monarchists' Union	N/A	1	1	2				
Party of National Unity and Political Union of Mountineers	N/A	1	1	2				
Society of the Revival of the Fatherland	N/A	1	1	2				
Union of Mountineers	N/A	1	1	2				

Table A8   (*Continued*)

Party	1992				1995			
	PR vote (%)*	PR seats	SMD seats	All seats	PR vote (%)	PR seats	SMD seats	All seats
Citizens' Union					23.71	90	17	107
Union of Revival					6.84	25	6	31
Progress Block					1.37	0	4	4
Socialist Party					3.79	0	4	4
Solidarity Block					2.15	0	3	3
Reformers' Union – National Concord					2.89	0	2	2
United Republican Party					1.69	0	1	1
State Justice Union					0.92	0	1	1
Lemi Organization					0.41	0	1	1
Independents					—	—	29	29
Other	N/A	0	0	0	44.06	0	0	0
All	100	150	80	230	100	146**	73	219

Party	1999			
	PR vote (%)	PR seats	SMD seats	All seats
Citizens' Union	41.75	85	47	132
Revival	25.18	51	7	58
Industry Will Save Georgia	7.08	14	1	15
Labour Party	6.59	0	2	2
Independents	—	—	16	16
Other	19.40	0	0	0
All	100	150	73	223

* These figures are first-preference votes.

Table A9 Hungary: Orszaggyules

Party	1990					1994				
	PR vote (%)	*PR seats*	*SMD vote (%)*	*SMD seats*	*All seats*	*PR vote (%)*	*PR seats*	*SMD vote (%)*	*SMD seats*	*All seats*
Democratic Forum	24.73	50	23.93	114	164	11.74	33	12.03	5	38
Alliance of Free Democrats	21.39	57	21.73	35	92	19.74	53	18.62	16	69
Independent Smallholders	11.73	33	10.67	11	44	8.82	25	7.88	1	26
Socialist Party	10.89	32	10.18	1	33	32.99	60	31.27	149	209
FIDESZ	8.95	20	4.75	1	21	7.02	20	7.70	0	20
Christian Democratic People's Party	6.46	18	5.80	3	21	7.03	19	7.37	3	22
Agrarian Alliance	3.13	0	2.81	1	1	2.10	0	2.45	1	1
Joint candidates	—	—	1.39	4	4	—	—	0.12	1	1
Independents	—	—	6.91	6	6					
Other	12.72	0	11.83	0	0	10.56	0	12.56	0	0
All	100	210	100	176	386	100	210	100	176	386

Table A9 (Continued)

Party	1998					2002				
	PR vote (%)	PR seats	SMD vote (%)	SMD seats	All seats	PR vote (%)	PR seats	SMD vote (%)	SMD seats	All seats
Democratic Forum	—	—	7.32	17	17					
Alliance of Free Democrats	7.57	22	10.2	2	24	5.57	17	6.77	2	19
Independent Smallholders	13.15	36	13.3	12	48					
Socialist Party	32.92	80	29.82	54	134	42.05	100	40.5	78	178
FIDESZ–Civic Party	29.48	58	21.75	90	148					
Agrarian Alliance										
Party of Justice and Life	5.47	14	5.58	0	14					
FIDESZ–Democratic Forum						41.07	93	39.43	95	188
Joint candidates						—	—		1	1
Independents	—		1.70	1	1					
Other	11.41	0	10.33	0	0	11.31	0	13.30	0	0
All	100	210	100	176	386	100	210	100	176	386

Table A10   Latvia: Saeima

Party	1993 Vote (%)	1993 Seats	1995 Vote (%)	1995 Seats	1998 Vote (%)	1998 Seats	2002 Votes (%)	2002 Seats
Latvia's Way	32.41	36	14.71	17	18.15	21		
National Independence Movement	13.35	15						
Harmony for Latvia	12.01	13						
Farmer's Union	10.65	12						
Equal Rights Movement	5.76	7						
Homeland and Freedom	5.35	6	11.99	14				
Christian Democratic Union	5.01	6						
Democratic Centre Party	4.77	5						
Saimnieks			15.22	18				
Popular Movement for Latvia			14.97	16				
Latvia's Unity			7.18	8				
Farmer's Union, Christian Democratic Union, Latgale Democratic Party			6.36	8				
National Conservative Party, Green Party			6.35	8				

Table A10 (Continued)

Party	1993 Vote (%)	1993 Seats	1995 Vote (%)	1995 Seats	1998 Vote (%)	1998 Seats	2002 Votes (%)	2002 Seats
Socialist Party			5.61	5				
National Harmony Party			5.58	6				
Popular Party					14.20	16	16.71	21
For Homeland and Freedom, National Independence Movement					21.30	24	5.39	7
Social Democratic Alliance					14.73	17		
New Party					12.88	14		
New Era					7.35	8	23.93	26
For Human Rights and a United Latvia							18.94	24
Latvia First							9.58	10
Green, Farmer's Union							9.46	12
Other	10.69	0	12.03	0	11.39	0	15.99	0
All	100	100	100	100	100	100	100	100

Table A11 Lithuania: Seimas

Party	1992					1996				
	PR vote (%)	PR seats	SMD vote (%)	SMD seats	All seats	PR vote (%)	PR seats	SMD vote (%)	SMD seats	All seats
Democratic Labour Party	43.98	36	34.98	37	73	10.01	10	11.21	2	12
Sajudis	21.17	17	18.79	13	30					
Joint List of LKDP, LPKTS and LDP	12.61	10	12.11	8	18					
Social Democratic Party	6.05	5	9.05	3	8	6.94	7	7.28	5	12
Joint List of LKDS and LTJS	3.55	0	1.33	1	1					
Centre Movement/Union	2.52	0	2.49	2	2	8.67	9	6.81	4	13
Union/Electoral Action of Lithuanian Poles	2.14	2	1.92	2	4	3.13	0	2.78	1	1
Joint List of LTS and NP	1.99	0	5.18	4	4					
Homeland Union						31.34	33	28.65	37	70
Christian Democratic Party						10.43	11	13.24	5	16
National Party 'Young Lithuania'						4.01	0	1.68	1	1

Table A11 (Continued)

Party	1992					1996				
	PR vote (%)	PR seats	SMD vote (%)	SMD seats	All seats	PR vote (%)	PR seats	SMD vote (%)	SMD seats	All seats
Women's Party						3.86	0	2.78	1	1
Christian Democratic Union						3.24	0	1.58	1	1
Joint List of LTS and LDP						2.20	0	3.82	3	3
Liberal Union						1.93	0	2.65	1	1
Peasants' Party						1.75	0	2.22	1	1
Union of Political Prisoners and Deportees						1.57	0	1.89	1	1
Independents	—	—	4.03	1	1	—	—	4.58	4	4
Other	5.99	0	10.12	0	0	10.92	0	8.83	0	0
All	100	70	100	71	141	100	70	100	67*	137*

* Four seats remained vacant following the election.

Table A11 (Continued)

Party	2000					
	PR vote (%)	PR seats	SMD vote (%)	SMD seats	All seats
Social Democratic Coalition of Algirdas Brazauskas	31.08	28	20.04	23	51
Liberal Union	17.25	16	15.65	18	34
New Union (Social Liberals)	19.64	18	15.41	11	29
Homeland Union	8.62	8	7.14	1	9
Peasants' Party	4.08	0	6.61	4	4
Centre Union	2.86	0	6.13	2	2
Union/Electoral Action of Lithuanian Poles	1.95	0	2.75	2	2
Christian Democratic Party	3.07	0	4.76	2	2
'Young Lithuania', New Nationalists Women's Party	1.15	0	1.14	1	1
Christian Democratic Union	4.19	0	2.27	1	1
Union of Moderate Conservative	2.01	0	2.87	1	1
Liberty Union	1.27	0	1.58	1	1
Union of Modern Christian Democrats	—	—	1.22	1	1
Independents	—	—	4.23	3	3
Other	2.83	0	8.20	0	0
All	100	70	100	71	141

Table A12   Macedonia: Sobranie

Party	1994 Vote (%)	1994 Seats	1998 PR vote (%)	1998 PR seats	1998 SMD vote (%)	1998 SMD seats	1998 All seats	2002 Vote (%)	2002 Seats
Social Democratic Union (and allies)	29.49	87	25.14	10	25.77	17	27	40.46	60
Internal Macedonian Revolutionary Organization (and allies)	14.30	0	38.83	15	34.61	47	62	24.41	33
Ethnic Albanian parties and coalitions including PDP, DPA, NDP	12.48	14	19.26	8	16.77	17	25	9.68	10
Democratic Union for Integration (ethnic Albanian)								11.85	16
Democratic Party	11.01	0							
Democratic Party of Macedonia	2.05	1							
Liberal Party of Macedonia	1.52	5							
Social Democratic Party of Macedonia	1.22	1							
Socialist Party of Macedonia (and allies)	0.67	1	4.70	0	6.86	1	1	2.12	1
Party for the Total Emancipation of Roma	0.66	1							
Social Democratic Union	0.42	1							
Social Democratic Union and Liberal Party joint candidates	0.40	1							
Democratic Party of Macedonian Turks	0.35	1							
Coalition of the Liberal Democratic Party and the Democratic Party of Macedonia			6.99	2	10.39	2	4		
Union of Macedonian Roma			—	—	0.32	1	1		
Independents	13.80	7	—	—	1.02	0	0		
Other	11.63	0	5.08	0	4.26	0	0	11.48	0
All	100	120	100	35	100	85	120	100	120

Table A13 Moldova: Parlamentul

Party	1994		1998		2001	
	Vote (%)	*Seats*	*Vote (%)*	*Seats*	*Vote (%)*	*Seats*
Democratic Agrarian Party	43.18	56				
Party of Socialists and 'Unity' Block	22.00	28				
Block of Peasants and Intellectuals	9.21	11				
Alliance of the Popular Christian Democratic Front/Popular Christian Democratic Party	7.53	9			8.24	11
Party of Communists			30.01	40	50.07	71
Democratic Convention of Moldova			19.42	26		
Electoral Block for a Democratic and Prosperous Moldova			18.16	24		
Party of Democratic Forces			8.84	11		
Braghis Alliance					13.36	19
Party of Rebirth and Conciliation					5.79	0
Democratic Party of Moldova					5.02	0
Other	18.08	0	23.57	0	17.52	0
All	100	104	100	101	100	101

Table A14   Poland: Sejm

Party	1991 Vote (%)	1991 Seats	1993 Vote (%)	1993 Seats	1997 Vote (%)	1997 Seats	2001 Vote (%)	2001 Seats
Democratic Union	12.32	62						
Alliance of the Democratic Left (and allies)	11.99	60	20.41	171	27.13	164	41.04	216
Catholic Electoral Action	8.74	49						
Civic Centre Alliance	8.71	44						
Peasant Party	8.67	48	15.40	132	7.31	27	8.98	42
Confederation for Independent Poland	7.26	46	5.77	22				
Liberal Democratic Congress	7.49	37						
Peasant Alliance	5.47	28						
Solidarity/Solidarity Electoral Action	5.05	27			33.83	201	5.6	0
Friends of Beer Party	3.27	16						
Christian Democracy	2.36	5						
Union of Political Realism	2.26	3						
Labour Solidarity	2.06	4						
Democratic Party	1.42	1						
German Minority	1.18	7						
Party of Christian Democrats	1.12	4						
Democratic Social Movement	0.46	1						
Party X	0.47	3						
'Piast' Peasant Election Alliance	0.37	1						

Movement for Silesian Autonomy	0.36	2						
Krakow Coalition of Solidarity with the President	0.25	1						
Podhalan Union	0.24	1						
Polish Western Union	0.23	4						
Great Poland and Poland	0.21	1						
Peasant Unity	0.17	1						
Electoral Committee of Orthodox Believers	0.12	1						
Solidarity '80	0.11	1						
Union of Great Poles	0.08	1						
Alliance of Women Against Life's Hardships	0.02	1						
Democratic Union			10.59	74				
Labour Union			7.28	41				
Non-Party Reform Block			5.41	16				
German Minority of Opole Silesia			0.44	3	0.39	2		
Germans of Katowice Province			0.21	1				
Freedom Union					13.37	60		
Movement for Rebuilding Poland					5.56	6		
Civic Platform							12.68	65
Self-Defence							10.20	53
Law and Justice							9.50	44
League of Polish Families							7.87	38
Other	7.54	0	34.49	0	12.41	0	3.77	0
All	100	460	100	460	100	460	100	460

Table A15   Romania: Camera Deputatilor*

Party	1990 Vote (%)	1990 Seats	1992 Vote (%)	1992 Seats	1996 Vote (%)	1996 Seats	2000 Vote (%)	2000 Seats
National Salvation Front	66.31	263	10.19	43				
Democratic Alliance of Hungarians in Romania	7.23	29	7.46	27	6.64	25	6.80	27
National Liberal Party	6.41	29					6.89	30
Romanian Ecological Movement	2.62	12						
National Peasants' Party	2.56	12						
Alliance for Romanian Unity	2.12	9						
Democratic Agrarian Party	1.83	9						
Ecological Party	1.69	8						
Socialist Democratic Party	1.05	5						
Social Democratic Party	0.53	2						
Democratic Group of the Centre	0.48	2						
Democratic Party of Labour	0.38	1						
Party of Free Change	0.34	1						
Party of National Reconstruction	0.32	1						
Party of Young Free Democrats	0.32	1						
Liberal Union 'Bratianu'	0.27	1						
Democratic National Salvation Front/Party of Social Democracy (and allies)			27.72	117	21.52	91	36.61	155
Democratic Convention			20.01	82	30.17	122		
Party of Romanian National Unity			7.72	30	4.36	18		
Greater Romania Party			3.89	16	4.46	19	19.48	84
Socialist Party of Labour			3.04	13				
Social Democratic Union					12.93	53		
Democratic Party							7.03	31
Other	5.54	0	19.97	0	19.92	0	23.19	0
All	100	385	100	328	100	328	100	327

* These data do not include seats reserved for ethnic minorities.

Table A16 Russia: Duma

Party	1993					1995				
	PR vote (%)	PR seats	SMD vote (%)	SMD seats	All seats	PR vote (%)	PR seats	SMD vote (%)	SMD seats	All seats
Liberal Democratic Party	23.93	59	3.59	5	64	11.18	50	3.71	1	51
Russia's (Democratic) Choice	16.19	40	8.08	30	70	3.86	0	2.93	9	9
Communist Party	12.95	32	4.14	16	48	22.30	99	8.02	58	157
Women of Russia	8.49	21	0.69	2	23	4.61	0	0.59	3	3
Agrarian Party	8.31	21	6.45	12	33	3.78	0	3.81	20	20
Yabloko	8.21	20	4.15	3	23	6.89	31	2.98	14	45
Unity and Concord (PRES)	7.06	18	3.21	1	19	0.36	0	0.45	1	1
Democratic Party	5.76	14	2.53	1	15					
Movement for Democratic Reforms	4.26	0	2.33	4	4					
Civic Union	2.01	0	3.57	1	1					
Russia's Future	1.31	0	0.92	1	1					
Dignity and Charity	0.73	0	1.00	2	2					
Our Home is Russia						10.13	45	1.95	10	55
Communists and Working Russia						4.53	0	1.47	1	1
Congress of Russian Communities						4.31	0	2.82	5	5
Party of Workers' Self-Government						3.98	0	0.64	1	1
Forward Russia!						1.94	0	1.23	3	3
Power to the People						1.61	0	2.11	9	9

Table A16 (Continued)

Party	1993					1995				
	PR vote (%)	PR seats	SMD vote (%)	SMD seats	All seats	PR vote (%)	PR seats	SMD vote (%)	SMD seats	All seats
Pamfilova-Gurov-Lysenko, Republican Party						1.60	0	0.74	2	2
Trade Unions and Industrialists						1.55	0	0.95	1	1
Block of Ivan Rybkin						1.11	0	1.41	3	3
Block of Stanislav Govorukhin						0.99	0	0.99	1	1
My Fatherland						0.72	0	0.48	1	1
Common Cause						0.68	0	0.24	1	1
Transformation of the Fatherland						0.49	0	0.34	1	1
Party of Economic Freedom						0.13	0	0.33	1	1
Block of Independents						0.12	0	0.51	1	1
Block '89						0.06	0	0.29	1	1
Independents	—	—	58.63	141	141	—	—	56.78	77	77
Other	0.79	0	0.71	0	0	13.07	0	4.23	0	0
All	100	225	100	219*	444*	100	225	100	225	450

* Six seats remained vacant following the election.

Communist Party	24.29	67	15.56	47	114
Inter-Regional Movement 'Unity'	23.32	64	2.46	9	73
Fatherland – All Russia	13.33	37	9.94	29	66
Union of Right Forces	8.52	24	3.55	5	29
Zhirinovsky Block	5.98	17	1.54	0	17
Yabloko	5.93	16	5.69	5	21
Our Home is Russia	1.19	0	2.98	8	8
Political Movement in Support of the Army	0.58	0	0.83	2	2
All People's Union	0.37	0	1.23	2	2
Pensioners' Party	1.95	0	0.81	1	1
Congress of Russian Communities and Boldyrev Movement	0.61	0	0.81	1	1
Block of General Andreii Nikolayev and Academician Svyatoslav Fyodorov	0.56	0	1.20	1	1
Socialist Party	0.24	0	1.16	1	1
Spiritual Heritage Socio-Political Movement	0.10	0	1.08	1	1
Independents	—	—	48.97	112	112
Other	13.03	0	7.88	0	0
All	100	225	100	224*	449*

* One seat remained vacant following the election.

Table A17   Slovakia: Narodna rada

Party	1990 Vote (%)	1990 Seats	1992 Vote (%)	1992 Seats	1994 Vote (%)	1994 Seats	1998 Vote (%)	1998 Seats	2002 Vote (%)	2002 Seats
Public Against Violence	29.35	48								
Christian Democratic Movement	19.21	31	8.89	18	10.08	17			8.25	15
Slovak National Party	13.94	22	7.93	15	5.40	9	9.07	14		
Communist Party/Party of the Democratic Left (and allies)	13.35	22	14.70	29	10.42	18	14.66	23		
Hungarian Coalitions	8.66	14	7.42	14	10.19	17	9.13	15	11.16	20
Democratic Party	4.40	7								
Party of Greens	3.49	6								
Movement for Democratic Slovakia (and allies)			37.26	74	34.97	61	27.00	43	19.50	36
Democratic Union					8.57	15				
Association of Workers					7.35	13				
Democratic Coalition							26.33	42		
Party of Civil Understanding							8.02	13		
Democratic and Christian Union									15.09	28
Smer									13.46	25
Communist Party									6.32	11
New Citizen Alliance									8.01	15
Other	7.60	0	23.80	0	13.02	0	5.79	0	18.21	0
All	100	150	100	150	100	150	100	150	100	150

Table A18   Slovenia: Drzavni Zbor*

Party	1990 Vote (%)	1990 Seats	1996 Vote (%)	1996 Seats	2000 Vote (%)	2000 Seats
Liberal Democratic Party	23.46	22	25.05	25	36.23	34
Christian Democrats	14.51	15	9.61	10		
United List	13.58	14	9.03	9	12.07	11
National Party	10.02	12	4.01	4	4.38	4
People's Party	8.69	10	19.38	19		
Democrats	5.01	6				
Greens	3.70	5				
Social Democratic Party	3.34	4	16.13	16	15.80	14
Democratic Party of Pensioners			4.32	5	5.16	4
Peoples' Party and Christian Democrats					9.53	9
New Slovenia					8.66	8
Party of Slovene Youth					4.33	4
Other	17.69	0	12.47	0	3.84	0
All	100	88	100	88	100	88

* These data do not include seats reserved for ethnic minorities.

Table A19   Ukraine: Verkhovna Rada

Party	1994		1998				
	*Vote (%)**	*Seats*	*PR vote (%)*	*PR seats*	*SMD vote (%)**	*SMD seats*	*All seats*
Communist Party	12.72	86	24.65	84	14.69	38	122
Popular Movement (Rukh)	5.15	20	9.40	32	6.34	14	46
Socialist Party	3.09	14					
Peasant Party	2.74	19					
Republican Party	2.52	8					
Congress of Ukrainian Nationalists	1.25	5					
Democratic Party	1.08	2					
Party of Democratic Rebirth	0.83	4					
National Assembly	0.51	1					
Labour Party	0.40	4					
Social Democratic Party	0.36	2					
Christian Democratic Party	0.35	1	1.30	0	0.81	2	2
Conservative Republican Party	0.34	2					
Civic Congress	0.25	2					
Socialist/Peasant Block			8.56	29	4.49	5	34
Party of Greens			5.44	19	0.83	0	19
Popular Democratic Party			5.01	17	4.17	12	29
Hromada			4.68	16	3.72	7	23
Progressive Socialist Party			4.05	14	0.98	2	16

Socialist Democratic Party (United)	17	3	1.90	14	4.01		
Agrarian Party	8	8	3.29	0	3.68		
Party of Reforms and Order	3	3	1.92	0	3.13		
Working Ukraine	1	1	0.52	0	3.06		
National Front	5	5	2.71	0	2.72		
Together block (Labour and Liberal parties)	1	1	1.31	0	1.89		
Forward Ukraine!	2	2	0.55	0	1.74		
Block of Democratic Parties–NEP	1	1	1.16	0	1.23		
Social Liberal Union	1	1	0.48	0	0.91		
Party of Regional Revival	2	2	0.87	0	0.91		
Union	1	1	0.16	0	0.70		
Fewer Words	1	1	0.28	0	0.17		
Independents	116	116	45.95	—	—	66.48	168
Other	0	0	2.87	0	12.76	1.93	0
All	450	225	100	225	100	100	338**

Table A19   *(Continued)*

Party	2002				
	PR vote (%)	PR seats	SM vote (%)*	SM seats	Total seats
Our Ukraine	24.49	70	14.52	41	111
Communist Party	20.76	59	10.36	7	66
For a United Ukraine	12.23	35	16.36	66	101
Yulia Tymoshenko Block	7.54	22	0.06	0	22
Socialist Party	7.14	20	3.77	2	22
Social-Democratic Party (united)	6.52	19	2.44	5	24
Democratic Party–Democratic Union	0.91	0	1.42	4	4
Unity	1.13	0	2.81	3	3
Naval Party	0.12	0	0.17	1	1
Party of National Economic Development	—	—	0.22	1	1
Independents	—	—	41.53	92	92
Other	19.16	0	6.34	0	0
All	100	225	100	222**	447

* Vote shares are defined here in terms of party membership.
** A total of 112 seats remained vacant following the election (all but approximately 50 of these were filled in a series of by-elections that took place over the course of the next three years).
*** Two seats remained vacant following the election.

Table A20 Yugoslavia: Vece Gradjana

Party	2000	
	Vote (%)	*Seats*
Democratic Opposition of Serbia	43.86	58
Left Coalition	32.95	44
Socialist People's Party of Montenegro	2.23	28
Serbian Radical Party	8.73	5
Serbian People's Party of Montenegro	N/A	2
Vojvodina's Hungarian Union	N/A	1
Serbian Renewal Movement	5.12	0
Other	N/A	0
All	100	138

Appendix B: Data Sources

The majority of the data employed in the analyses undertaken in this volume is collected in the database of the Project on Elections and Political Transformation in Post-Communist Europe, which can be accessed at www.essex.ac.uk/elections. The sources of the data collected in the Database are provided there. The references contained in this Appendix are additional material not found in the Database; this material is divided into three sections. The first section lists sources of social and economic data used in the quantitative analyses undertaken in the preceding chapters. The second section provides sources of electoral data, and the third section gives sources of data on political parties. The second and third sections are broken down by country.

Social and economic data

GDP: United Nations Monthly Bulletin of Statistics on-line version at www.esa.un.org/unsd; *UN Statistical Yearbook*, New York: United Nations, various editions; International Monetary Fund World Economic Outlook Database (available at www.imf.org).

Population density: calculated from voter registration data (see below) and country area data found in the *UN Statistical Yearbook*, New York: United Nations, various editions.

Electoral data

Albania

Legislation

1991 elections: Krenar Loloci, 'Electoral Law in Eastern Europe: Albania', *East European Constitutional Review* (1994), pp. 42–50; *Chronicle of Parliamentary Elections and Developments* 25 (1990–91), pp. 29–31.

1992 elections: 'Law on Elections for the People's Assembly of the Republic of Albania', 4 February 1992, F. Clifton White Resource Center, IFES, Washington, DC, document provided to the archive by the International Republican Institute.

1997 elections: 'Law on Elections for the People's Assembly of the Republic of Albania', 4 February 1992, F. Clifton White Resource Center, IFES, Washington, DC, document provided to the archive by the International Republican Institute; 'For the Changes in the Law No 7556, Date 4/2/1992 ' The Elections for the Parliament of the Republic of Albania', 2 January 1996, F. Clifton White Resource Center, IFES, Washington, DC.

2001 elections: 'Law on Elections for the People's Assembly of the Republic of Albania' with 1992 and 1997 amendments, 16 May 1997, www.ifes.org.

Results:

1991 elections: 'Albania', *Chronicle of Parliamentary Elections and Developments* 25 (1990–91), pp. 29–31; 'Albania Elections: Vote Totals by Zone (Constituency), March 31, 1991', Clifton White Resource Center, IFES, Washington, DC.

1992 elections: 'Albania', *Chronicle of Parliamentary Elections and Developments* 26 (1991–92), pp. 33–4; '1992 Results for Albania', Clifton White Resource Center, IFES, Washington, DC.

1997 elections: IPU Parline database at www.ipu.org; Elections around the World (Derksen) database at www.electionworld.org;.

2001 elections: Albanian Central Electoral Commission Website at www.kqz.org.al; IPU Parline database at www.ipu.org; Elections around the World (Derksen) database at www.electionworld.org.

Notes: 2001 – the Democratic-Party-led 'Union for Victory' coalition is treated as a single party as it fielded a joint list and ran joint candidates in most districts. SMD district-level results are missing for district 8; single-member district vote totals are calculated on the basis of the other 99 districts.

Armenia

Legislation

1995 elections: IPU Parline database at www.ipu.org.
1999 elections: see www.essex.ac.uk/elections.

Results

1995 elections: IPU Parline database at www.ipu.org; NCSEER Post Communist Elections Project Home Page at www.wws.princeton.edu/~jtucker/pcelections.html.
1999 elections: Central Electoral Commission website at www.elections.am; The website of the Armenian office of the International Foundation for Electoral Systems at www.ifes.am.

Bosnia and Herzegovina

Legislation

1996 elections: 'OSCE Mission to Bosnia and Herzegovina Provisional Electoral Commission Rules and Regulations: Decisions until July 16, 1996', *Sluzbeni List* 5, 22, 1996.
1998 elections: 'Rules and Regulations – Elections 12–13 September, 1998', OSCE Mission to Bosnia and Herzegovina, Sarajevo, 1998.
2000 elections: OSCE Mission to Bosnia and Herzegovina website at www.oscebih.org; Association of Election Officials in Bosnia and Herzegovina, *Elections and Development of a Draft Election Law in Bosnia and Herzegovina*, Technical Series No. 1/2001, Sarajevo: Association of Election Officials in Bosnia and Herzegovina, 2001.
2002 elections: 'Election Law of BiH', available at the website of the OSCE Mission to Bosnia and Herzegovina, www.oscebih.org.

Results

1996 elections: 'Election Results', *Sluzbeni List* 5, 32, 1996.
1998 elections: Website of the OSCE Mission to Bosnia and Herzegovina, www. oscebih.org.
2000 elections: Website of the OSCE Mission to Bosnia and Herzegovina, www. oscebih.org.
2002 elections: Bosnian Permanent Electoral Commission website at www. izbori.ba.

Bulgaria 2001

(additional source): 'Zakon za politicheskite partii', 28 March 2001.

Croatia

Legislation

1992 elections: 'Law on Political Organizations' 24 April 1990; 'Law on Political Parties', 24 August 1993; 'Law on the Election of Representatives in the Parliament (Sabor) of the Republic of Croatia', 25 April 1992, available in English in Siber, 1997.
1995 elections: Kasapovic, 1996; 'Organisation for Security and Co-operation in Europe Office for Democratic Institutions and Human Rights Observation of the Parliamentary Elections in the Republic of Croatia, 29 October 1995', *OSCE Documents 1973–99*, CD-ROM, Organisation for Security and Co-operation in Europe, Prague.
2000 elections: 'Law on Elections of Representatives to the Croatian State Parliament', 29 October 1999, Croatian Central Electoral Commission.

Results

1992 elections: Ivan Siber (ed.), *The 1990 and 1992/93 Sabor Elections in Croatia: Analyses, Documents and Data*, Berlin: Sigma, 1997.
1995 elections: Mirjana Kasapovic, '1995 Parliamentary Elections in Croatia', *Electoral Studies* 15, 2 (1996), pp. 269–82; NCSEER Post Communist Elections Project Home Page at www.wws.princeton.edu/ ~jtucker/pcelections.html.
2000 elections: Adam Carr's Psephos database at http://psephos.adam-carr.net.

The Czech Republic 2002

Czech Electoral Commission website at www.volby.cz.

Georgia

Legislation

1992 elections: Lincoln Allison, Alexander Kukhianidze, and Malkhaz Matsaberizde, 'The Georgian Election of 1992', *Electoral Studies* 12, 2 (1993), pp. 174–9; *Chronicle of Parliamentary Elections and Developments* 27 (1992–93), pp. 95–7.
1995 elections: Lincoln Allison, 'The Georgian Elections of November 1995', *Electoral Studies*, 1996; *Chronicle of Parliamentary Elections and Developments* 30 (1995–96), pp. 91–4.
1999 elections: see www.essex.ac.uk/elections.

Results

1992 elections: Lincoln Allison, Alexander Kukhianidze, and Malkhaz Matsaberizde, 'The Georgian Election of 1992', *Electoral Studies* **12**, 2 (1993), pp. 174–9; *Chronicle of Parliamentary Elections and Developments* **27** (1992–93), pp. 95–7; NCSEER Post Communist Elections Project Home Page at www.wws. princeton.edu/~jtucker/pcelections.html.

1995 elections: Lincoln Allison, 'The Georgian Elections of November 1995', *Electoral Studies*, 1996; *Chronicle of Parliamentary Elections and Developments* **30** (1995–96), pp. 91–4; NCSEER Post Communist Elections Project Home Page at www.wws.princeton.edu/~jtucker/pcelections.html.

1999 elections: Website of the Georgian office of the International Foundation for Electoral Systems at www.ifes.ge; 'Georgia Parliamentary Elections 31 October and 14 November 1999' Organization for Security and Co-operation I Europe, Warsaw, 7 February, 2000 available at www.osce.org/ohihr/.

Hungary 2002

Central Electoral Commission website at www.election.hu.

Latvia 2002

Central Electoral Commission website at www.velesanas-2002.cvk.lv.

Note: the 2002 results employed in this analysis are provisional.

Macedonia

Legislation

1994 elections: 'Law on Election and Recall of Representatives and Councillors', Skopje, October 1994; from the F. Clifton White Resource Center, International Foundation for Election Systems, Washington, DC.

1998 elections: 'Law on the Election of Members for the Parliament of Macedonia', 1998 downloaded from www.izbori98.gov.mk.

2002 elections: 'Law on Election of Members of the Parliament of Macedonia, 2002, Macedonian Central Electoral Commission Website at www.dik.mk.

Results

1994 elections: *Statistical Yearbook of the Republic of Macedonia, 1996*, Statistical Office of the Republic of Macedonia, Skopje, 1996.

1998 elections: *Parlamentarni izbori '98, Konechni rezultati od 'Parlamentarnite Izbori '98'*, State Electoral Commission, Skopje, 1999.

2002 elections: Macedonian Central Electoral Commission Website at www. dik.mk; International Foundation for Electoral Systems; Election Guide database at www.electionguide.org; W. Derksen's Elections Around the World database at electionworld.org.

Slovakia 2002

Legislation and results are taken from the Central Electoral Commission website at www.civil.gov.sk.

Slovenia

Legislation

1992 elections: 'Law on Elections to the National Assembly', 1992, held at the F. Clifton White Resource Center, International Foundation for Election Systems, Washington, DC.
1996 elections: 'Electoral System in Slovenia', Central Electoral Commission website at www.sigov.si/elections/system.htm; Inter-Parliamentary Union Parline database at www.ipu.org.
2000 elections: 'National Assembly Elections Act', available at the Central Electoral Commission website at www.sigov.si/elections.

Results: 1992–2000: Website of the Central Electoral Commission at www.sigov.si/elections.

Ukraine 2002

Legislation

'Zakon Ukraïny pro vybory narodnykh deputativ', 18 October 2001, available at www.rada.gov.ua.

Results

Central Electoral Commission's website at www.cvk.ukrpack.net.

Note: In the Ukrainian 1994 and 1998 data for single-member district races, party affiliation is understood in terms of membership, rather than nomination, as many party affiliates found it easier to have themselves nominated as independent candidates.

Yugoslavia

Legislation

'The Law on the Election of Federal Deputies to the Chamber of Citizens in the Federal Assembly', available on the website of the Centre for Free Elections and Democracy at www.cesid.org.

Results

Yugoslav Federal Government website at www.gov.yu; International Foundation for Election Systems Election Guide at www.ifes.org/eguide/.

Data on parties

Szajkowski, Bogdan, *Political Parties of Eastern Europe, Russia and the Successor States*, Harlow: Longman, 1994.
Alan Day, Richard German and John Campbell (eds), *Political Parties of the World*, London: Cartermill, 1996.
Richard Rose, Neil Munro and Tom Mackie, *Elections in Central and Eastern Europe Since 1990*, Strathclyde: Centre for the Study of Public Policy, University of Strathclyde, 1998.

'Notes on Recent Elections' section of *Electoral Studies*, various issues.

These general sources were in some cases supplemented by sources listed in the bibliography and for individual countries by the following.

Armenia

'Republic of Armenia Parliamentary Election 30 May 1999: Final Report' Organization for Security and Co-operation in Europe, Warsaw, 30 July 1999, available at www.osce.org/odihr/.
National Democratic Institute, 'The May 30, 1999 Parliamentary Elections in Armenia', available at www.ifes.am.

Estonia

Vello Pettai and Marcus Kreuzer, 'Party Politics in the Baltic States: Social Bases and Institutional Context', *East European Politics and Societies* **13**, 1 (1999), pp. 148–89.

Georgia

'Georgia Parliamentary Elections 31 October and 14 November 1999' Organization for Security and Co-operation in Europe, Warsaw, 7 February, 2000' available at www.osce.org/ohihr/.
'Political Parties in Georgia', European Forum website at www.europeanforum.bot-consult.se.

Latvia

Vello Pettai and Marcus Kreuzer, 'Party Politics in the Baltic States: Social Bases and Institutional Context', *East European Politics and Societies* **13**, 1 (1999), pp. 148–89.

Lithuania

Vello Pettai and Marcus Kreuzer, 'Party Politics in the Baltic States: Social Bases and Institutional Context', *East European Politics and Societies* **13**, 1 (1999), pp. 148–89.

Poland

Frances Millard, *Polish Politics and Society*, New York and London: Routledge, 1999.

Russia

Yu. K. Abramov and T. Yu. Golovin (eds), *Politicheskie partii i dvizhennya Rossii 1998: yezhogodnik*, Moscow: Press Ltd., 1998.
O. K. Zastrozhnoi (ed.), *Obshcherossiiskie izbiratel'nye ob"edineniya: nakanune vyborov deputatov Gosudarstvennoi Dumy Federal'novo Sobraniya Rossiiskoi Federatsii tret'evo sozyva: spravochnik*, Moscow: Ves' Mir, 1999. Grigorii V. Golosov,

'Political Parties in the 1993–96 Elections' in Vladimir Gel'man and Grigorii V. Golosov (eds), *Elections in Russia, 1993–96: Analyses, Documents and Data*, Berlin: Sigma, 1999.

Ukraine

Politychni partiï Ukraïny, Kiev: KIS, 1998.

Appendix C: Data on Party System Evolution

This Appendix provides detailed notes on the assumptions and methods behind the data presented and analysed in Chapter 6. Information on data sources can be found in the second and third sections of Appendix B.

System changes: Calculations of indices are based on the most comparable figures. Thus the figures for Albania 1997–2001 are based on SMD volatility only. The PR component of the Bulgarian 1990 mixed system is used to calculate volatility figures for the 1990–91 elections (given that a fully PR system was used in 1991). For similar reasons, the Croatian score for 1995–2000 is based on the PR component of the 1995 ballot only. As far as Macedonia is concerned, the 1994–98 score is based on the SMD ballot whereas the 1998–2002 score is based on the PR ballot. Finally, the single-member component of the Ukrainian 1998 mixed system is used in calculating volatility between the 1994 and 1998 election (given that a fully single-member system was employed in 1994).

In absolute majority systems in two rounds (the single-member races in Hungary and Lithuania 1992 and 1996, as well as the Ukrainian election of 1994), results from the first round are employed in calculating volatility, given that the first round is the only one in which all seats were contested.

Independent candidates were discarded from the vote totals and percentages were recalculated on the basis of the remaining votes.

Decision rules used to determine the continuity of parties between elections: Coalition partners are considered to have retained their identity, meaning that the parties that make up the coalition are considered to have contested two consecutive elections, if they contested the first election as separate parties and the second election as a coalition, or vice versa. In this case the votes of the relevant parties are added together in both elections.

In the case of mergers: Mergers that result in a party which contains the original names (substantially unchanged, in the sense that they are still identifiable) of the parties which merged are treated like a coalition, as continuity of identity is indicated by this name. Mergers that involve party A absorbing party B, such that the resulting political organization retains the name of party A and party B's name is lost entirely, are treated as the extinction of party B (and party A are considered to have maintained continuity of identity). Mergers that result in the creation of a new party with a new name substantially different from that of either of its component parts are considered to be a new party, and the parties that merged to form it are considered extinct.

In the case of splits: If the resultant parties both (all) acquire new names following the split, they are considered new parties and the party which spawned them are treated as extinct. If, as is most commonly the case, a splinter group breaks away from an existing party and forms a new party, the new party is treated as such, and the remaining rump party is normally treated as being continuous with the party as it was before the split. If a party splits and both factions claim ownership of the original name, then the decision of the judicial and/or other body which adjudicates in the dispute is observed, and the party which loses the right to the original name is considered a new party.[1]

If a party is grouped with different coalition partners from one election to the next, continuity is not assumed, as such shifting coalitions indicate lack of consistent identifiability.

In the case of name changes: Parties that change their name without experiencing either a split or a merger are considered to have maintained continuity.

In some cases individual parties experience a number of the above identity changes, either simultaneously or over time. Where possible, the above rules are applied to consecutive changes. When there is possible ambiguity as to how the schema has been applied in practice, this is indicated in the form of notes.

No attempt is made to make a clear distinction between parties, coalitions, and other types of electoral contender (with the exception of independents which are excluded, as indicated above).

Notes on individual countries: cases which cannot be determined unambiguously according to the above rules and exceptions.

Albania

The Workers' Party in 1991 is considered continuous with the Socialist Party in 1992.

Bosnia and Herzegovina

The Joint List BiH in 1996 is considered to be continuous with the SDP in 1998.

The Coalition for a Single and Democratic Bosnia and Herzegovina in 1998 is considered to be continuous with the Party of Democratic Action in 2000.

The SNSD–DSP Coalition in 2000 is considered to be continuous with the Union of Independent Social Democrats in 2002.

Bulgaria

Between 1990 and 1997 there were three main forces in Bulgarian electoral politics: the Bulgarian Socialist Party (BSP), the Union of Democratic Forces (SDS) and the Movement for Rights and Freedoms (DPS). In 1997 each of these parties formed a coalition with other smaller parties that had previously part of different coalitions. Nevertheless, the continuity of the three main parties will be assumed.

The Czech Republic

The Left Bloc of 1992 is assumed to be continuous with the Communist Party of Bohemia and Moravia (KSCM) in 1996 (not the Left Bloc party).

Estonia

The Left Alternative in 1992 is considered to be continuous with the Justice Alliance in 1995.

Secure Home in 1992 is considered to be continuous with the Coalition Party-Rural Union (KMU) in 1995.

The Popular Front in 1992 is considered to be continuous with the Estonian Centre Party + the Estonian Entrepreneurs' Party (EEE) in 1995.

Our Home is Estonia (MKE) in 1995 is considered to be continuous with the Russian Party in Estonia (VEE) in 1999.

Georgia

The National Democratic Party in 1995 is considered to be continuous with the National Democratic Alliance – Third Way in 1999.

Hungary

The Hungarian Socialist Workers' Party (MSZMP) in 1990 is considered to be continuous with the Hungarian Workers' Party (MP) in 1994.

Joint FIDESZ–MPP + MDF candidates are counted together with FIDESZ–MPP, whereas joint MDF + FIDESZ–MPP candidates are counted together with the MDF.

Latvia

The United List of the Latvian Farmer's Union (LZS), Latvian Christian Democratic Union (LKDS), and Latgale Democratic Party in 1995 is considered to be continuous with the Latvian Farmer's Union (LZS) + the Latvian Christian Democratic Union (LKDS) in 1993.

The coalition of the Latvian National Conservative Party and the Latvian Green Party in 1995 is considered to be continuous with the Latvian National Independence Movement (LNNK) + the Green List (ZS) of 1993.

Macedonia

The SDSM coalition in 1994 is considered to be continuous with the SDSM in 1998, which is in turn considered to be continuous with the Together for Macedonia coalition in 2002.

VMRO–DPMNE in 1994 is considered to be continuous with the VMRO–DA coalition in 1998.

Moldova

The Alliance of Democratic Forces Electoral Bloc (AFD) in 1998 is considered to be continuous with the National Liberal Party (PNL) in 2001.

The Electoral Bloc for a Democratic and Prosperous Moldova (PMDP) in 1998 is considered to be continuous with the Democratic Party of Moldova (PDM) in 2001.

Poland

Solidarity Electoral Action (AWS) in 1997 is considered to be continuous with Solidarity + Fatherland + the Coalition for the Republic + the Non-Party Reform

Bloc + the Confederation for an Independent Poland + the Centre Alliance + the Peasant Alliance.

The Union of Political Realism (UPR) in 1993 is considered to be continuous with the Union of the Right of the Republic in 1997.

Romania

The Democratic National Salvation Front (FDSN) is considered to be continuous with the Romanian Party of Social Democracy (PDRS) in 1996.

Russia

Russia's Choice (VR) in 1993 is considered to be continuous with Russia's Democratic Choice – United Democrats (DVR-OD) in 1995.

The Congress of Russian Communities (KRO) in 1995 is considered to be continuous with the Congress of Russian Communities (KOR) + Movement of Yuri Boldyrev in 1999.

The Liberal Democratic Party of Russia (LDPR) in 1995 is considered to be continuous with the Zhirinovski Block in 1999.

Slovakia

The Movement for a Democratic Slovakia (HZDS) in 1992 is considered to be continuous with the Movement for a Democratic Slovakia and Peasants' Party of Slovakia (HZDS + RSS) in 1994.

The Common Choice block in 1994 is considered to be a coalition of the SDL, the SDSS and the SZS.

The DS in 1994 is considered to be continuous with the DS + the ODU.

Slovenia

The Unity List of 1992 is considered to be continuous with the United List of Social Democrats in 1996.

Ukraine

The Ukrainian Christian Democratic Party (UkhDP) in 1994 is considered to be continuous with the Forward Ukraine! block in 1998.

Our Ukraine in 2002 is considered to be continuous with Rukh, the Party of Reforms and Order the National Front, Razom, and Forward Ukraine in 1998.

For a United Ukraine in 2002 is considered to be continuous with the Popular Democratic Party, Working Ukraine, and the Agrarian Party in 1998.

The Yuliya Tymoshenko Block in 2002 is considered to be continuous with Hromada in 1998.

The Socialist Party in 2002 is considered to be continuous with the Socialist/Peasant block in 1998 on the list vote.

The Democratic Union in 2002 is considered to be continuous with NEP in 1998.

The Nataliya Vitrenko Block in 2002 is considered to be continuous with the Progressive Socialist Party in 1998.

Notes

1 Electoral Systems and Post-Communist Transition

1. See especially Duverger, 1959; Rae, 1971; Katz, 1980, 1997; Powell, 1982, 2000; Lijphart, 1994; Cox, 1997; Farrell, 2001; Lijphart and Grofman, 1984; Grofman and Lijphart, 1986; and Taagepera and Shugart, 1989.
2. Major comparative works include Alexander, 1979, 1989; Gunlicks, 1993; Gallagher and Marsh, 1988; Katz and Mair, 1992, 1994; Alexander and Shiratori, 1994.
3. But see Bohrer, 1997; Taagepera, 1998b; Blais and Dion, 1990; Reilly and Reynolds, 1999.
4. Lijphart, 1992; McGregor, 1993; Holmes, 1994; Kuusela, 1994; Geddes, 1996; Ishiyama, 1996; Jasiewicz, 1998; Lewis, 1998; Elster *et al.*, 1998: 111–30; Moser, 1999; Kitschelt *et al.*, 1999: 32–5, 53–5; Birch, 2000.
5. E.g. Gabel, 1995, Moser, 1995, 1997; Toka, 1995; Benoit, 1996, 1999; Gebethner, 1996; Iordanova, 1997.
6. Kitschelt, 1992, 1995; Cotta, 1994; Waller, 1994; Lewis, Lomax, and Wightman, 1994.
7. See Furtak, 1990 for an overview of the electoral systems in the communist world in the late 1980s.
8. In the former Soviet area, Turkmenistan and Kazakhstan have also retained single-member systems. They are, however, outside the case set considered here (see below).
9. The only other electoral formula to be used in the region was the single transferable vote employed in the Estonian parliamentary elections of 1990 but subsequently abandoned in favour of list-PR.
10. For an overview of the distribution of compulsory voting at the millenium, see IDEA, 2002: 105–10.
11. Much ink has been spilt on the élite-dominated nature of post-communist politics. See, for example, Agh, 1994; Kopecky, 1995; Lewis, 2000.
12. See, for example, Pzreworski, 1991; Shugart and Carey, 1992; Lijphart and Waisman, 1996; Linz and Stepan, 1996; Kitschelt *et al.*, 1999.
13. There is ideological justification for this as well: PR embeds the notion of party-based competition and hence ideological pluralism in the political system.
14. The separate development of the two literatures has most likely been due to the different types of data on which they have relied. While the study of district format and seat allocation rules has benefited from readily accessible cross-national data, campaign finance data have been less reliable, less comparable, and harder to come by. Studies of finance have thus been largely confined to single country analyses and in many cases they have been based on qualitative rather than quantitative data. The extensive database employed in the present study affords a rare opportunity to develop a range of comparable indicators of campaign finance regulatory structures across the states in question.

2 An Overview of Post-Communist Electoral Systems: Design and Measurement

1. The Slovenian republican elections of 1990 (outside the dataset considered here) were also conducted under a 2.5 per cent threshold, which was abolished for the first elections held in independent Slovenia in 1992.
2. From a bargaining perspective, all systems can be conceptualized as mixed systems, with pure PR and pure SMD outcomes being special cases in which one system wins entirely, and all other cases being the result of bargains among the proponents of each type.
3. An additional feature characteristic of the region is the existence of dedicated seats for ethnic minorities in Romania, Slovenia, and Croatia, but these represent relatively small proportions of the total number of parliamentary seats in these states, and are therefore of little relevance to the concerns of this study.
4. This phenomenon has also been observed in the new democracies of Southern Europe (van Biezen, 2000).
5. The only state in the region to prohibit private finance is outside the set of cases considered here; in the Belarussian elections of 1995 only state financing of electoral campaigns was allowed.
6. Other scholars split mixed systems up into those compensatory systems that are classified as PR systems, and those in which the two component parts are independent, which are classified as 'semi-proportional' (Reynolds and Reilly, 1997). It has also been argued that both compensatory and parallel systems are part of a broader category of mixed system that includes those in which some districts elect deputies according to one formula and some according to another (Massicotte and Blais, 1999; cf. Blais and Massicotte, 1996).

3 Electoral Participation

1. For a fuller description of voting practices under communism, see Birch *et al.*, 2002, chapter 1.
2. Some cross-national analyses use the total voting age population as a denominator. This approach has the advantage that it allows the researcher to control for alternative registration procedures or differential effectiveness of the registration process, which can in some cases exhibit noteworthy variation (cf. Pérez-Liñán, 2001). The disadvantage is that in some countries substantial proportions of the eligible electorate are non-citizens, who usually do not have voting rights (See Powell, 1986: Appendix 3 for a more extended discussion of these considerations). In the post-communist states examined here, registration is in virtually all cases automatic for the vast majority of the electorate, obviating the need to control for registration system design. There is also little reason to suspect great variations in the capacity of the state to implement registration effectively. There are, however, substantial variations in the proportion of the population who are citizens of the states in which they reside. Estonia and Latvia have numerous non-citizen immigrants and descendents of immigrants living in their borders, which

makes the voting age population a poor indicator in these cases. It is for this reason that turnout will be measured as a proportion of the registered electorate.

3. The Western European average is calculated from data presented in IDEA, 1997: 51–82. Countries include Austria, Belgium, Denmark, Finland, France, Germany, Greece, Ireland, Italy, the Netherlands, Norway, Portugal, Spain, Sweden, and Switzerland.

4. At the individual level, Poland is not exceptional at all. Turnout has been found to be higher among the better educated and more urbanized sectors of the population than among less educated rural residents, and the most religious have been found to vote with greater frequency (Wade *et al.*, 1994: 104). These are patterns familiar to students of electoral participation, suggesting that the phenomenon is a polity-level one.

5. Another way of categorizing the various factors is according to how they affect turnout, for instance, by distinguishing factors that represent costs from those that represent benefits, or resources conducive to voting from instrumental and psychological factors. The first mode of classification will be employed here, for the simple reason that it enables us to single out the institutional variables that are the primary focus of this volume.

6. Duch found post-communist turnout to be poorly predicted by individual-level factors in general, but in some cases it was linked to education and in some cases to media exposure (Duch, 1998: 217).

7. Plausible counter-arguments focus on the claim that plurality electoral laws are likely to lead to a more decisive outcome in terms of government formation (at least in parliamentary systems), which ought to enhance the relevance of the electoral process in the eyes of the voters (Crewe, 1981; Jackman, 1986; Jackman and Miller, 1995). It has also been supposed that voters value the dyadic link with their representative under single-member systems, and that they are more likely to vote under such systems on this basis (Powell, 1980; Crewe, 1981). The weight of empirical evidence suggests that neither decisiveness nor the constituency link is as important as other factors in the average elector's vote calculus.

8. These final three links will be examined in greater detail in later chapters. For the purposes of the present analysis, these effects of electoral systems will be assumed, and the electoral system will be taken as a proxy for them.

9. The 'voter fatigue' argument might also be made *vis-à-vis* two-round elections, where it could be expected to apply particularly to the second round. To simplify matters we will be considering turnout in first rounds only.

10. In mixed systems the measure was calculated in terms of the weighted average of the differences in the two component parts of the system (where vote share data for both parts were available).

11. Once electoral system type is controlled, representational inclusion (discussed in detail in Chapter 4) has no additional effect on turnout.

12. Neither did any of the excluded variables discussed here prove significant in any of the cross-sectional models constructed.

13. These results also confirm Jackman and Miller's (1995: 480) finding that cultural factors are less important than institutional factors in shaping turnout in new democracies.

4   Representation Inclusion

1. Elsewhere elements of functional representation have persisted in the composition of upper chambers; in both Croatia and Slovenia this was the case well into the post-communist period.
2. See, for example, Birch, 2000; Moser, 2001a: chapters 3 and 4; Moser, 2001b; Matland and Montgomery, 2003.
3. We might hypothesize that district magnitude would have an impact in PR systems also, but Cox has shown that above a magnitude of 5, this effect is negligible (Cox, 1997: 100). Anckar's empirical investigation confirmed this hypothesis, finding no effect of magnitude on vote wastage (1997).
4. Another aspect of the electoral system that could in theory affect the ability of voters to vote strategically is the extent to which differing and contradictory incentives implied by it. A clever electoral 'engineer' could minimize the extent to which voters were able to act strategically by building cross-cutting incentives into the system. An example of such a situation is the Albanian mixed one-vote system used between 1991 and 1997. Under this system voters voted for candidates in SMDs, and their single votes were used to calculate both the first-round outcomes in the SMDs and the distribution of PR seats according to the party affiliation of the SMD candidates. The two-round system offered some voters the option of casting a 'sincere' vote in the first round and then voting strategically in the second round, but in practice the vast majority of SMD races in these three elections were decided in the first round, and by the time of the 1997 election most voters could have been expected to know that they were likely to have only one shot at determining the electoral outcome. A voter who supported a candidate from a party that had limited support in their district was thus faced with a dilemma; they could vote sincerely in the hopes of influencing the limited number of seats decided by PR, or vote strategically in the knowledge that they were 'better' represented at the local level (inasmuch as there were fewer voters per SMD deputy than PR deputy). The Albanian electoral system was exceptional in the region; the other mixed systems all offered voters two votes. There are more limited cross-cutting incentives built into the Hungarian systems, in as much as vote results at the district level affect higher-level seat allocation; see Duch and Palmer, 2002.
5. It might be possible to argue that a form of collective representation could be developed out of some individual vote choices in as much as voters were voting on the basis of the candidate's ethnicity, gender, and so on – but without knowledge of the basis of vote choice, it is difficult to make this assertion.
6. The Albanian mixed system employed between 1992 and 1997 was based on a single (SMD) vote, so in this case inclusion is calculated on the basis of the SMD vote alone, given that in all these elections only parties that won SMD seats won PR seats.
7. In the second and third elections this variable did have a slight (and barely significant) impact in line with expectations; see Table 4.3.

5   Party System Size and Shape

1. The literature on these processes is abundant, but special mention should be made of several comparative volumes, including Pridham and Lewis, 1996;

Olson and Norton, 1996; Dawisha and Parrott, 1997; Kitschelt *et al.*, 1999; Lewis, 2000, 2001.
2. This was a feature also of the second Italian elections based on a mixed system, held in 1996, in which lists included the Dini List, the Prodi List, and the Segni Pact. The common elements of regional political diversity and largely patronage-based politics may explain why we find this phenomenon in these two states.

6 Party System Stability and Change

1. Similar distinctions have been made or implied by several authors, including Mair, 1997; Toka, 1997; Kitschelt *et al.*, 1999; Colton, 2000; Markowski, 2001, though the concepts are measured differently in the present analysis (see below).
2. This may be what we are currently observing in Russia, where President Putin enjoys extremely high levels of support across much of the political spectrum for his alleged success in bringing 'order' to the violence-plagued country.
3. Mogens Pedersen defines volatility as 'the net change within the electoral party system resulting from individual vote transfers' (1979: 3).
4. Several writers have, however, noted that party system instability can coexist with stable electoral preferences (Crewe, 1985; Mair, 1997).
5. Prior to summing, any votes won by independents are excluded from the total vote and party vote shares are then recalculated on the basis of the revised denominator.
6. In Latin America electoral volatility has reached levels similar to those found in Eastern Europe (Mainwaring and Scully, 1995: 8). See also Coppedge, 1998: 559; Roberts and Wibbels, 1999.
7. Bartolini and Mair (1990) find that the opposite has been true throughout large portions of the history of Western European party competition, a result they explain with reference to the magnification in vote switching which results from tactical voting under systems with small districts and high thresholds. But the differences they find are small enough and inconsistent enough over time to warrant caution in interpreting them.
8. These include, for example, Russia's Choice and successors as well as Unity in Russia, the Popular Democratic Party and successors in Ukraine, together with a plethora of smaller parties.
9. Dummy variables were included in the replacement model to account for the possible effects of outliers Hungary and Croatia which exhibit unusual low replacements scores. Neither of these variables was significant, suggesting that the factors which shape replacement generally are relevant also in accounting for the low scores observed in these states.

7 Conclusion

1. The analysis in this section is confined to Russian and Ukrainian cases because these states have been the object of the greatest number of case studies; many of the observations made here are also applicable to Armenia and Georgia, on which less work has been done to date.

Appendix C: Data on Party System Evolution

1. It may at first seem inconsistent that continuity is attributed to parties that merge but not to those that split. But upon reflection, this is reasonable, If a party splits there is bound to be less continuity of organizational resources as the resultant splinter organizations will mostly have to establish new branches, publications, and so on whereas mergers allow for the consolidation of existing resources. Moreover, party supporters will find it easier to follow their party if it merges with another one than they will if it splits, in which case they will have to decide which group it supports.

Bibliography

Agh, Atilla, 'From Nomenklatura to Clientura: The Emergence of New Political Elites in East-Central Europe', in Geoffrey Pridham and Paul G. Lewis (eds), *Stabilising Fragile Democracies: Comparing New Party Systems in Southern and Eastern Europe*, New York and London: Routledge, 1996, pp. 44–68.

Alexander, Herbert E. (ed.), *Political Finance*, Beverly Hills, CA and London: Sage, 1979.

—— (ed.), *Comparative Politics Finance in the 1980s*, Cambridge: Cambridge University Press, 1989.

Alexander, Herbert E. and Rei Shiratori, *Comparative Political Finance among the Democracies*, Boulder, CO: Westview, 1994.

Barany, Zoltan D., 'Elections in Hungary', in Robert K. Furtak (ed.), *Elections in Socialist States*, New York and London: Harvester Wheatsheaf, 1990, pp. 71–97.

Barkan, Joel, 'Elections in Agrarian Societies', *Journal of Democracy* **6** (1995), pp. 106–16.

Bartolini, Stefano and Peter Mair, *Identity, Competition, and Electoral Availability: The Stabilisation of European Electorates 1885–1985*, Cambridge: Cambridge University Press, 1990.

Benoit, Kenneth, 'Hungary's "Two Vote" Electoral System', *Representation* **33**, 4 (1996).

—— 'Votes and Seats: The Hungarian Electoral Law and the 1994 Parliamentary Election', in Gabor Toka and Zsolt Enyedi (eds), *Elections to the Hungarian National Assembly 1994: Analyses, Documents and Data*, Berlin: Sigma, 1999, pp. 108–38.

Berezkin, A. V., V. A. Kolosov, M. E. Pavlovskaya, N. V. Petrov, and L. V. Smirnyagin, 'The Geography of the 1989 Elections of People's Deputies of the USSR (Preliminary Results)', *Soviet Geography* **30**, 8 (1989), pp. 607–34.

—— *Vesna 1989: geografiia i anatomiia parlamentskikh vyborov*, Moscow: Progress, 1990.

van Biezen, Ingred, 'Party Finance in New Democracies: Spain and Portugal', *Party Politics* **6**, 3 (2000), pp. 329–42.

van Biezen, Ingred and Petr Kopecky, 'On the Predominance of State Money: Reassessing Party Financing in the New Democracies of Southern and Eastern Europe', *Perspectives on European Politics and Society* **2**, 3 (2001), pp. 401–29.

Birch, Sarah, '*Nomenklatura* Democratization: Electoral Clientelism in Post-Soviet Ukraine', *Democratization* **4**, 4 (1997), pp. 40–62.

—— 'Elections and Representation in Post-Communist Eastern Europe', in Hans-Dieter Klingemann, Ekkehard Mochmann, and Kenneth Newton (eds), *Elections in Central and Eastern Europe: The First Wave*, Berlin: Sigma, 2000a.

—— *Elections and Democratization in Ukraine*, Basingstoke: Macmillan, 2000b.

—— 'Electoral Systems and Party Systems in Europe East and West', *Perspectives on European Politics and Society* **2**, 3 (2001), pp. 355–77.

—— 'Two-Round Electoral Systems and Democracy', *Comparative Political Studies*, **36**, 3 (2003), pp. 319–44.

Birch, Sarah, Frances Millard, Kieran Williams, and Marina Popescu, *Embodying Democracy: Electoral System Design in Post-Communist Europe*, Palgrave Macmillan, 2002.

Blais, André, *To Vote or Not To Vote*, Pittsburgh, PA: University of Pittsburgh Press, 2000.

Blais, André and R. K. Carty, 'Does Proportional Representation Foster Voter Turnout?', *European Journal of Political Research* **18** (1990), pp. 167–81.

Blais, André and Stéphane Dion, 'Electoral Systems and the Consolidation of New Democracies', in Diane Ethier (ed.), *Democratic Transition and Consolidation in Southern Europe, Latin America and Southeast Asia*, Basingstoke: Macmillan, 1990, pp. 250–65.

Blais, André and Louis Massicotte, 'Electoral Systems', in Lawrence LeDuc, Richard G. Niremi, and Pippa Norris (eds), *Comparing Democracies: Elections and Voting in Global Perspective*, Thousand Oaks: Sage, 1996, pp. 49–82.

Bohrer, Robert E. II, 'Deviations from Proportionality and Survival in New Parliamentary Democracies', *Electoral Studies* **16** (1997), pp. 217–26.

Broughton, David and Mark Donovan, *Changing Party Systems in Western Europe*, London and New York: Pinter, 1999.

Brunner, Georg, 'Elections in the Soviet Union', in Robert K. Furtak (ed.), *Elections in Socialist States*, New York and London: Harvester Wheatsheaf, 1990, pp. 20–52.

Budge, Ian, 'Electoral Volatility: Issue Effects and Basic Change in 23 Post-War Democracies', *Electoral Studies* **1** (1982), pp. 147–68.

Burg, Steven L. and Paul S. Shoup, *The War in Bosnia-Herzegovina: Ethnic Conflict and International Intervention*, Armonk, NY and London: ME Sharpe, 1999.

Burnell, Peter and Alan Ware (eds), *Funding Democratization*, Manchester: Manchester University Press, 1998.

Campbell, Angus, Philip Converse, W. Miller, and Donald Stokes, *The American Voter*, New York: Wiley, 1960.

Carey, John M. and Mathhew Soberg Shugart, 'Incentives to Cultivate a Personal Vote: A Rank Ordering of Electoral Formulas', *Electoral Studies* **14**, 4 (1995), pp. 417–39.

Carstairs, Andrew McLaren. *A Short History of Electoral Systems in Western Europe*, London: George Allen and Unwin, 1980.

Carson, George Barr, Jr., *Electoral Practices in the USSR*, London: Atlantic Press, 1956.

del Castillo, Pilar, 'Financing of Spanish Political Parties', in Herbert E. Alexander (ed.), *Comparative Political Finance in the 1980s*, Cambridge: Cambridge University Press, 1989, pp. 172–99.

Centro de Asesoria y Promoción Electoral and Instiuto de Investigaciones Juridicas [CAPEIIJ], *Legislaición Electoral Comparada: Colombia, Mexico, Panamá, Venezuela y Centroamérica*, San José, Costa Rica: Capel, 1986, pp. 179–244.

Colton, Timothy J., *Transitional Citizens: Voters and What Influences Them in the New Russia*, Cambridge, MA: Harvard University Press, 2000.

Coppedge, Michael, 'The Dynamic Diversity of Latin American Party Systems', *Party Politics* **4**, 4 (1998), pp. 547–68.

Cotta, Maurizio, 'Building Party Systems after the Dictatorship: The East European Cases in Comparative Perspective', in Geoffrey Pridham and Tatu Vanhanen (eds), *Democratization in Eastern Europe: Domestic and International Perspectives*, London and New York: Routledge, 1994, pp. 99–127.

Cotta, Maurizio 'Structuring the New Party Systems after the Dictatorship: Coalitions, Alliances, Fusions and Splits During the Transition and Post-Transition Phase', in Geoffrey Pridham G. Lewis (eds), *Stabilising Fragile Democracies: Comparing New Party Systems in Southern and Eastern Europe*, London and New York: Routledge, 1996.

Cox, Gary, *Making Votes Count: Strategic Coordination in the World's Electoral Systems*, Cambridge: Cambridge University Press, 1997.

Cox, Gary and Mathew D. McCubbins, 'Institutions and Public Policy in Presidential Systems', in Stephen Haggard and Mathew D. McCubbins (eds), *Presidents, Parliaments, and Policy*, Cambridge: Cambridge University Press, 2001, pp. 64–102.

Crewe, Ivor, 'Electoral Participation', in David Butler, Howard R. Penniman, and Austin Ranney (eds.), *Democracy at the Polls: A Comparative Study of Competitive National Elections*, Washington and London: American Enterprise for Public Policy Research, 1981, pp. 216–63.

—— 'Introduction: Electoral Change in Western Democracies: A Framework for Analysis', in Ivor Crewe and David Denver (eds), *Electoral Change in Western Democracies: Patterns and Sources of Volatility*, London and Sydney: Croom Helm, 1985, pp. 1–22.

Crewe, Ivor and David Denver (eds), *Electoral Change in Western Democracies: Patterns and Sources of Volatility*, London and Sydney: Croom Helm, 1985.

Crewe, Ivor, Tony Fox, and James Alt, 'Non-Voting in British General Elections, 1966–October 1974', in Colin Crouch (ed.), *British Political Sociology Yearbook* 3, London: Croom Helm, 1977, pp. 38–109.

Dahl, Robert A., *Democracy and its Critics*, New Haven and London: Yale University Press, 1989.

Dalton, R. J., *Citizen Politics: Public Opinion and Political Parties in Advanced Western Democracies*, 2nd edn, Chatham, NJ: Chatham House, 1996.

Dawisha, Karen, 'Democratization and Political Participation: Research Concepts and Methodologies', in Karen Dawisha and Bruce Parrott (eds), *The Consolidation of Democracy in East-Central Europe*, Cambridge: Cambridge University Press, 1997, pp. 40–65.

Dawisha, Karen and Bruce Parrott (eds), *The Consolidation of Democracy in East-Central Europe*, Cambridge: Cambridge University Press, 1997.

Downs, Anthony, *An Economic Theory of Democracy*, New York: Harper and Row, 1957.

Duch, Raymond, 'Participation in the New Democracies of Central and Eastern Europe: Cultural versus Rational Choice Explanations', in Samuel Barnes and Janos Simon (eds), *The Postcommunist Citizen*, Budapest: Erasmus Foundation and Institute for Political Science of the Hungarian Academy of Sciences, 1998, pp. 195–227.

Duch, Raymond and Harvey D. Palmer, 'Strategic Voting in Post-Communist Democracy?' *British Journal of Political Science* 32, 1 (2002), pp. 63–91.

Duverger, M., *Political Parties: Their Organisation and Activity in the Modern State*, 2nd edn, London: John Wiley, 1959.

Ekiert, Grzegorz, 'Democratisation Processes in East Central Europe: A Theoretical Reconsideration', *British Journal of Political Science* 21 (1991), pp. 285–313.

Elster, Jon, Claus Offe, and Ulrich K. Preuss, *Institutional Design in Post-Communist Societies: Rebuilding the Ship at Sea*, Cambridge: Cambridge University Press, 1998.

Etzioni-Halevy, Eva, *Political Manipulation and Administrative Power*, London: Routledge and Kegan Paul, 1979.

Evans, Geoffrey and Stephen Whitefield, 'Explaining the Formation of Electoral Cleavages in Post-Communist Democracies', in Hans-Dieter Klingemann, Ekkhard Mochmann, and Kenneth Newton (eds), *Elections in Central and Eastern Europe: The First Wave*, Berlin: Sigma, 2000, pp. 36–67.

Farrell, David M., *Comparing Electoral Systems*, Basingstoke: Macmillan, 1997.

—— *Electoral Systems: A Comparative Introduction*, Basingstoke: Palgrave, 2001.

Fiorina, Morris, *Retrospective Voting in American National Elections*, New Haven: Yale University Press, 1981.

Franklin, Mark N., 'Electoral Participation', in Lawrence LeDuc, Richard G. Niemi, and Pippa Norris (eds), *Comparing Democracies: Elections and Voting in Global Perspective*, Thousand Oaks, CA, London and New Delhi: Sage, 1996, pp. 216–35.

Friedgut, Theodore H., *Political Participation in the USSR*, Princeton, NJ: Princeton University Press, 1979.

Furtak, Robert K, *Elections in Socialist States*, New York and London: Harvester Wheatsheaf, 1990.

Gabel, Matthew J., 'The Political Consequences of Electoral Laws in the Hungarian 1990 Elections', *Comparative Politics* (1995), pp. 205–14.

Gallagher, M. and M. Marsh (eds), *Candidate Selection in Comparative Perspective: The Secret Garden of Politics*, London, 1988.

Ganev, Venelin I., 'Focus: A Symposium on Bulgaria: Introduction', *East European Constitutional Review* 10, 4 (2001), pp. 48–50.

Gebethner, S., 'Proportional Representation versus Majoritarian Systems: Free Elections and Political Parties in Poland, 1989–1991', in Arend Lijphart and Carlos Waisman (eds). *Institutional Design in New Democracies: Eastern Europe and Latin America*, Boulder, CO: Westview, 1996, pp. 59–76.

Geddes, Barbara, 'Initiation of New Democratic Institutions in Eastern Europe and Latin America', in Arend Lijphart and Carlos H. Waisman (eds), *Institutional Design in New Democracies: Eastern Europe and Latin America*, Boulder, CO: Westview, 1996, pp. 15–42.

Gel'man, Vladimir, 'The Iceberg of Russian Political Finance', in Peter Burnell and Alan Ware (eds), *Funding Democratization*, Manchester: Manchester University Press, 1998, pp. 158–79.

Golosov, Grigorii V., 'Russian Political Parties and the 'Bosses': Evidence from the 1994 Provincial Elections in Western Siberia', *Party Politics* 3, 1 (1997), pp. 5–21.

Gray, Mark and Miki Caul, 'Declining Vote Turnout in Advanced Industrial Democracies, 1950 to 1997: The Effects of Declining Group Mobilization', *Comparative Political Studies* 33, 9 (2000), pp. 1091–122.

Grofman, Bernard and Arend Liphart (eds), *Electoral Laws and their Political Consequences*, New York: Agathon Press, 1986.

Grzymala-Busse, Anna M., *Redeeming the Communist Past: The Regeneration of Communist Parties in East Central Europe*, Cambridge: Cambridge University Press, 2002.

Gunlicks, A. B., *Campaign and Party Finance in North America and Western Europe*, Boulder, CO: Westview, 1993.

Hayward, Fred. M., *Elections in Independent Africa*. Boulder, CO: Westview, 1987.

Haerpfer, Christian and Richard Rose, 'Support for Parliaments and Regimes in the Transition Toward Democracy in Eastern Europe', *Legislative Studies Quarterly* 19, 1 (1994), pp. 5–32.

Herron, Erik S., 'Mixed Electoral Rules and Party Strategies: Responses to Incentives by Ukraine's Rukh and Russia's Yabloko', *Party Politics* **8**, 6 (2002), pp. 719–33.

Hibbing, J. R. and S. C. Patterson, 'Public Trust in the New Parliaments of Central and Eastern Europe', *Political Studies* **42**, 4 (1994), pp. 570–92.

Hill, Ronald J., *Soviet Politics, Political Science, and Reform*, Oxford: Martin Robertson, 1980.

Holmes, Stephen (ed.), 'Designing Electoral Regimes: Introduction', *East European Constitutional Review* **3**, 2 (1994), pp. 39–77.

Höpken, Wolfgang, 'Elections in Yugoslavia', in Robert K. Furtak (ed.), *Elections in Socialist States*, New York and London: Harvester Wheatsheaf, 1990, pp. 119–41.

Ikstens, Janis, Michael Pinto-Duschinsky, Daniel Smilov, and Marcin Walecky, 'Political Finance in Central and Eastern Europe: An Interim Report', *Österreichische Zeitschrift für Politikwissenschaft* 2002/1, pp. 21–40.

Inkeles, Alex (ed.), *On Measuring Democracy: Its Consequences and Concomitants*, New Brunswick and London: Transaction, 1991.

International Institute for Democracy and Electoral Assistance [IDEA], *Voter Turnout Since 1945: A Global Report*, Stockholm: International IDEA, 2002.

Iordanova, Marina, 'Electoral Law and the Electoral System', in Georgi Karasimeonov (ed.), *The 1990 Election to the Bulgarian Grand National Assembly and the 1991 Election to the Bulgarian National Assembly: Analyses, Documents and Data*, Berlin: Sigma, 1997, pp. 34–43.

Ishiyama, John T, 'Electoral Systems Experimentation in the New Eastern Europe: The Single Transferable Vote and the Additional Member System in Estonia and Hungary', *East European Quarterly* **29**, 4 (1996), pp. 487–507.

—— ' "Red versus Expert": Candidate Recruitment and Communist Party Adaptation in Post-Soviet Politics', *Party Politics* **4**, 3 (1998), pp. 297–318.

—— 'Candidate Recruitment, Party Organisation and the Communist Successor Parties: The Cases of the MSzP, the KPRF and the LDDP', *Europe-Asia Studies* **52**, 5 (2000), pp. 875–96.

Jackman, Robert W., 'Political Institutions and Voter Turnout in Industrial Democracies', *American Political Science Review* **81**, 2 (1986), pp. 405–23.

Jackman, Robert W. and Ross A. Miller, 'Voter Turnout in the Industrial Democracies During the 1980s', *Comparative Political Studies* **27**, 4 (1995), pp. 467–92.

Jacobson, Gary C., 'Public Funds for Congressional Campaigns: Who Would Benefit?' in Herbert E. Alexander (ed.), *Political Finance*, Beverly Hills, CA and London: Sage, 1979, pp. 99–128.

Jasiewicz, Krzysztof, 'Elections and Voting Behaviour', in Stephen White, Judy Batt, and Paul G. Lewis (eds), *Developments in Central and East European Politics*, Basingstoke: Macmillan, 1998, pp. 166–87.

Jones, Mark P. *Electoral Laws and the Survival of Presidential Democracies*, Notre Dame and London: Notre Dame University Press, 1995.

Jowitt, Ken, 'Soviet Neotraditionalism: The Political Corruption of a Leninist Regime', *Soviet Studies* **35**, 3 (1983), pp. 275–97.

Karklins, Rasma, 'Soviet Elections Revisited: Voter Abstention in Non-Competitive Voting', *American Political Science Review* **80**, 2 (1986), pp. 449–69.

Katz, Richard, S., *A Theory of Parties and Electoral Systems*, Baltimore and London: Johns Hopkins University Press, 1980.

—— 'Intraparty Preference Voting', in Bernard Grofman and Arend Liphart (eds), *Electoral Laws and their Political Consequences*, New York: Agathon Press, 1986, pp. 85–103.

—— 'Party Organizations and Finance', in Lawrence LeDuc, Richard G. Niemi, and Pippa Norris (eds), *Comparing Democracies: Elections and Voting in Global Perspective*, 1996, pp. 107–33.

—— *Democracy and Elections*, New York and Oxford: Oxford University Press, 1997.

Katz, Richard S. and Peter Mair (eds), *Party Organizations: A Data Handbook on Party Organizations in Western Democracies, 1960–1990*, London, Thousand Oaks and New Delhi: Sage, 1992.

—— and —— (eds), *How Parties Organize: Change and Adaptation in Party Organizations in Western Democracies*, London, Thousand Oaks and New Delhi: Sage, 1994.

—— and ——, 'Changing Models of Party Organization and Party Democracy: The Emergence of the Carter Party', *Party Politics* 1, 1 (1995), pp. 5–28.

Kim, Jae-On and Mahn-Geum Ohn, 'A Theory of Minor Party Persistence: Election Rules, Social Cleavage, and the Number of Political Parties,' *Social Forces* 70, (1992), pp. 575–99.

King, Charles, *The Moldovans: Romania, Russia and the Politics of Culture*, Stanford, CA: Hoover Institution Press, 2000.

Kitschelt, Herbert, 'The Formation of Party Systems in Eastern Europe', *Politics and Society* 20 (1992).

——, 'Formation of Party Cleavages in Post-Communist Democracies: Theoretical Proposition', *Party Politics* 1, 4 (1995), pp. 447–72.

Kitschelt, Herbert, Zdenka Mansfeldova, Radoslaw Markowski, and Gabor Toka, *Post-Communist Party Systems: Competition, Representation and Inter-Party Cooperation*, Cambridge: Cambridge University Press, 1999.

Klingemann, Hans-Dieter, Ekkehard Mochmann, and Kenneth Newton (eds). *Elections in Central and Eastern Europe: The First Wave*, Berlin: Sigma, 2000.

Kolarova, Rumyana and Dimitr Dimitrov, 'Bulgaria', *East European Constitutional Review*, 3, 2 (1994).

—— and —— 'The Roundtable Talks in Bulgaria', in Jon Elster (ed.), *The Roundtable Talks and the Breakdown of Communism*, Chicago and London: University of Chicago Press, 1996, pp. 178–212.

Kopecky, Petr, 'Developing Party Organizations in East-Central Europe: What Type of Party is Likely to Emerge?', *Party Politics* 1, 4 (1995), pp. 515–34.

Kostadinova, Tatiana, 'Do Mixed Electoral Systems Matter?: A Cross-National Analysis of their Effects in Eastern Europe', *Electoral Studies* 21 (2002), pp. 23–34.

Krasovec, Alenka, 'Party and State in Democratic Slovenia', in Paul Lewis (ed.), *Party Development and Democratic Change in Post-Communist Europe: The First Decade*, London and Portland, OR: Frank Cass, 2001, pp. 93–106.

Kuusela, K, 'The Founding Electoral Systems in Eastern Europe, 1989–1991', in G. Pridham and T. Vanhanen (eds), *Democratization in Eastern Europe: Domestic and International Perspectives* London and New York: Routledge, 1994, pp. 128–50.

Laakso, Markku U. and Rein Taagepera, ' "Effective" Number of Parties: A Measure with Application to Western Europe', *Comparative Political Studies* 12, 3 (1979), pp. 3–27.

Lawson, Kay, 'Political Parties and Linkage', in Kay Lawson (ed.), *Political Parties and Linkage: A Comparative Perspective*, New Haven, CT and London: Yale University Press, 1980, pp. 3–24.

—— 'Cleavages, Parties, and Voters', in Kay Lawson, Andrea Rommele and Georgi Karasimeonov (eds), *Cleavages, Parties and Voters; Studies from Bulgaria, the Czech Republic, Hungary, Poland, and Romania*, Westport, CT and London: Praeger, 1999, pp. 19–34.

Lewis, Paul G., (ed.), *Party Structure and Organization in East-Central Europe*, Cheltenham: Edward Elgar, 1996.

—— 'Party Funding in Post-Communist East-Central Europe', in Peter Burnell and Alan Ware (eds), *Funding Democratization*, Manchester: Manchester University Press, 1998, pp. 137–57.

—— *Political Parties in Post-Communist Eastern Europe*, London and New York: Routledge, 2000.

—— (ed.), *Party Development and Democratic Change in Post-Communist Europe: The First Decade*, London and Portland, OR: Frank Cass, 2001.

Lewis, Paul, Bill Lomax, and Gordon Wightman, 'The Emergence of Multi-Party Systems in East-Central Europe: A Comparative Analysis', in Geoffrey Pridham and Tatu Vanhanen (eds), *Democratization in Eastern Europe: Domestic and International Perspectives*, New York: Routledge, 1994, pp. 151–88.

Leyes, Colin, 'Models, Theories, and the Theory of Political Parties', *Political Studies* 7 (1959), pp. 127–46.

Lijphart, Arend, 'Democratization and Constitutional Choices in Czecho-Slovakia, Hungary, and Poland, 1989–1991', *Journal of Theoretical Politics* 4, 2 (1992), pp. 207–23.

—— *Electoral Systems and Party Systems: A Study of Twenty-Seven Democracies, 1945–1990*, Oxford: Oxford University Press, 1994.

—— 'Constitutional Choices for New Democracies', in Larry Diamond and Marc F. Plattner (eds), *The Global Resurgence of Democracy*, 2nd edn, Baltimore and London: Johns Hopkins University Press, 1996, pp. 162–74.

—— *Patterns of Democracy: Government Forms and Performance in Thirty-Six Countries*, New Haven and London: Yale University Press, 1999.

Lijphart, Arend and Bernard Grofman (eds), *Choosing an Electoral System: Issues and Alternatives*, New York: Praeger, 1984.

Lijphart, Arend and Carlos H. Waisman (eds), *Institutional Design in New Democracies: Eastern Europe and Latin America*, Boulder, CO: Westview, 1996.

Linz, Juan J., 'The Perils of Presidentialism', in Larry Diamond and Marc F. Plattner (eds), *The Global Resurgence of Democracy*, 2nd edn, Baltimore: Johns Hopkins University Press, 1996, pp. 124–42.

—— 'Introduction: Some Thoughts on Presidentialism in Postcommunist Europe', in Ray Taras (ed.), *Postcommunist Presidents*, Cambridge: Cambridge University Press, 1997, pp. 1–14.

Linz, Juan L. and Alfred Stepan, *Problems of Democratic Transition and Consolidation: Southern Europe, South America, and Post-Communist Europe*, Baltimore and London: Johns Hopkins University Press, 1996.

Lipset, Seymour M. and Stein Rokkan, 'Cleavage Structures, Party Systems and Voter Alignments', in Seymour M. Lipset and Stein Rokkan (eds), *Party Systems and Voter Alignments: Cross-National Perspectives*, New York: The Free Press, 1967, pp. 1–64.

Loloci, Krenar, 'Electoral Law in Eastern Europe: Albania', *East European Constitutional Review* (1994), pp. 42–50.

McDonald, Ronald and J. Mark Ruhl, *Party Politics and Elections in Latin America*, Boulder, CO, San Francisco, and London: Westview, 1989.

McGrath, Troy, 'The Legacy of Leninist Enforced De-Participation', in Peter Lentini (ed.), *Elections and Political Order in Russia: The Implications of the 1993 Elections to the Federal Assembly*, Budapest: Central European University Press, 1995, pp. 226–45.

McGregor, J., 'How Electoral Laws Shape Eastern Europe's Parliaments', *RFE/RL Research Report* **2**, 4 (1993), pp. 11–18.

Mainwaring, Scott and Timothy R. Scully, *Building Democratic Institutions: Party Systems in Latin America*, Stanford, CA: Stanford University Press, 1995.

Mair, Peter, 'Party Organizations: From Civil Society to the State', *How Parties Organize: Change and Adaptation in Party Organizations in Western Democracies*, Richard S. Katz and Peter Mair (eds), London and Thousand Oaks: Sage, 1994, pp. 1–22.

—— 'What is Different about Post-Communist Party Systems?', Studies in Public Policy Number 259, Centre for the Study of Public Policy, University of Strathclyde, 1996.

—— *Party System Change: Approaches and Interpretations*, Oxford: Oxford University Press, 1997.

Mair, Peter, and Ingred van Biezen, 'Party Membership in Twenty European Democracies, 1980–2000', *Party Politics* **7**, 1 (2001), pp. 5–21.

Markowski, Radoslaw, 'Political Parties and Ideological Spaces in East Central Europe', *Communist and Post-Communist Studies* **30**, 3 (1997), pp. 221–54.

—— 'Party System Institutionalization in New Democracies: Poland – A Trend-Setter with No Followers', in Paul G. Lewis (ed.), *Party Development and Democratic Change in Post-Communist Europe: The First Decade*, London and Portland, OR: Frank Cass, 2001, pp. 55–77.

Massicotte, Louis and André Blais, 'Mixed Electoral Systems: A Conceptual and Empirical Survey', *Electoral Studies* **18**, 3 (1999), pp. 341–66.

Matic, Andrej Auersperger, 'Electoral Reform as a Constitutional Dilemma', *East European Constitutional Review* **9**, 3 (2000), pp. 77–81.

Matland, Richard, 'Women's Representation in National Legislatures: Developed and Developing Countries', *Legislative Studies Quarterly* (1998).

Millar, James R. (ed.), *Politics, Work, and Daily Life in the USSR: A Survey of Former Soviet Citizens*, Cambridge: Cambridge University Press, 1987.

Miller, William L., Stephen White, and Paul Heywood, *Values and Political Change in Post-Communist Europe*, Basingstoke: Macmillan, 1998.

Mishler, William and Richard Rose, 'Trust, Distrust and Skepticism: Popular Evaluations and Poltical Institutions in Post-Communist Societies', *Journal of Politics* **59**, 2 (1997), pp. 418–51.

Montgomery, Kathleen, 'Electoral Effects on Party Behaviour and Development', *Party Politics* **5**, 4 (1999), pp. 507–23.

Moser, Robert G., 'The Impact of the Electoral System on Post-Communist Party Development: The Case of the 1993 Russian Parliamentary Elections', *Electoral Studies* **14**, 4 (1995), pp. 377–98.

—— 'The Impact of Parliamentary Electoral Systems in Russia', *Post-Soviet Affairs* **13**, 3 (1997), pp. 284–302.

Moser, Robert G. 'Electoral Systems and the Number of Parties in Post-Communist States', *World Politics* **51**, 3 (1999), pp. 359–84.

—— *Unexpected Outcomes: Electoral Systems, Political Parties, and Representation in Russia*, Pittsburgh: University of Pittsburgh Press, 2001a.

—— 'The Effects of Electoral Systems on Women's Representation in Post-Communist States', *Electoral Studies* **20**, 3 (2001b), pp. 353–70.

Nassmacher, Karl-Heinz, 'Structure and Impact of Public Subsidies to Political Parties in Europe: The Examples of Austria, Sweden and West Germany', in Herbert E. Alexander (ed.), *Comparative Political Finance in the 1980s*, Cambridge: Cambridge University Press, 1989, pp. 236–67.

Nishikawa, Misa and Erik S. Herron, 'Contamination Effects and the Number of Parties in Mixed-Superposition Electoral Systems', *Electoral Studies* **20** (2001), pp. 63–86.

Nohlen, Dieter, *Wahlsysteme der Welt: Daten und Analysen*, Munich and Zurich: Piper, 1978.

—— 'Sistemas Electorales y Gobernabilidad', in Dieter Nohlen (ed.), *Elecciones y Sistemas de Partidos en America Latina*, San José, Costa Rica: Instituto Interamericano de Derechos Humanos, 1993, pp. 391–424.

Nohlen, Dieter, Michael Krennerich, and Bernhard Thibaut, *Elections in Africa: A Data Handbook*, Oxford: Oxford University Press, 1999.

Norris, Pippa, 'Legislative Recruitment', in Lawrence LeDuc, Richard G. Niemi, and Pippa Norris (eds), *Comparing Democracies: Elections and Voting in Global Perspective*, Thousand Oaks and London: Sage, 1996, pp. 184–215.

—— *Democratic Pheonix: Reinventing Political Activism*, Cambridge: Cambridge University Press, 2002.

Norris, Pippa and Joni Lovenduski, *Political Recruitment: Gender, Race, and Class in the British Parliament*, Cambridge: Cambridge University Press, 1995.

O'Donnell, G., P. Schmitter, and L. Whitehead (eds), *Transitions from Authoritarian Rule*, **4**, Baltimore and London: Johns Hopkins University Press, 1986.

Olson, David M., 'Party Formation and Party System Consolidation in the New Democracies of Central Europe', *Political Studies* **46**, 3 (1998) pp. 432–64.

Olson, David M. and Philip Norton (eds), *The New Parliaments of Central and Eastern Europe*, London and Oregon: Frank Cass, 1996.

Ordeshook, Peter and Olga Shevtsova, 'Ethnic Heterogeneity, District Magnitude, and the Number of Parties', *American Journal of Political Science* **38** (1994), pp. 100–23.

Paltiel, Khayyam Z., 'The Impact of Election Expenses Legislation in Canada, Western Europe and Israel', in Herbert E. Alexander (ed.), *Political Finance*, Beverly Hills, CA and London: Sage, 1979, pp. 15–39.

Pammett, Jon H. and Joan DeBardeleben, 'The Meaning of Elections in Transitional Democracies: Evidence from Russia and Ukraine', *Electoral Studies* **15**, 3 (1996), pp. 363–81.

Panebianco, A., *Political Parties: Organization and Power*, Cambridge: Cambridge University Press, 1988.

Pedersen, Mogens, 'The Dynamics of European Party Systems: Changing Patterns of Electoral Volatility', *European Journal of Political Research* **7** (1979), pp. 1–26.

Pérez-Liñán, A., 'Neoinstitutional Accounts of Voter Turnout: Moving Beyond Industrial Democracies', *Electoral Studies* **20**, 2 (2001), pp. 281–98.

Pettai, Vello and Marcus Kreuzer, 'Institutions and Party Development in the Baltic States', in Paul Lewis (ed.), *Party Development and Democratic Change in Post-Communist Europe: The First Decade*, London and Portland, OR: Frank Cass, 2001, pp. 107–25.

Powell, G. Bingham, 'Voting Turnout in Thirty Democracies: Partisan, Legal, and Socio-Economic Influences', in Richard Rose (ed.), *Electoral Participation: A Comparative Analysis*, Beverly Hills and London: Sage, 1980, pp. 5–34.

—— *Contemporary Democracies: Participation, Stability, and Violence*, Cambridge: Harvard University Press, 1982.

—— 'American Turnout in Comparative Perspective', *American Political Science Review* 80, 1 (1986), pp. 17–37.

—— *Elections as Instruments of Democracy: Majoritarian and Proportional Visions*, London and New Haven: Yale University Press, 2000.

Pravda, Alex, 'Elections in Communist Party States', in Guy Hermet, Richard Rose, and Alain Rouquié (eds), *Elections without Choice*, London: Macmillan, 1978, pp. 169–95.

Pridham, Geoffrey and Paul G. Lewis (eds), *Stabilising Fragile Democracies: Comparing New Party Systems in Southern and Eastern Europe*, London, and New York: Routledge, 1996.

Przeworski, Adam, *Democracy and the Market: Political and Economic Reforms in Eastern Europe and Latin America*, Cambridge: Cambridge University Press, 1991.

Radcliffe, Benjamin, 'The Welfare State, Turnout, and the Economy; A Comparative Analysis', *American Political Science Review* 86, 2 (1992), pp. 444–54.

Rae, Douglas, *The Political Consequences of Electoral Laws*, 2nd edn, New Haven and London: Yale University Press, 1971.

Raina, Peter, 'Elections in Poland', in Robert K. Furtak (ed.), *Elections in Socialist States*, New York and London: Harvester Wheatsheaf, 1990, pp. 98–142.

Randall, Vicky and Lars Svasand, 'Party Institutionalization in New Democracies', *Party Politics* 8, 1 (2002), pp. 5–29.

Reilly, Benjamin, *Democracy in Divided Societies: Electoral Engineering for Conflict Management*, Cambridge: Cambridge University Press, 2001.

Reilly, Ben and Andrew Reynolds, *Electoral Systems and Conflict in Divided Societies*, Papers on International Conflict Resolution No. 2. Washington, DC: National Academy Press, 1999.

Reynolds, Andrew, 'The Case for Proportionality', *Journal of Democracy* 6 (1995), pp. 117–24.

—— *Electoral Systems and Democratization in Southern Africa*, Oxford: Oxford University Press, 1999.

Reynolds, Andrew and Ben Reilly (eds), *The International IDEA Handbook of Electoral System Design*, Stockholm: International IDEA, 1997.

Riker, William, 'The Two-Party System and Duverger's Law: An Essay on the History of Political Science', *American Political Science Review* 76 (1982), pp. 753–66.

Roberts, Kenneth M. and Erik Wibbels, 'Party Systems and Electoral Volatility in Latin America: A Test of Economic, Institutional, and Structural Explanations', *American Political Science Review* 93, 3 (1999), pp. 575–90.

Rokkan, Stein, *Citizens, Elections, Parties: Approaches to the Comparative Study of the Processes of Development*, Oslo: Universitetsforlaget, 1970.

Roper, Steven D., 'The Influence of Romanian Campaign Finance Laws on Party System Development and Corruption', *Party Politics* 8, 2 (2002), pp. 175–92.

Rosenstone, Steven and Mark Hansen, *Mobilization, Participation and Democracy in America*, New York: Macmillan, 1993.

Rose, Richard, 'Mobilizing Demobilized Voters in Post-Communist Societies', *Party Politics* **1**, 4 (1995), pp. 549–64.

Rose, Richard and Christian Haerpfer, 'New Democracies Barometer IV: A Ten Nation Survey', Studies in Public Policy 262, Strathclyde: Centre for the Study of Public Policy, University of Strathclyde, 1996.

Rose, Richard and William T. Mishler, 'Mass Reaction to Regime Change in Eastern Europe: Polarization or Leaders and Laggards?', *British Journal of Political Science* **24**, 2 (1994), pp. 159–82.

Rose, Richard, Neil Munro and Stephen White, 'Voting in a Floating Party System: The 1999 Duma Election', *Europe-Asia Studies* **53**, 3 (2001), pp. 419–43.

Rose, Richard, Neil Munro, and Tom Mackie, *Elections in Central and Eastern Europe Since 1990*, Strathclyde: Centre for the Study of Public Policy, University of Strathclyde, 1998.

Rose, Richard, William Mishler, and Christian Haerpfer, *Democracy and its Alternatives: Understanding Post-Communist Societies*, Baltimore, MD: Johns Hopkins University Press, 1998.

Rouquié, Alain, 'Clientelist Control and Authoritarian Contexts', in Guy Hermet, Richard Rose, and Alain Rouquié (eds), *Elections without Choice*, London and Basingstoke: Macmillan, 1978, pp. 9–35.

Rule, Wilma and Joseph F. Zimmerman (eds), *US Electoral Systems: Their Impact on Minorities and Women*, Westport, CT: Greenwood, 1992.

Rustow, Dankwart A., 'Transitions to Democracy: Toward a Dynamic Model', *Comparative Politics* (1970), pp. 337–63.

Sartori, Giovanni. 'Political Development and Political Engineering.' In *Public Policy* **27** (eds) John D. Montgomery and Albert O. Hirschman, Cambridge, MA: Harvard University Press, 1968, pp. 261–98.

—— *Parties and Party Systems*, Cambridge: Cambridge University Press, 1976.

Schmidt, Steffan, 'Patrons, Brokers, and Clients: Party Linkages in the Colombian Systems', in Kay Lawson (ed.), *Political Parties and Linkage: A Comparative Perspective*, New Haven, CT and London: Yale University Press, 1980.

Shugart, Matthew Soberg, 'Executive–Legislative Relations in Post-Communist Europe', *Transition* **2** 25, (13 December 1996), pp. 6–11.

Shugart, Matthew Soberg and John M. Carey, *Presidents and Assemblies: Constitutional Design and Electoral Dynamics*, Cambridge: Cambridge University Press, 1992.

Shugart, Matthew Soberg and Martin P. Wattenberg (eds), *Mixed-Member Electoral Systems: The Best of Both Worlds?*, Oxford: Oxford University Press, 2001.

Shvetsova, Olga, 'A Survey of Post-Communist Electoral Institutions, 1990–1998', *Electoral Studies* **18** (1999), pp. 397–409.

Slider, Darrell, 'The Soviet Union', *Electoral Studies* **9**, 4 (1990), pp. 295–302.

Stepan, Alfred and Cindy Skach, 'Constitutional Frameworks and Democratic Consolidation: Parliamentarism and Presidentialism', *World Politics* **46** (1993), pp. 1–22.

Szajkowski, Bogdan, 'The Albanian Election of 1991', *Electoral Studies* **11**, 2 (1992), pp. 157–61.

Szczerbiak, Aleks, 'Cartelisation in Post-Communist Politics: State Party Funding in Post-1989 Poland', *Perspectives on European Politics and Society* 2, 3 (2001), pp. 431–51.

Taagepera, Rein, 'The Baltic States', *Electoral Studies* 9, 4 (1990), pp. 303–11.

—— 'Effective Number of Parties for Incomplete Data', *Electoral Studies* 16, 2 (1997), pp. 145–51

—— 'Nationwide Inclusion and Exclusion Thresholds of Representation', *Electoral Studies* 17, 4 (1998a), pp. 405–18.

—— 'How Electoral Systems Matter for Democratization', *Democratization* 5, 3 (1998b), pp. 68–91.

Taagepera, Rein and Matthew Soberg Shugart, *Seats and Votes: The Effects and Determinants of Electoral Systems*, New Haven and London: Yale University Press, 1989.

Thomas, Susan, *How Women Legislate*, Oxford: Oxford University Press, 1993.

Toka, Gabor, 'Seats and Votes: Consequences of the Hungarian Election Law', in Gabor Toka (ed.), *The 1990 Election to the Hungarian National Assembly: Analyses, Documents and Data*, Berlin: Sigma, 1995, pp. 41–66.

—— 'Political Parties and Democratic Consolidation in East Central Europe', Studies in Public Policy 279, Strathclyde: Centre for the Study of Public Policy, University of Strathclyde, 1997.

Turner, Arthur W., 'Postauthoritarian Elections: Testing Expectations about "First" Elections', *Comparative Political Studies* 26, 3 (1993), pp. 330–49.

Uhlander, Carol, 'Rational Turnout: The Neglected Role of Groups', *American Journal of Political Science* 33 (1989), pp. 390–422.

Verba, Sidney and Norman H. Nie, *Participation in America: Political Democracy and Social Equality*, London and New York: Harper and Row, 1972.

Verba, Sidney, Norman H. Nie, and Jae-on Kim, *Participation and Political Equality: A Seven-Nation Comparison*, Cambridge: Cambridge University Press, 1978.

Verba, Sidney, Kay Schlozman, and Henry Brady, *Voice and Equality*, Cambridge, MA: Harvard University Press, 1995.

Vorozheikina, Tatiana, 'Clientelism and the Process of Democratization in Russia', in Luis Roniger and Ayse Gunes-Ayata (eds), *Democracy, Clientelism, and Civil Society*, Boulder and London: Lynne Reiner, 1994, pp. 105–20.

Wade, Larry L., Alexander J. Groth, and Peter Lavelle, 'Estimating Participation and Party Voting in Poland: The 1991 Parliamentary Elections', *East European Politics and Societies* 8, 1 (1994), pp. 94–121.

Waller, Michael, 'Groups, Parties, and Political Change in Eastern Europe from 1977', in Geoffrey Pridham and Tatu Vanhanen (eds), *Democratization in Eastern Europe: Domestic and International Perspectives*, London: Routledge, 1994, pp. 38–62.

Weissberg, R., 'Collective v. Dyadic Representation in Congress', *American Political Science Review* 72 (1978), pp. 535–47.

White, Stephen, Richard Rose, and Ian McAllister, *How Russia Votes*, Chatham, NJ: Chatham House, 1997.

Wightman, Gordon, 'Conclusions', in Gordon Wightman (ed.), *Party Formation in East-Central Europe: Post-Communist Politics in Czechoslovakia, Hungary, Poland and Bulgaria*, Aldershot: Edward Elgar, 1995, pp. 217–37.

Wildavsky, Aaron B. 'A Methodological Critique of Duverger's *Political Parties*', *Journal of Politics* 21 (1959), pp. 303–18.

Willerton, John P. Jr., 'Elite Mobility in the Locales: Towards a Modified Patronage Model', in David Lane (ed.), *Elites and Political Power in the USSR*, Aldershot: Edward Elgar, 1988.
Wyman, Matthew, Stephen White, Bill Miller, and Paul Heywood, 'The Place of "Party" in Post-Communist Europe', *Party Politics* **1**, 4 (1995), pp. 535–48.
—— 'Public Opinion, Parties and Voters in the December 1993 Russian Elections', *Europe-Asia Studies* **47**, 4 (1995), pp. 591–614.

Index

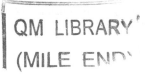